Ancient Peoples and Places
THE UPPER AMAZON

General Editor
DR GLYN DANIEL

ABOUT THE AUTHOR

From Berkeley High School, Donald Lathrap proceeded to the University of California at Berkeley in 1946, to study Anthropology. In 1950, he was appointed Assistant Archaeologist of the University of California Survey. After attending Harvard University Graduate College, he took up the post of Instructor to the University of Illinois, Urbana, in 1959, was promoted to Assistant Professor in 1962 and Associate Professor in 1964; he has been Professor there since 1968. From 1956 onwards, he has engaged in a series of field surveys in eastern Peru, in all but the first of which he has been assisted by his wife, Joan, who is also a trained anthropologist. A Member of the executive committee of the Society of American Archaeology and Associate of the American Academy for the Advancement of Science, Professor Lathrap has contributed articles to a number of scientific journals and anthologies.

THE UPPER AMAZON

Donald W. Lathrap

75 PHOTOGRAPHS
42 LINE DRAWINGS
15 MAPS

 THAMES AND HUDSON

NAZARETH COLLEGE LIBRARY

THIS IS VOLUME SEVENTY IN THE SERIES
Ancient Peoples and Places
GENERAL EDITOR: DR GLYN DANIEL

First published 1970
© *Donald W. Lathrap 1970*
All rights reserved. No part of this publication
may be reproduced, stored in a retrieval system, or
transmitted, in any form or by any means, electronic,
mechanical, photocopying, recorded or otherwise,
without the prior permission of the Publishers.
Filmset by Keyspools Ltd, Golborne, Lancs and
printed in Great Britain by The Camelot Press Ltd, Southampton
Not to be imported for sale into the U.S.A.
500 02067 1

CONTENTS

	LIST OF ILLUSTRATIONS	8
	CHRONOLOGICAL CHART	14, 15
	ACKNOWLEDGMENTS	16
I	INTRODUCTION	17
II	THE UPPER AMAZON AS A SETTING FOR CULTURAL DEVELOPMENT	22
	The river system of the Amazon Basin	22
	The vegetation cover	31
	The fauna of the tropical forest	35
	The soils and their agricultural potential	36
III	TROPICAL FOREST CULTURE	45
	The definition of Tropical Forest Culture	45
	The nature of the Tropical Forest agricultural system	47
	Technological aspects of Tropical Forest Culture	60
	The origin of Tropical Forest Culture	63
IV	LANGUAGES OF THE UPPER AMAZON: CLUES TO PAST MIGRATIONS AND ANCIENT DEMOGRAPHY	68
	The Arawakan stock	70
	Tupi-Guaranian	78

	Panoan and its affinities	79
	Gĕ and Cariban	81
	Equatorial	83
V	THE EARLY TROPICAL FOREST CULTURES OF THE UPPER AMAZON	84
	Early Tutishcainyo	84
	Late Tutishcainyo	89
	Shakimu	92
	The Alto Pachitea	95
	The Cave of the Owls	102
	The Huánuco Basin	103
	The bend of the Marañón	107
	Ecuador	109
	The more distant cultural relationships of the early Tropical Forest Cultures of the Upper Amazon	110
VI	THE BARRANCOID PEOPLES AND THEIR MIGRATIONS	113
	Northern Barrancoid	113
	Hupa-iya	117
	Barrancoid styles of the Central Amazon	120
	Naranjal and the modern Campa	121
	Eastern Bolivia and the Upper Xingú	123
	Summary	127
VII	DISPLACED PERSONS	128
	Yarinacocha	129
	Pacacocha	131
	Enoqui and the modern Amuesha	135

VIII	FURTHER INVASIONS OF THE UCAYALI BASIN	136
	Cumancaya	136
	Caimito, Napo, and the Polychrome Tradition	145
IX	RIDGED FIELDS	160
X	THE CARIB EXPANSION OUT OF THE AMAZON BASIN	164
XI	TERRACING AND THE EASTERN SLOPES OF THE ANDES	171
XII	THE PRESENT ETHNOGRAPHIC PICTURE IN THE UCAYALI BASIN	180
	The Shipibo and Conibo	180
	The Cocama	185
	The Panoan-speaking tribes of the forest	186
	BIBLIOGRAPHY	191
	SOURCES OF ILLUSTRATIONS	204
	THE PLATES	209
	NOTES ON THE PLATES	241
	INDEX	251

ILLUSTRATIONS

PLATES
1. The Ucayali River below Pucallpa
2. Air view of the Ucayali River flood plain
3. Canoe travel on Yanayacu
4. Ox-bow lake of Yarinacocha
5. The Imaríacocha lake
6. The easternmost range of the Peruvian Andes
7. Tropical rain-forest of the Río Pisqui
8. Terrain and vegetation of the eastern Peruvian Andes
9. Pottery sherd, Early Shakimu Complex
10. Cup, Early Shakimu Complex
11. Top part of bottle, Early Shakimu Complex
12. Bowl, Early Shakimu Complex
13. Sherds of bowl, Cave of the Owls Fine Ware
14. Fragments of bowls, Cave of the Owls Fine Ware
15. Excised sherds of the Pangotsi Complex
16. Fragment of roller stamp, Nazaratequi Complex
17. Examples of incised decoration, Nazaratequi Complex
18. The Crossed Hands, Kotosh ruin
19. The ruin of Kotosh
20. Junction of the Tabaconas and Chinchipe Rivers
21. Necklace of shell beads, Huayurco site
22. Bottle of burnished black-ware, Huayurco site

PLATES	23	*Adorno* off stone bowl, Huayurco site
	24	Sherd with appliqué decoration, Huayurco site
	25	Small onyx bowl, Huayurco site
	26, 27	Sculptured stone bowls, Huayurco site
	28	Sherds of the Hupa-iya Complex
	29	Decorated spindle whorls, Hupa-iya Complex
	30	*Adornos* of the Hupa-iya Complex
	31	Vessel of Yarinacocha Complex
	32	*Adornos* from Cumancaya Complex vessels
	33	Fragment of scraped *olla*, Cumancaya Complex
	34	Fragment of *olla* with incised decoration, Cumancaya Complex
	35	Fragment of corrugated *olla*, Cumancaya Complex
	36	Large corrugated burial urn, Cumancaya Tradition
	37	Small ceramic head from Aspusana River
	38	Zoned bichrome sherd from Aspusana River
	39	Ceramic colander and pestle, Cumancaya Complex
	40	Zoned bichrome bowl, Naneini Complex
	41	Bowl with human face in appliqué, Caimito Complex
	42	*Olla* with broad-line incision and appliqué, Caimito Complex
	43	Frog effigy, Caimito Complex
	44	Miniature four-lobed bottle, Caimito Complex
	45, 46	Air views of ridged fields in Eastern Bolivia
	47	Central structure of the ruin of Capash
	48	The ruins of Gran Pajatén
	49	Mosaic masonry at Gran Pajatén
	50	Detail of mosaic masonry, Gran Pajatén
	51	Ceramic figurine, Tantamayo style

PLATES	52	Pitcher of the Killke series from Cuzco
	53	Double wall of the ruined city of Trenchera
	54	General view of Trenchera ruins
	55	Field maize at Painaco
	56	Large funerary urn, Calchaqui region
	57	Shipibo water jar
	58	Pisquibo drinking vessel
	59	Shipibo *cushma* (men's garment)
	60	Conibo drinking vessel
	61	Conibo food bowl
	62	Pisquibo manioc-beer strainer
	63	Shipibo rocker pestel with trough mortar
	64	Young Shipibo woman in fiesta attire
	65	Shipibo women making manioc beer
	66, 67	Pisquibo cooking pots
	68	Hearth in Pisquibo cook-house
	69	Cocamilla water jar
	70	Cocamilla bowl
	71	Ticuna water jar
	72	Cooking-pot of Isconahua band
	73	Drinking vessel of Isconahua band
	74	Vessel of Cashibo band
	75	Small bowl from cache, Lower Utoquinea River
FIGURES	1	Map: *Archaeological sites in the Upper Amazon Basin, p. 23*
	2	Map: *Geological features of the Amazon Basin, p. 27*
	3	Map: *Vegetation cover of the Amazon Basin, p. 33*
	4	Map: *Distribution of Macro-Arawakan and Macro-Tupi-Guaranian languages, p. 71*
	5	Maps: *Stages of population dispersal pertaining to Macro-Arawakan, pp. 76, 77*

FIGURES

6 Map: Other linguistic stocks in the Amazon Basin, p. 81
7 Early Tutishcainyo vessel shapes and decoration, pp. 86, 87
8 Cat design, Early Tutishcainyo Complex, p. 89
9 Late Tutishcainyo vessel shapes and decoration, pp. 90, 91
10 Early Shakimu vessel forms and decoration, p. 93
11 Unrolled design from Early Shakimu bowl, p. 94
12 Late Shakimu vessels, p. 95
13 Vessel forms, Cobichaniqui Complex, p. 97
14 Pangotsi vessel forms, p. 99
15 Nazaratequi vessel forms, pp. 100, 101
16 Map: Distribution of early ceramic complexes, p. 111
17 Sherds in the Barrancoid Tradition, p. 115
18 Vessel shapes and decoration typical of Hupa-iya Complex, p. 118
19 Vessel shapes and decoration, Naranjal Complex, p. 122
20 Vessel forms and decoration, Lower Mound Verlarde Complex, p. 124
21 Sherds of Lower Mound Velarde Complex, p. 125
22 Map: Sites producing ceramics in Barrancoid Tradition, p. 126
23 Vessels of Yarinacocha Complex, p. 130
24 Vessels of Pacacocha Complex, p. 132
25 Bat-head adornos, Nueva Esperanza Complex, p. 133
26 Typical vessels, Enoqui Complex, p. 134
27 Vessels of Cumancaya Complex, p. 137
28 Pedestal bowl, Cumancaya Complex, pp. 138, 139
29 Decorated sherds from a Cumancaya burial, p. 139
30 Painted designs from the Southern Mato Grosso, p. 141
31 Design layouts from Mojocoya Trichrome Style vessels, p. 143
32 Pottery from urn burials on the Río Palacios, p. 144
33 Vessel forms of Caimito Complex, p. 146

FIGURES

34 Unrolled design from burial urn, Caimito Complex, p. 147
35 Incised-excised designs, Caimito Complex, p. 148
36 Ceramic objects of Caimito Complex, p. 149
37 Polished stone axehead, Caimito Complex, p. 150
38 Napo Phase burial urn and three sherds, pp. 152, 153
39 Pottery from urn burials, Upper Mount Velarde Complex, p. 158
40 Map: Extent of raised agricultural fields in South America, p. 162
41 Incised and excised sherds of late prehistoric cultures, p. 166
42 Late prehistoric ceramics with appliqué decoration, p. 167
43 Map: Late sites characterized by vessels having triangular incision and strip appliqué decoration, p. 169
44 Vessels from the Peruvian and Bolivian Andes, p. 172
45 Map: Sites dominating the crest and eastern slopes of the Andes, p. 174
46 Red-slipped ware from Chullpa Pampa, p. 175
47 Vessel shapes demonstrable for Chacra de Giacomotti, p. 177
48 Cast bronze axe from Río Pisqui, p. 178
49 Map: Recent distribution of aboriginal groups in the Ucayali Basin, p. 181
50 Band designs from Shipibo and Pisquibo cooking pots, p. 183
51 Impressions from modern carved wooden roller seals, p. 185
52 Sherds of the Tournavista Complex, pp. 186, 187
53 Fine-line incised sherds from the Tournavista to Pucallpa road, p. 188
54 Paintings by Isconahua women, p. 189

A mis compadres,
Catalino Augustín Cumapa y Manuel Rengifo Barbarán,
sin cuya ayuda este libro no se hubiera realizado.

AD	HUANUCO BASIN	HUALLAGA VALLEY	ALTO PACHITEA	CENTRAL UCAYALI BASIN	RIO NAPO
1500	Chupachu	Monzón Coarse Wares	Enoqui	Caimito	Napo
1000			Naneini	Cumancaya	
				Nueva Esperanza	
		Aspusana		Cashibocaño	Tivacundo
500	Higueras			Pacacocha	
				Yarinacocha	
0			Nazaratequi		
				Hupa-iya	Yasuní
	Kotosh Sajara-patac				
500				Late Shakimu	
				Early Shakimu	
	Kotosh Chavín				
1000	Kotosh Kotosh		Pangotsi		
	G			Late Tutishcainyo	
1500		Cave of the Owls Fine Ware	Cobichaniqui		
	Kotosh Waira-jirca H				
2000 BC	Mito			Early Tutishcainyo	

UPPER AMAZON		TEFÉ		MANAUS	ITACOATIARA	LOWLAND BOLIVIA	
							Mound Masicito
Pirapitinga	Santa Luzia	Miracanguera				Upper Velarde	
São Joaquim		Tefé					Lower Velarde
			Japurá	Paredão	Guarita	Chimay	
				Guarita			
		Caiambé		Manacapurú			
					Itacoatiara		

Chronological Chart

▨▨▨▨ Major discontinuity in Ceramic Tradition

Acknowledgments

In the thirteen years that I have been working in the Upper Amazon, I have been assisted by many persons and institutions. The following list can be only a partial expression of my indebtedness to others. The Shipibo of San Francisco de Yarinacocha have been considerate hosts and dedicated assistants. Sr Roger Mori of Pucallpa has aided each of the sessions of field work in many ways. My Peruvian colleagues have been invariably enthusiastic and supportive; in particular Dr Jorge C. Muelle, Dr Toribio Mejía Xesspe, Dr Julio Espejo Nuñez, Dr Duccio Bonavia, and Sr Pedro Rojas Ponce.

Financial support for the various sessions of research has come from The American Museum of Natural History, The National Science Foundation, the Fulbright-Hays Commission, and the Graduate Research Board of the University of Illinois.

In the field I have been most ably assisted by my wife, Joan W. Lathrap. Several graduate students at the University of Illinois have assisted me in these projects, and have undertaken major programs of independent research also contributing to this book, notably William L. Allen and Thomas P. Myers.

At various times Gerardo Reichel-Dolmatoff, Irving Rouse, John H. Rowe, Clifford Evans, and Betty J. Meggers have made collections and illustrations available to me and have discussed various aspects of these problems with me.

In the actual preparation of the manuscript I have been greatly assisted by my wife, Joan W. Lathrap, Mr Scott Raymond, Mrs John Douglas, Mrs Douglas Butterworth, and Miss Lynne Wolf. Dr F. K. Lehman made helpful suggestions concerning Chapter IV.

The editorial assistance of Mr E. C. Peters and Dr G. H. S. Bushnell is most gratefully acknowledged, as is the work on design and layout done by Miss Cecilia Fellner. D.W.L.

CHAPTER I

Introduction

On the lower Ucayali in eastern Peru there is a fast-growing town called Juancito. Most of the inhabitants still gain their livelihood by farming *chacras*, agricultural fields prepared by the slash-and-burn agricultural system, which lie a kilometre or so back in the surrounding jungle. Tobacco and rice are two of the important cash crops. In matters of dress and custom the people are not noticeably different from the inhabitants of the two large cities of eastern Peru, Iquitos and Pucallpa. They consider themselves to be typical representatives of Peruvian culture and would be offended if called Indians. Yet, a generation ago most of the inhabitants of Juancito or their ancestors were classified as Cocamas, descendents of the great Tupían-speaking nation which dominated the mainstream of the Upper Amazon at the time of first European contact. A few of the women of Juancito still make pottery in a much debased style, which only dimly reflects the complex ceramic tradition of their ancestors; and in case of sickness a shaman who has conserved the religious and medicinal lore of the Cocama will be consulted. In spite of these vestiges of their old culture, or perhaps because of them, the townspeople of Juancito are even less tolerant of their Indian neighbours than is the average Peruvian citizen.

Immediately across the Ucayali from Juancito, and with a clear view of the town's two well-tended plazas, stands the Conibo colony of Painaco. As Shipibo-Conibo communities go, it is a very old one and was extant in the 1840's when the French explorer Castelnau mapped this section of the Ucayali River. At that time its location was central to the large block of down-river Conibo; at present it is the northernmost Conibo town and the northernmost community where any vestiges of

17

Shipibo-Conibo culture are preserved. Fifteen years ago it was a large town, and houses extended in an unbroken chain along two kilometres of river bank. Today only two small clusters of houses remain, separated by a trackless stretch of second-growth jungle. In spite of its demographic decline, Painaco remains something of a ceremonial and religious centre for all of the Shipibo-Conibo, and within the last three years Indian families from a couple of hundred kilometres up-stream came here to have their daughters put through a properly conducted puberty ceremony. Fragments of the great wooden gong, used to beat out the welcome to the guests and to describe in conventional drum language the progressively more drunken frenzy of the participants, are still lying around the village. Painaco is in many respects the most conservative and most interesting of Shipibo-Conibo communities, but if the present demographic trends continue it will have ceased to exist in another ten years.

The decline of Painaco is not symptomatic of a general decline in Shipibo-Conibo population. During the last twenty years these Indians have more than doubled their numbers. Painaco does seem to have more than its share of endemic sickness, but the greater part of its population loss is due to emigration rather than to death. Family by family its inhabitants have moved up-stream along the Ucayali, usually far up-stream to the Conibo colonies on Imaríacocha or to those on the Upper Ucayali well above the junction of the Ucayali and Pachitea.

The motivations underlying this continuing emigration are various, and each Conibo family carefully weighs the pros and cons of the move before making it. They are well aware that they are exchanging rich, for much poorer agricultural land. The deep alluvial soils around Painaco will produce an abundant yield of any of the major crops known to the Conibo; while the upland soils around Imaríacocha, although adequate for a few crops of manioc and pineapples, will scarcely support bananas or maize. On the other hand, good fishing can still be had at

Introduction

Imaríacocha, but the waters around Painaco have been nearly fished-out by the rapidly increasing population of Juancito. A full day's journey is required to reach an isolated lake where a decent catch of fish can be made, and to the Conibo a day without fresh fish is a day of starvation. The balancing of good farm land on the one hand against good fishing on the other might lead to a decision to stay on at Painaco a little longer; but there are other pressures to emigrate. The houses of the Conibo are continually being robbed by their neighbours from Juancito. Several of the matrons of Painaco indicated that this pilfering was the reason they had given up making pottery. A trip to Juancito exposes the Conibo to the most violent kinds of ridicule and vituperation. His costume, habits, and intelligence will all be subjected to the most scathing comments. These continual attacks on his identity as an Indian are a major factor driving him up-stream.

One might view the continuing depopulation of Painaco as a simple example of acculturation, of the disappearance of Indian culture in the face of superior western technology. Viewed in these terms it is of little significance to our understanding of the prehistory of the Upper Amazon Basin. I think that these events are better viewed as a struggle between the more numerous and better organized ex-Cocama, who are also taking greater advantage of western technology, against the less numerous and more divisive Conibo, who incidentally retain with pride their identity as Indians. The struggle is for a rare commodity in the Amazon Basin, good agricultural land; and, as is usual, the victory is going to the group with greater numbers, greater cohesiveness, and a more efficient technology.

This competition for agricultural land has been going on for a long time, and began several millennia before Orellana's voyage of discovery down the Amazon in 1542. The groups who have lost the battle have been many, and they have been pushed further up-stream and off the major rivers into the intervening expanses of jungle. Earlier the struggle was marked by all-out warfare and a flamboyant development of cannibalism and headhunting; but the weapons of today, petty theft, ridicule, and economic exploitation are still effective.

This fight for the limited supply of productive farm land has been the most important single force in the culture history of the Amazon Basin, and more than any other factor is clearly visible in the archaeological record. The results of these continuing population pressures and population expansions are equally visible if one confines one's examination to tribal distributions at the period of first white contact. Thus Julian Steward writes: 'Culturally, the Chuncho (the people of the Upper Amazon) belong with the Tropical Forest peoples. They appear to represent a series of migratory waves that had spent their force against the barrier of the Andes, where representatives of many widely distributed linguistic families . . . and members of isolated linguistic families; . . . subsided into comparative isolation.' It is the more obvious and significant of these waves of migration that form the subject-matter of this book, and offer the organizing principle around which its outline was constructed. All lines of evidence indicating such migrations will be examined, and the population pressures and economic factors which caused them will be discussed. An understanding of these demographic and economic factors must be based in a detailed consideration of the Amazon Basin as a habitat for man.

There is an extreme Balkanization of Amazon Basin cultures such as we might expect as a result of the multiple migrations discussed above, and markedly dissimilar cultures have existed in adjacent areas for long periods of time. Only the more obvious, major migrations and the cultural traditions carried by these migrations can be considered. Wherever possible an attempt is made to trace the fate of the particular peoples and cultural tradition up to the period of white contact. These waves of migration are seen mainly from the vantage point of the Central

Introduction

Ucayali Basin, the area for which we have the most data, but an attempt is made to accommodate all available evidence from the Upper Amazon Basin and to relate the culture history of the Upper Amazon to that of adjacent areas. As more data become available from other areas of the Amazon Basin, the picture will certainly grow more complex than the one to be presented here. It is doubtful if the culture history of the tropical forests of South America will ever be successfully encompassed in a really simple developmental model.

CHAPTER II

The Upper Amazon as a Setting for Cultural Development

THE TWO PERVASIVE environmental features of the Upper Amazon Basin are the network of tremendous rivers which drain the area and the nearly continuous canopy of jungle which covers it. No other area of tropical forest approaches in extent the forests of the Upper Amazon and no other river system of the world carries anything approaching the volume of water that passes each year down the Amazon. Since man's entry into this region these two factors have been pre-eminent in affecting his way of life.

THE RIVER SYSTEM OF THE AMAZON BASIN

In terms of its total length, that is the distance from its mouth to the source of its longest tributary, the Amazon is slightly shorter than either the Nile or the Mississippi-Missouri; but in terms of the volume of water which passes through them, all other rivers of the world are comparatively puny. The annual discharge of the Amazon is five times that of the Congo and twelve times that of the Mississippi. The average flow of water through its mouth is 12,860,000,000 litres (2,829 million gallons) per second.

The nomenclature of the Amazon River is confusing. According to Peruvians, the Amazon comes into being at the point in north-eastern Peru where the Marañón and the Ucayali join. According to Brazilians, the river which crosses the Peruvian border at Tabatinga is the Solimões and the Amazon proper is born at the confluence of the Solimões and the Negro, the greatest northern tributary of the Amazon. Because of a Peruvian bias, and to simplify terminology I will refer to this whole stretch of river as the Upper Amazon. It is best to consider that the Upper

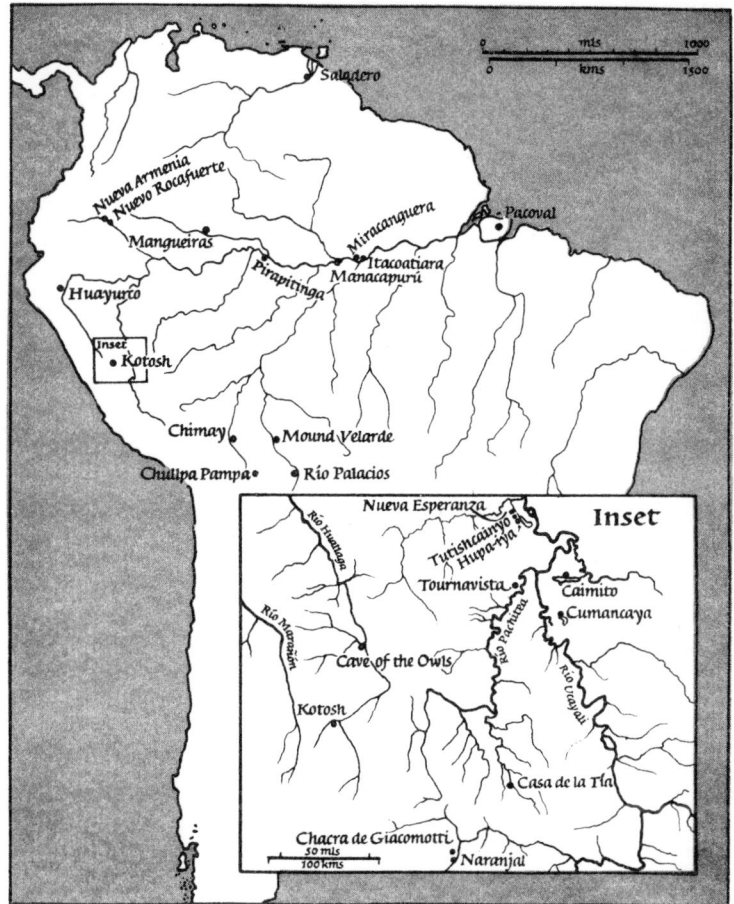

Fig. 1 The location of some of the more important archaeological sites in the Upper Amazon Basin. The Central Ucayali Basin is indicated in larger scale

Amazon ends and the Middle Amazon begins, not at the mouth of the Negro but down-stream at the mouth of the Río Madeira, the greatest southern tributary. Below the mouth of the Madeira, the Amazon is entrenched in a relatively narrow valley, seldom more than 100 kilometres wide. This narrow trough is bounded by two uplands consisting of extremely ancient and extremely hard rock, the Highland of Guiana to the north and the Brazilian Highland to the south. Above the mouth of the Madeira, the valley of the Amazon widens rapidly so that at the foot of the Andes the basin is about 2,000 kilometres wide from north-west to south-east. The major tributaries of the Upper Amazon are great rivers in their own right.

The degree to which the network of huge rivers forming the Amazon system was the major avenue for communication and travel cannot be overemphasized. The typical tribes of the tropical forests of South America were canoe travellers. Lowie has stated the case clearly: 'The very wide distribution of certain traits in the area is correlated with navigation. Thanks to their mobility, the canoeing tribes were able to maintain themselves in the midst of boatless populations, to travel with ease over periodically inundated tracts, and to diffuse their arts and customs over enormous distances. The combination of this technological factor with natural conditions has produced the extraordinary levelling of culture ("acculturation" in German parlance) . . .'

The system of waterways of which Lowie speaks actually extends far beyond the limits of the Amazon watershed. To the north the Amazon system is connected to the Orinoco by a level channel called the Casiquiare Canal which drains into both the Upper Orinoco and the Upper Río Negro. In the wet season the upper tributaries of the Essequibo, Guyana's greatest river, are connected to the headwaters of the Río Branco, a tributary of the Negro, by a sheet of water covering the Rupunini Savannah. To the south the annual innundation of the Llanos de Mojos and the Gran Chaco merge the basins of the Río Madeira and the Río Paraguay into a vast, freshwater sea opening up a net of waterways extending to the La Plata Estuary. To the Indian with developed water craft most of the tropical and part of the temperate areas of South America were connected by easily travelled highways.

Cultural Development

It is also important to note that for ethnic groups without developed watercraft the Amazon river system offers a series of formidable barriers to further expansion or movement. Even such upper tributaries as the Ucayali are more than a kilometre wide, and in its course below Manaus the Amazon in places attains a width of 15 kilometres, about half as wide as the Straits of Dover.

In order to understand the present characteristics of the Amazon Basin and of its rivers and soils, one must briefly examine its geological history. Along its eastern edge the Amazon Basin is bounded by the Guiana Highlands to the north and the Brazilian Highlands to the south. Though the two uplands are separated by the trough of the Lower Amazon, they are similar in their history and petrological characteristics. Both are the result of very ancient upward displacement through faulting and have been tectonically stable for many millions of years. In their long history as exposed uplands the two areas have been subjected to extreme erosion and have been swept bare of all but the most resistant rock. Most of their surface consists of extremely metamorphosed crystalline rock of Pre-Cambrian age. In more limited areas the Pre-Cambrian basement series is still capped by deep beds of slightly younger, but still very ancient, sedimentary rocks. These highly indurated sandstones occur as table-lands rising vertically a thousand metres or more above the surrounding country. This table-land topography has its most spectacular development in the Sierra Pacaraima and Roraima, a series of elongated mesas paralleling the border between Brazil and Venezuela and extending slightly into Guyana. Here are some of the tallest sheer cliffs in the world and what is generally conceded to be the world's highest waterfall, Angel Falls.

It would appear that for a long time after eastern South America rose up, the rivers in what is now the Amazon Basin drained westward into the Pacific Ocean. It was the relatively recent upthrust of the Andes which dammed this drainage system and

Plate 1

Fig. 2

The Upper Amazon

temporarily created a huge freshwater sea. Rapid erosion of the steep unconsolidated eastern slope of the Andes filled this freshwater sea with a mass of unconsolidated sands and silts, the depth of which is unknown. These unconsolidated alluvial deposits cover almost all of the huge triangle of land bounded by the Río Japurá on the north, the Río Madeira on the southeast, and the face of the Andes to the west. Their precise dating in geological terms is difficult since their bedding is discontinuous and irregular and their fossil content is essentially nil, but they probably range from Pliocene into early Pleistocene. Ultimately the present mouth of the Amazon was established and the Amazon and its tributaries began to cut valleys into this huge plain. The present inner valleys of the Amazon and its tributaries were cut at a time when sea level was much lower than it is now, probably at the peak of the glacial advances during the Pleistocene. As far up-stream as Manaus the bed of the Amazon is below sea level and the river's whole delta has been lost in the submerging of its mouth. This change in relative sea level has affected the behaviour of the Amazon and its tributaries as far up as Pucallpa, and they are now filling their inner valleys rather than cutting them deeper. In part it is the inundation of the Lower Amazon Valley which causes the extremely slight gradient of the river and its major tributaries: Pucallpa on the Central Ucayali is more than 4,500 kilometres from the mouth of the Amazon yet its elevation above sea level is little over 160 metres.

Fig. 2

The topographical maps of South America suggest that the whole vast triangle of land which comprises the Upper Amazon Basin is a unit in terms of its morphology. This cartographic convention masks what is the single most important distinction for the student of human ecology in the tropical lowlands of South America: the distinction between the active flood plain of the Amazon and its major tributaries, and the vast areas of more ancient alluvial deposit laid down when the Amazon Basin was a freshwater sea. As noted above, the active flood

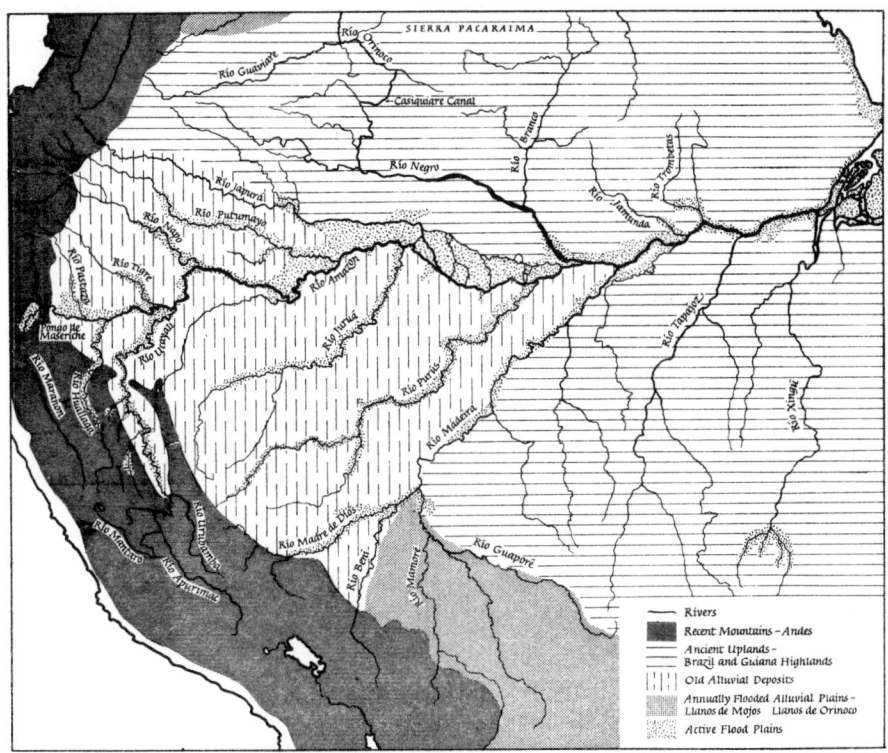

Fig. 2 Landforms and other significant geological features of the Amazon Basin and adjacent areas

plain is incised into these ancient alluvial deposits. The bluffs bounding it are nowhere a particularly impressive feature, ranging in height from 10 to 20 metres, but the economic potential of the two zones is vastly different and the line of demarkation is a sharp one. In terms of its agricultural potential, and in terms of protein resources such as fish and game, the flood plain is an infinitely more attractive habitat for man. This was true in 2000 BC and is true today, as is demonstrated by any maps of the modern population distribution in the Amazon Basin.

Plate 4

The Upper Amazon

Considering the magnitude of the Amazon River system the extent of the flood plain is remarkably restricted, relatively much smaller than that of the Mississippi River system. It has been calculated that the total area of unconsolidated sediments laid down in the Amazon Basin since the rise of the Andes is about 3,106,800 sq. kilometres (1,930,470 sq. miles); but the area of the active flood plain is only about one tenth of this. While the flood plain is the area most attractive for human occupation, only a part of it is available for human utilization. Much is occupied by the beds of the rivers and much more is in side channels, ox-bow lakes, and swampy regions that are above water for only a small part of the year, if at all. Thus 140,000 to 160,000 sq. kilometres (87,000 to 99,000 sq. miles) is probably an accurate estimate of the recent alluvial lands available to man in the Amazon Basin. It is this scarcity of recent alluvium that has been so dominant a factor affecting the evolution of culture in the Amazon Basin.

Plates 2, 3

With the exception of the Negro and its tributaries almost all the affluents of the Upper Amazon rise in the High Andes. The highland valleys along their upper courses are often broad and open, but as these rivers cut through the eastern ranges of the Andes they are typically entrenched in narrow steep-sided canyons 2,000 metres deep or more. Usually the river occupies the whole floor of the canyon and there are only occasional small patches of level ground along the stream beds. The orientation of these canyons is typically determined by the tectonic structure of the Andes and most run in a north-northwesterly direction. Of these northward-flowing rivers only the Marañón and the Huallaga have developed moderate expanses of flood plain in their lower canyons. Once they have broken through the easternmost barrier of the Andes the courses of the Amazon's tributaries assume the classic pattern of meandering rivers. Their valleys, the active flood plains of the rivers, range between 10 and 80 kilometres wide. The bluffs of old alluvial deposits bounding the

Plate 8

Plate 20

Plate 2

Cultural Development

flood plains set the limits to the continually changing meanders of the rivers.

When such a river has changed its course the derelict channel remains as a crescent-shaped expanse of open water known as an ox-bow lake. The flood plain of an actively meandering river is a complex of ox-bow lakes, some new and intact, many partially destroyed by later meander loops, and many partially or completely filled by alluvial deposition.

Plate 2

The processes of geomorphological evolution are usually thought of as imperceptible in terms of human life span, but this is not true of actively meandering rivers such as the Ucayali. In the twelve years that the author has been familiar with the course of the Central Ucayali two major loops have been cut off, the whole lower course of a tributary river has been pre-empted and widened, and the river has moved away more than a kilometre from what was originally planned as the port of the city of Pucallpa.

The highest land within the flood plain is always immediately adjacent to the active channel of the river. During flooding, the river dumps most of its load of sand and mud immediately adjacent to its course so that natural levees are built up. The areas within the expanding loops of the meanders are marked by a series of high ridges parallel to each other and to the expanding, convex bank of the river. These ridges, or point-bar formations, frequently appear as regular as a ploughed field when viewed from the air. There is an interesting succession of vegetation on these point-bar formations: those most recently vacated by the river support dense stands of the bamboo-like *caña brava*; slightly older ridges, a short distance back from the present river course, carry nearly pure stands of immature balsa trees; while older ridges still further back from the river carry a progressively more mature cover of tropical forest. This pattern of differential vegetation cover is striking when viewed from above and is a great aid in interpreting air photographs.

Plate 1

Derelict natural levees and the ridges of the point-bar formations are the preferred sites for human habitation within the flood plain. During years when the flooding is of less than average intensity these lands may escape inundation altogether while in years of severe flooding a pile dwelling with a floor a metre or so above the ground is usually enough to assure a dry hearth.

The meander topography described above is typical of most of the major tributaries of the Upper Amazon once they have entered the lowlands. Where the main stream of the Amazon is concerned the situation is rather different. A short distance below the Peruvian town of Nauta, where the Marañón and Ucayali join, the Amazon stops meandering and assumes a far less circuitous course which might best be likened to a three-strand braid. The multiple channels of the river surround huge, lenticular islands. Sternberg has demonstrated that the land forms along the Upper Amazon are less labile than those in the flood plains of the meandering tributaries, though the form and position of these islands is subject to gradual modification by the river. The interior section of the islands is low and swampy, and human occupation is concentrated on the natural levees at their edges.

The vast areas of unconsolidated sediments which stretch between the flood plains of the major tributaries of the Amazon are usually referred to as an upland plain. This designation is somewhat misleading, for while there are no hills rising above the average elevation, there are likewise few areas of really level ground. Since the surface of these unconsolidated sediments is seldom more than 40 metres above the elevation of the closest flood plains, it would be inaccurate to speak of these surfaces as being deeply dissected, but they are certainly intricately dissected by dendrites of small canyons which carry no water except during the heaviest rains. A cross-country hike on such a plain involves an inordinate amount of scrambling up and down the steep and frequently slippery sides of these arroyos. This shallow

Cultural Development

but intricate relief is effectively masked by the continuous mantle of tropical forest vegetation so that in air views of these old alluvial uplands they appear more or less level.

Most writers describing the Amazon Basin have emphasized the contrast between the white-water rivers and the black-water rivers. Nowhere is this distinction more evident than at Manaus where the Río Negro, the type specimen of a black-water river, meets the muddy, opaque waters of the Upper Amazon. For many kilometres below the juncture the two streams do not merge or mix, and one can see the dark blue, transparent waters of the Negro and the turbid waters of the Amazon flowing side by side. We have already noted the causal factor which differentiates these two kinds of streams. The black-water rivers drain the obdurate surfaces of the Guiana and Brazilian highland and are thus almost free of sediments. The white-water rivers are those that drain the eastern slope of the Andes bringing down millions of tons of sediment from those steep and largely unconsolidated slopes. The minor tributaries of the Amazon which rise entirely on the old alluvial plain more closely resemble the black-water rivers in their load of sediment. All the waters of the Amazon Basin are rich in aquatic life ranging from minute crustacea up to some of the largest freshwater fish known, but it is the white waters which are richest both in number and density of species and this inequality in the distribution of riverine resources has certainly affected the distribution of Pre-Columbian populations.

THE VEGETATION COVER

Even today the Upper Amazon Basin supports a continuous-stand rain-forest broken mainly by the major rivers. *Chacras*, fields cleared for agricultural use, occur along the major streams and for a short distance back from their shores. More recently such clearings have appeared along the few roads penetrating the area, but as yet these scarcely mar the interminable canopy of tree tops. As viewed from the air the traces of man's existence

Fig. 3

are dwarfed by the tremendous stretches of intervening jungle, which appears as an even and homogeneous cover. Some of the more common species of trees bear spectacular masses of yellow, red or violet flowers which in season break the monotony of the expanse of tree tops, but when viewed from above, the overwhelming impression given by the forest is that of evenness and uniformity, and the smaller topographic features are masked by the vegetation.

In contrast to the dense intertwining of the upper canopy of the forest, the floor of the forest, 150 feet or so below, has relatively sparse vegetation which in stands of mature trees offers little obstacle to travel. Most of the light is filtered out by the tree tops so that the forest floor presents a sombre aspect of muted greens and dark browns disturbed only occasionally by the dazzling blue of a huge Morpho butterfly. Here again one's initial impression is of uniformity, an impression which from the botanical point of view is erroneous. The forests of the Amazon Basin are characterized by a tremendous range of species. An acre of land may contain 30 or 40 species of mature trees, and one may have to walk a considerable distance to find two that are alike. Since these trees vary tremendously in the quality of the wood, and in the uses to which their wood can be put, a considerable knowledge of forestry was required of the aboriginal inhabitants. Only a small percentage of the total array of species yielded valuable wood, and certain of the economically important trees, such as those in the genera *Protium* and *Hymenea* which produce the resin used for glazing much Upper Amazon pottery, were sufficiently sporadic or restricted in their distribution to necessitate trade among far-flung tribes or villages for the purpose of obtaining essential raw materials. Large *cedros, Cedrela,* the most desirable tree for canoe-making, are quickly used up in densely populated areas.

The tropical forest of the Amazon Basin offered a wide range of useful materials for construction, with certain species of palm

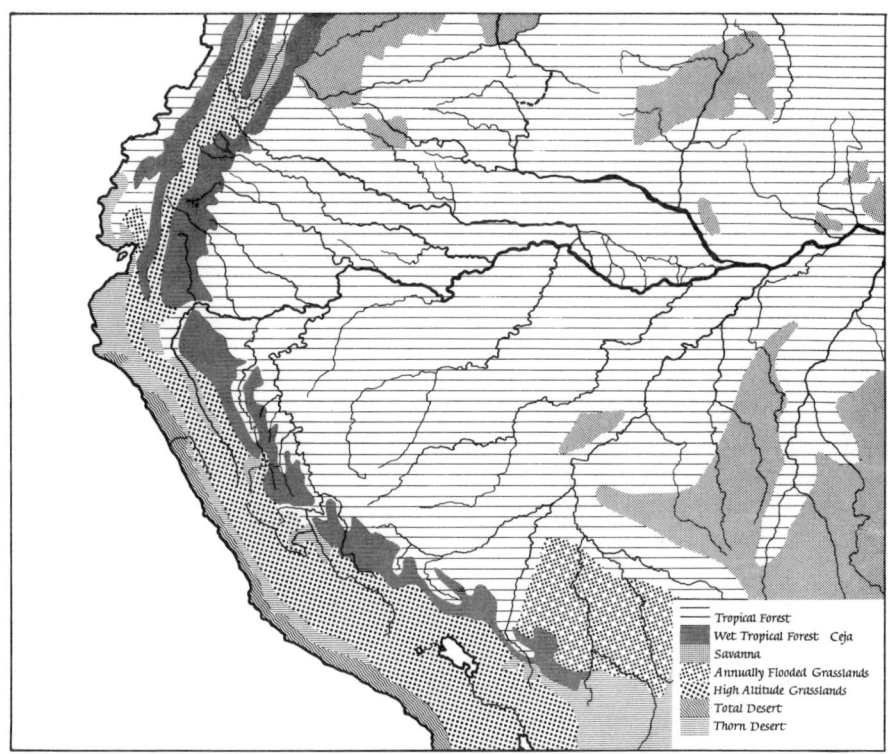

Fig. 3   Simplified map of the vegetation cover of the Amazon Basin

making excellent thatch and the bark of various vines providing an excellent substitute for rope. There were also a number of natural sources of raw materials for manufacturing. Several species of trees yielded bark suitable for making into bark cloth. Rubber was a fairly minor product from the Indians' point of view but has become very important to modern civilization. Through a complete knowledge of the properties of the wild plants of the Amazon Basin the Indians were able to extract a wide range of powerful poisons for hunting, fishing, and warfare. Equally remarkable was the formidable array of narcotics

The Upper Amazon

derived from wild plants which played an important role in the religious and aesthetic life of the aborigines. On the other hand, with the important exception of the fruit of several wild or semi-domesticated palms, the tropical forest was less bountiful in terms of naturally occurring vegetable foods, offering far less than either the hardwood forests of the Northern Hemisphere or the thorn forests of the arid tropics.

Though there are certain species of trees which are confined to the active flood plain of the major rivers, the differences between the jungle on the flood plains and the jungle on the old alluvium between the major rivers are not obvious.

The continuous nature of the tropical forest cover of the Amazon has been stressed. The most notable exceptions are the considerable expanses of high grass in the Llanos de Mojos of eastern Bolivia and in the Río Branco Basin of northern Brazil. As is indicated elsewhere such open grasslands are maintained by the sharp annual alternation between flooding and total drought.

Plates 7, 8

The forest on the steep eastern slopes of the Andes differs from the tropical forest on the floor of the Amazon Basin in being less tall and far denser. The extremely heavy rainfall on these exposed slopes supports a tangled growth of low trees, tree ferns, fuschias, and orchids. The trees carry a heavy load of moss and epiphitic plants mainly of the family *Bromeliaceae*. This type of vegetation cover is best developed between 600 to 2,000 metres elevation and is usually referred to as *ceja*.

Plate 6

Plate 19

As rainfall on the eastern Andes is largely the result of westward-moving air masses striking the abrupt eastern escarpment of the cordillera, there is a very marked rain shadow effect in the intermontane basins. The exposed eastern slopes of any ridge or mountain receive almost daily precipitation while the western slopes, and all areas lying behind and below the second or third ridge of the Andes, receive very little rain. Basins such as the Huánuco and Cochabamba valleys show dramatic contrasts in vegetation cover, with the valley floor and westward-facing slopes supporting a sparse cover of cactus and thorn forest, while exposed eastern slopes have typical *ceja*. The boundaries between the two vegetation zones are razor sharp and one can literally jump out of a fuschia tree and land in a patch of cactus.

Plate 19

THE FAUNA OF THE TROPICAL FOREST

The fauna of the tropical forest of South America is a fascinating subject in its own right. Here are to be found more primitive and isolated species of birds than in any other part of the world, and many of the mammals are strange in form and of habit. One could write at length on the Indians' relationship with the fauna they encounter, but for purposes of this book it is only necessary to stress the great differences in faunal resources between the riverine flood plains and the jungles on the old alluvial deposits away from the rivers.

The fishing resources of the major rivers and especially of the ox-bow lakes adjacent to the major rivers are truly phenomenal. The paiche, *Arapaima gigas,* is among the largest species of freshwater fish of the world. Its coarse flesh dries well and was a major article of commerce long before the arrival of the Europeans. There is a tremendous range of catfish and armoured catfish: all are relatively common and most provide excellent food. The pirañha, though something of a menace, is also very tasty and a major source of food where it occurs in quantity. There are a number of highly nutritious species, such as the *boca chica*, which occur seasonally in unbelievable quantities. In short, the fishing resources were sufficient to supply the protein requirements of relatively dense populations.

A wide range of aquatic turtles was an important source of food both for their meat and for their eggs. Caimans were also much used for meat by some groups, and were relatively abundant. The completely aquatic manatee, or sea cow, was common throughout much of the Amazon Basin and its meat was everywhere in demand. Several other major game animals, especially the capybara and other of the giant South American rodents, are semi-aquatic and can be hunted most efficiently from canoes. Much of the larger and more edible avifauna is also riverine in its habitat.

By way of contrast the jungles away from the major rivers have meagre game resources. The fishing potential of the smaller tributaries is limited. Monkeys are relatively common but are hard to hunt since they live in the upper canopy of the jungle. Persistent hunting of a particular group of monkeys will cause it to move off. The animals whose habitat is the floor of the jungle are either solitary and relatively rare, such as the tapir, or migratory and undependable in their occurrence, such as the two species of peccary. The extreme fragility of the game resources in the jungles away from the rivers was a dominant factor affecting human utilization of these areas.

THE SOILS AND THEIR AGRICULTURAL POTENTIAL

Fig. 2

Widely varying statements have been published concerning the fertility of the soils in the Amazon Basin, and concerning the possibility that these soils might in the future support dense, agriculturally based populations. Some authors have argued that the lush vegetation covering the area is a clear indication of high soil fertility. Others have alleged that the extreme infertility of its soils is the explanation for the low population densities supposedly typical of the Amazon Basin in Pre-Columbian times. Since all the prehistoric societies to be considered in this book had an economy based mainly on agriculture, the agricultural potential of the available soils is a basic consideration.

The way in which soil characteristics set limits on expanding human populations is a complex subject. If we are interested in the carrying capacity of a particular area of land, we must ask, 'How many calories can be produced per acre?' With this as our frame of reference, a whole new series of questions becomes

Cultural Development

relevant. What were the staple crops available to the population in which we are interested? What were the characteristics of the available soils in relation to the specific nutritional demands of the staple crops? What area around a particular habitation did their system of transportation permit the people to farm effectively? Within this radius, how much of the surface was suitable for farming of one kind or another, and how much was totally unsuited to any kind of farming? Given the demands of particular crops on particular kinds of soil and/or the degree to which the intrusion of weeds became an insurmountable problem, how long can a particular crop be grown on a particular plot of land before it has to be fallowed? What was the total pattern of agricultural practices known to the group which tended to improve or maintain the productive capacity of a plot of land? Could the existing patterns of social and political control muster sufficient manpower to make the most effective agricultural practices feasible? Finally, one must ask what percentage of the minimum daily diet came from agriculture and what percentage was obtained by fishing, hunting, and gathering?

Each of the factors indicated could be discussed at length, but two of them are of particular significance to the argument of this book. It cannot be emphasized too strongly that soils are not desirable or fertile in any absolute sense but only in terms of the total demands of the staple crops of the group being studied; and it cannot be assumed that people outside the modern western tradition of scientific agriculture were incapable of improving the agricultural potential of initially unpromising settings, or of maintaining the fertility of soils over a long period of continuous cropping.

The demands which various cultivated plants make upon their environment are widely variable. Certain major crops such as rice and taro in the Old World, and *Xanthosoma* and arrowroot in the New World, flourish under conditions of inundation during most of their growing season. Other crops such as beans and maize are highly intolerant of flooded or water-logged soils after they have germinated. Many crops, especially maize, are highly sensitive to drought during the latter part of their growing season and need either a dependable pattern of summer rains or controlled irrigation; while others, such as manioc, are extremely drought-resistant, and after enduring a rainless period of a year or more will become productive shortly after normal rains resume. Some crops, notably peanuts, require very loose, friable, sandy soils to attain maximum fruition, while others will tolerate, indeed flourish on hard, heavy clays.

Maize feeds heavily on nitrogen, and tends to deplete rapidly the nitrogen available in the soils on which it is grown. Other plants, such as manioc, extract far less nitrogen each year and so permit longer periods of cultivation on a particular plot without fallowing or artificial fertilization. Each major crop has its unique requirements in terms of the other major nutritive elements in the soil, so that the carrying capacity of any acre of ground must be reckoned in terms of the total requirements of the crop or rotation of crops grown on it.

Most groups outside the western tradition of scientific agriculture are good practical agronomists, are aware of the situations in which their important staples thrive, and are also aware of how long a period of cropping a particular kind of soil can take. The group which is seriously agricultural in its orientation will have a wide range of crops at its disposal and will thus be able to make the most of a variety of soils and locations, none of which are outstanding in terms of any absolute standards of soil fertility.

Within the tropical and temperate zones there are probably few areas of the earth's surface where agricultural potential cannot be vastly improved by a maximum use of ingenuity and labour. Students of the culture history of the New World should always keep in mind that schemes of soil reclamation and improvement making the best intensive use of labour were employed by various Pre-Columbian groups. The *chinampas* which

Cultural Development

furnished the subsistence basis for the Aztec Empire in Mexico are justly famous in this regard. Equally impressive was the enormous additional amount of the agricultural land made available in the Central Andes through the semi-terracing and terracing of the steep slopes. The geographical range of the agricultural terracing in the Central Andes, requiring vast numbers of man hours in their construction, is only gradually becoming appreciated, especially the distance to which such land utilization extended down the eastern slopes of the Andes and penetrated the regions now covered by *ceja* vegetation. The extent to which other forms of intensive land reclamation were significant to the agricultural development of the Amazon Basin will be considered in a later chapter.

Within the floor of the Amazon Basin recent alluvial soils are largely confined to the relatively limited flood plains of the Amazon and its major tributaries. The recent alluvial soils are usually high in nutritive materials and of a good, friable structure. The continual meandering of the river courses ensures that most of these soils have been re-sorted not long before, so that the effects of downward leaching are minimized. The increment of fresh silts off the eastern slope of the Andes and the masses of organic muck and raft vegetation left by the annual flooding also serve to maintain a high level of fertility. On the best strips of recent alluvium a banana plantation will thrive for a period of 15 to 25 years. Maize, which is often taken as a kind of absolute gauge of soil fertility, also does well on these soils.

Plate 55

The annual flooding which maintains the fertility of the recent alluvial soils also sets certain limits on their utilization. The highest natural levees and point-bar formations, flooded only during the wettest years, are desirable for crops such as manioc which require a long maturation period between planting and harvesting. Such rarely flooded lands will be put to most use.

The annual cycle of flooding also produces a bonus of a particular kind of agricultural land. The difference between flood stage and low water is far more dramatic on the tributaries of the Amazon than on the Amazon itself. The tributaries are long and the incidence of heaviest rains varies markedly from one watershed to another, so that each of the tributaries dumps the crest of its flood into the Amazon at a different time, all of which tends to lower the crest of the flood in the Amazon and to extend the period of high water over a longer span of time.

On the major tributaries, such as the Ucayali, the difference between high and low water may be as much as 10 to 18 metres. The crest of the flood passes rapidly, however, and much of the river bed is dry for the greater part of the year. Vast flats of silty soils are exposed in the river beds, and are available as farm lands without the work of clearing the forests. Such lands are ideal for any crop with a short maturation period and a preference for light sandy soils. Peanuts are ideal in such situations, and thousands of acres of river bed are planted with these even before the river has completely subsided. Since the recent introduction of rice, it has also been cultivated extensively on such locations.

Other pockets of recent alluvial land are found to the west of the Amazon Basin proper along the upper reaches of various tributaries of the Amazon in valleys enclosed by the more easterly ranges of the Andes. Some, such as the valley of the Huallaga below Tingo María and the Chanchamayo Basin, are less than 700 metres above sea level and are heavily watered. These support dense tropical rain-forest when not cultivated. Others, such as the Huánuco Basin on the upper Huallaga in Peru and the Cochabamba Basin in Bolivia, lie considerably higher, between 2,000 and 3,000 metres. These latter basins are so thoroughly in the rain-shadow of the eastern ranges of the Andes, that they receive little rainfall and are watered mainly by the rivers which run through them. The archaeological record indicates that the unleached soils of these basins have been exploited for a very long time.

Plate 19

Cultural Development

There is one further area of rapidly accumulating alluvial deposits which lies within the Amazon and which differs somewhat in character from the limited strips of soils within the flood plains. This is the expanse of lowlands called the Llanos de Mojos, in north-eastern Bolivia. Here the run-off from the north-eastern flank of the Bolivian Andes is partially blocked and deflected to the north by the western extension of the Brazilian Highlands. This partial damming of the floodwaters means that their load of silt is dropped more quickly than is the case with most Amazonian tributaries, so that the whole Llanos can be considered as a vast alluvial fan along the north-eastern foot of the Bolivian Andes. The whole of the Llanos de Mojos is subjected to shallow flooding during the rainy season, December to April, and a huge inland sea is produced. As the rainfall on the eastern slopes of the Andes decreases, the rivers contract to within their beds and the flat lands between the rivers become extremely dry. As was noted earlier, this annual alternation between complete inundation and total drought maintains a cover of tall grasses over most of the Llanos, with forest being confined to mounds of human origin and the natural levees along the stream courses. The potential fertility of these recent alluvial soils and their considerable extent should be noted, though they presented formidable obstacles to the Pre-Columbian farmer, and are not now used for agricultural purposes. Before these lands could be brought under cultivation, the heavy sods resulting from the grass cover had to be broken, and the annual fluctuation between total immersion and total aridity had to be controlled or at least mitigated.

The Llanos de Orinoco lies outside the Amazon Basin, but deserves mention because of the way it duplicates the soil conditions of the Bolivian Llanos, and because the Pre-Columbian cultures of this area were clearly related to those of the Amazon Basin. Here several seasonally flooding rivers draining the south-eastern slope of the Venezuelan and Colombian Andes are partially dammed by the Guiana Highlands and again a huge nearly level, alluvial fan has built up, which is under water for four months of the year and bone dry at the height of the intervening dry season. This, once again, results in high grasslands, offering the same opportunities and challenges to the Pre-Columbian agronomists. The major difference between the two Llamos is in the time of the flooding, which on the Llanos de Orinoco occurs from June to September.

So much for the actively accumulating, alluvial soils in the Amazon Basin; it is now necessary to examine the soils developing on the adjacent uplands which are undergoing varying degrees of dissection and erosion.

As might be expected, the hard rocks of the Guiana Highlands and the Brazilian Highlands develop only thin soil covers at a very slow rate. The chemical composition of these rocks is such that they weather mainly to pure silicon sands, rather than to soils with an appreciable nutritive content. Some geographers have dismissed these soils as completely without agricultural value. There may be limited exceptions to that generalization, but most of the Indian groups living on the two highlands confined their farming to the narrow strips of alluvial soils along the flood plains of the major rivers. These alluvia of the black-water rivers are far less extensive and of much lower fertility than those of the white-water rivers.

Along the base of the Peruvian Andes and extending out for a considerable distance into the floor of the Amazon Basin are exposures of more recent sedimentary rocks and those of volcanic origin. The amount and quality of the soils developing in these areas depends on the angle of the surface and the nature of the rocks weathering to produce soil. Where the slope is not great and the underlying mother-material is limestone or recently extruded lava, soils of high fertility will result. The extent and nature of the various kinds of soils along the Andean foothills needs more study. Even on the very steep slopes of the eastern face of the Andes a considerable build-up of soil and humus is facilitated by the dense and matted *ceja* vegetation. Man's ability to farm these slopes depends on his capacity to control erosion when this has been cleared.

The remaining group of soils comprises those developing on the vast area of old alluvial deposits which cover ninety per cent of the Amazon Basin. Where the situation has not been recently modified by man, these soils support an exuberant growth of tropical rain-forest. Once cleared they will support moderately productive agriculture for a short period of time, but if they are not permitted to return to jungle their quality deteriorates rapidly. It is characteristic of these soils that they are intensively leached. The heavy rains which percolate through them tend to remove all soluble materials from the upper layers of the soils and deposit them in the lower levels as hard beds or pans. Since erosion proceeds very slowly on these surfaces, fresh materials which might weather to form less mature and more fertile soils are not readily exposed, and leaching is the predominant process affecting the character of the soils.

Though the tropical forest produces quantities of litter, bacterial action and the swarms of ants which roam the floor of the forest rapidly reduce the organic materials lying there and humus formation is minimal. Once the forest is removed, the thin layer of humus is quickly depleted under cultivation.

A number of trees and vines of the Amazon Basin have a tendency to concentrate silicon in their leaves, stems, and bark. Thus the silica constituent in the soils is progressively removed and what remains is altered in the direction of pure metallic oxides. It is mainly iron oxides that are dissolved near the surface and re-deposited a foot or more below as ironpans. All these processes work to produce the kind of heavy, infertile, red clays known as laterites, and the progressive laterization of the soils is accelerated when the forest is cleared for agriculture, exposing the surface to full sunlight and the full force of the tropical rains. All agronomists who have considered the subject have agreed that these soils present a bleak prospect for continued agricultural use. They can, however, be used effectively in swidden (slash-and-burn) agriculture if the forest is allowed to regenerate itself between each period of cultivation. During the first year after these soils have been cleared of their cover of jungle, and the ash of the burned vegetation has been added, they will yield a crop of maize, which, while not admirable in terms of maize production in the Midwest of the United States, is significant in terms of subsistence agriculture. In a year or two the yield has greatly decreased; but fertility can be prolonged if the crop used is manioc, which is far less demanding on all of the nutritive elements in the soil.

The tropical forest farmer living on the bluff of old alluvium adjacent to the active flood plain, could simultaneously farm the limited but excellent recent alluvial soils in an intensive and continuous manner and the poor but essentially unlimited soils of the old alluvial deposits using slash-and-burn agriculture, with a long fallow period for any particular plot. The varying requirements of the wide range of cultigens at his disposal could be related effectively to the different soils available, maximizing productivity. Whenever one is discussing the carrying capacity of the soils of the Amazon Basin, one should remember that for a very long time the staple has been manioc, one of the most productive and least demanding crops ever developed by man.

CHAPTER III

Tropical Forest Culture

THE WAY OF LIFE of the earliest-known Indians of the Upper Amazon Basin followed a cultural pattern designated Tropical Forest Culture. There is at the present time little to suggest that the region was previously occupied by peoples other than these. Likewise I find little convincing evidence that the Amazon Basin was extensively invaded by peoples from other areas and of cultural patterns differing appreciably from Tropical Forest Culture. From before 2000 BC till AD 1500 the culture history of the Upper Amazon Basin is best understood in terms of the working-out of the economic and demographic potential of the Tropical Forest cultural pattern or tradition.

THE DEFINITION OF TROPICAL FOREST CULTURE

It has become fashionable among writers on South American culture history to contrast the way of life of the Indians of the Amazon Basin with that of the Pre-Columbian inhabitants of the Caribbean Coast of South America. At the time of the first Spanish explorers, certain features pointing to complex culture were widespread among the Circum-Caribbean groups. Among the traits frequently cited are: large communities (1,000 people or more); chiefs with more than nominal authority; chiefs whose authority extended beyond the face-to-face community; developed patterns of warfare; a religious system with a highly conceptualized hierarchy of deities; the representation of deities through carved wood or stone idols; special temple structures to house such idols; a professional priesthood to maintain the temples and to perform religious ceremonies. All these characteristics have been taken to be representative of a cultural tradition designated 'Circum-Caribbean' and of an evolutionary level of culture, the 'Circum-Caribbean level', intermediate between the high civilizations of the Andean and Mesoamerican zones and the simple level of cultural development characteristic of the surviving tribes of the Amazon Basin.

As the concept of a Circum-Caribbean level of culture became crystallized, that of a Tropical Forest level of culture gradually sharpened as a contrastive, taxonomic unit. It was defined mainly in negative terms, and societies were so classified if they lacked all of the features of cultural complexity mentioned above. Groups such as the surviving Wai Wai living on the infertile Guiana Highlands were taken as typical representatives of Tropical Forest Culture, and it was argued that such small and simple social units as the Wai Wai were the only kind of social unit which could develop in the harsh environment of the Amazon Basin.

Once such a theory of extreme environmental determinism was formulated, it was an easy further step to conclude that any group in the Amazon Basin which exhibited any of the diagnostic features of the Circum-Caribbean level must of necessity have migrated there from outside or have been strongly influenced by adjacent areas of high civilization. Thus, the occurrence of powerful chiefs, social classes, temples, idols, and a priesthood in the Llanos de Mojos in Bolivia was taken as an example of late influence from the Andean area; while the clear archaeological evidence for large and complex social units on Marajó Island at the mouth of the Amazon was interpreted in terms of a migration from the highlands of the Northern Andes, even though no closely related culture has ever been found in the highlands there.

I do not accept the view postulated by certain other scholars that there was a sharp contrast in cultural level between the Circum-Caribbean peoples and the Tropical Forest peoples. Only by comparing the flourishing sixteenth-century inhabitants of the Circum-Caribbean area with the marginal and shattered tribes now surviving in the Amazon Basin does this contrast become evident. Those who make a point of it neglect the accounts of the earliest European explorers in the Amazon Basin who consistently noted dense populations, extensive political units, powerful chiefs or kings, priests, temples, and idols along the mainstream of the Amazon from its inception near Nauta to its mouth. These long-vanished riverine people, who were the most numerous inhabitants of the Amazon Basin around AD 1500, have the best claim to be regarded as typical representatives of Tropical Forest Culture; but it was the riverine peoples who were first destroyed by the combined effects of European diseases, missionization, and the slave trade.

Since there were vast differences in the level of cultural complexity between the riverine groups and the groups inhabiting the interfluvial uplands, Tropical Forest Culture must be defined in terms of shared cultural elements rather than as a uniform level of cultural achievement. The most crucial part of this shared cultural content lies in the sphere of economics. Tropical Forest Culture is a way of life supported by intensive root-crop agriculture. Wherever possible, there is a maximum exploitation of the food resources of the rivers, lakes, and coasts; while the hunting of land mammals and birds in the jungles away back from the major bodies of water was definitely of secondary importance.

THE NATURE OF THE TROPICAL FOREST AGRICULTURAL SYSTEM

Our understanding of the age and origin of Tropical Forest Culture is inextricably bound up with our understanding of the age and origin of the major cultivated plants which were basic to the agricultural system. It must be admitted that the amount of evidence available on these questions is small. The most reliable kinds of data for demonstrating the presence of a cultivated plant in an ancient context are the actual remains of the plant itself. Such remains are common from archaeological sites in the arid parts of the world and are especially common in dry cave sites. Excavations in the dry refuse of sites along the coast of Peru and in dry caves in various parts of Mexico have yielded considerable direct evidence concerning the presence of particular crops. The Upper Amazon Basin is too humid to permit the preservation of vegetable remains in open sites; and while solution caverns are common in the beds of limestone along the foot-hills of the Andes, such caves are anything but dry.

The great majority of the more important food crops in the Amazon Basin are root crops. By root crops I mean any plant in which the edible section develops under the ground, whether it be from a tuber, a rhizome, or an actual root. The standard way of reproducing such plants is by planting cuttings from the stem tuber or root. The important root crops of South America have been under cultivation so long and have been so modified as the result of selective propagation, that they have lost the power to set seed. They can only be maintained by vegetative reproduction and are dependent on man for their survival. In these plants the flowering and seed-producing organs have become so degenerate, that they can be expected to leave little trace in the pollen record.

In areas where the edible parts of the major staples are small, hard seeds, the seeds or their equally identifiable chaff frequently leave indelible casts in the moist clay of unfinished pots. The edible parts of the South American root crops are large and soft, and thus unlikely to leave such traces. As a result of all these factors, evidence concerning the antiquity and point of origin of the various major crops supporting Tropical Forest Culture is mainly indirect.

Manioc was the most important staple in the Tropical Forest agricultural system. *Manihot utilisima* is a leggy bush with large, five-lobed, palmate leaves of a blue-green colour. It usually ranges from 5 to 8 feet in height. It is a member of the *Euphorbiaceae*, a family of plants of pan-Tropical distribution, mostly associated with semi-arid to arid environments; but the particular genus, *Manihot*, is confined to the New World, and is represented by a number of wild species ranging from Lower California to northern Argentina. The cultivated species has been so thoroughly modified by selective propagation, that its relationship to any one known wild species of *Manihot* is difficult to establish. Genetic studies, which might facilitate such a decision, have not progressed to the level of work on other important New World cultigens such as maize and cotton. The great cultural geographer, Carl O. Sauer, has always favoured some area in northern South America where large riverine flood plains, supporting tropical forest, abut on areas of relatively arid savannah. As we will see, the archaeological record by no means negates such an assumption.

As was indicated earlier, manioc is one of the most efficient food crops ever developed by man. In terms of calories per acre, its only peers are rice and the banana. Like a number of other important New World cultigens, such as maize and the white potato, it has become widespread in the Old World in Post-Columbian times, and is now the staple diet in much of Tropical Africa, and an important crop in parts of South East Asia and Indonesia. It has never held such a place in temperate climates, since it combines a long growing season (nearly a year from planting to harvest) with a complete intolerance of frost.

Though a most efficient food-producer, manioc does not yield a balanced diet: its calorie content resides almost entirely in carbohydrates. Where a manioc-based diet is not supplemented with animal protein or large quantities of high-quality vegetable protein, the protein deficiency disease, kwashiorkor (red baby), will be common and a major source of child mortality.

It has been customary to divide cultivated manioc into two basic kinds, the bitter and the sweet. In the past the two groups have even been classified as two distinct species, a position which is unjustified on genetic grounds. There can now be no doubt that the bitter group and the sweet group of manioc were both derived from the same wild ancestor and were developed and differentiated through selective propagation so as to be used for different culinary purposes. All manioc contains in its tissue a glucoside which, on exposure to air, breaks down to form, among other chemicals, a considerable quantity of HCN. In the sweet variety this glucoside is concentrated in the skin and bark, while in the bitter variety an appreciable quantity is found throughout the enlarged, starchy root stock, which is the valuable portion of the plant. The situation is actually far more complex than a binary distinction would suggest, since most Indian groups maintain a number of manioc varieties which differ in starch quality, colour, flavour, and length of time for maturation. These varieties frequently cross-cut the basic bitter-sweet dichotomy. In any particular strain of manioc, the amount and distribution of the glucoside in the plant and its edible root stock depends on a number of non-genetic factors, such as the age of the root stock and the weather that prevailed while it was developing, as well as on the ancestry of the strain.

There has been considerable speculation, much of it fanciful, about the historical relationship between the two strains of manioc. Among the ideas mooted are: that bitter manioc was the more primitive form and sweet manioc was selectively modified from it as an improvement; that bitter manioc was originally used as a fish poison—only later was it discovered that the pulpy mass, out of which the poisonous juice has been extracted, was edible; and that the bitter form is maintained because the glucoside acts as an effective deterrent to insects and wild animals such as peccaries and deer, which would otherwise make depredations on the manioc plantations.

Manioc juice does not make an effective fish poison since the HCN is slow in developing; and even though Prussic acid is extremely poisonous, it dissipates so rapidly as to be impracticable in this role. For the same reasons the unoxidized glucosides in bitter manioc fail to deter either insects or peccaries. Finally, all available evidence indicates that the bitter manioc was developed as an *improvement* on the sweet. Plants within the sweet group occasionally flower and produce viable seed while plants in the bitter group never do so, a difference which clearly indicates that the latter group is more modified genetically from the wild ancestor. The sweet group has a far wider distribution than the bitter, suggesting that its dispersal started sooner.

Because the bitter manioc takes far longer to process, and because it is potentially poisonous to man, it might be assumed that the sweet variety is preferable. A glance at the distinct culinary functions of the two groups shows why this is a mistake. Sweet manioc is used as a pot vegetable, simply peeled and then either boiled or baked. It is also reduced to a mash for the production of beer. The sweet manioc root stock does not keep and must be used within a few days after it has been dug from the ground.

The bitter group is used for the production of large discs of flat, unleavened bread and a 'flour' consisting of hard, globular pellets about 2 mm. in diameter. While raw, bitter manioc root stocks keep no better than sweet root stocks, the bread and flour produced by reducing it keep indefinitely and can be used to build up a large economic surplus.

The complicated procedures for processing bitter manioc, as well as the equipment used, are standardized over most of the range where it is important. These patterns are of interest to the archaeologist; for while manioc itself has no hard parts to be preserved in ancient middens, some of the highly specific equipment used in reducing has come down to us. The distribution of bitter manioc in time and space can thus be inferred from the archaeological record.

The bitter manioc was first peeled with a knife of shell or cane. A specialized grating board carved from a single piece of hardwood was used to reduce the peeled stock to pulp. Typically this grater consisted of a stool-like seat attached to a broad, longitudinally concave, rectangular grating surface. The teeth of the grater were set into the wood and fixed with a resin glue. In some cases the teeth were thorns or bone splinters (which are not preserved in archaeological deposits), but in many instances microblades of quartz or flint were used instead. Where quantities of microblades of exotic raw materials are found in sites on the alluvial plains of Tropical South America, one can be reasonably certain that the carved wooden grater boards were used, and that bitter manioc was the staple food.

Once reduced to a pulp, the manioc was placed in a remarkable press, usually known by its Tupían name *típití*. The *típití* is a long tube of twilled basketry which is open at its upper, and closed at its lower end. Once the press was filled with the wet pulp, it was forcibly elongated, thus exerting tremendous lateral pressure on the contents and causing the juice to be expelled. (A large-mouthed pot with broadly flaring rim was placed beneath to catch as much of the juice as possible. While the *típití* is not preserved in archaeological deposits the juice-catching pot, frequently called a buck pot, being of a highly specific form, can usually be recognized.

Fig. 18 k, l

Once the poisonous juices have been expressed, the pulp is placed on a broad, circular griddle of pottery which is typically supported over the fire by three cylindrical fire-dogs of fired clay. If the pulp is first compacted into a thin disc and turned only occasionally, rounds of unleavened bread are the result. If the pulp is put into the vessel as a loose mass and stirred continuously, small, hard pellets of flour are obtained. Fragments of both the fire-dogs and the large ceramic griddles usually known as comals are found in archaeological contexts and where at all common, fragments of the latter offer positive evidence that bitter manioc was the mainstay of the economy.

Plate 68

Figs. 15 g, 23 i, 24 f, 26 b

A finer flour could be obtained by soaking the pulp in water so that pure starch sank to the bottom and all of the fibrous material could be removed. This pure manioc starch was then heated on the griddle and dried to small pellets. The tapioca of commerce, the only form of manioc to be much used in temperate areas, is the result.

The juice expressed by the *tipití* is also used. It is thickened by long simmering over a slow fire. As the juice is transformed into a thick, highly flavoured syrup, all the HCN is either evaporated or converted to sugars. This syrup is the base of the standard main course, the pepper-pot, a stew to which vegetables (sweet potato, sweet manioc, cara, xanthosoma) are added with whatever meat or fish happens to be available.

The culturally significant difference between bitter manioc and sweet manioc does not consist in the presence of the glucoside in the root stock, but in the fact that not only is there more starch in the former than in the latter but this starch is of a quality more suitable to the production of flour and bread. It is likely that the increase in the glucoside in bitter manioc and the change in the quality and quantity of starch are brought about by the same mutation, though chemical and genetic studies should be made to verify this.

Bitter manioc is raised only where there is a reason to build up an economic surplus. Where maize is grown extensively, it typically replaces bitter manioc in this function, since maize can be prepared for long-term storage with a far smaller expenditure of labour. The presence of bitter manioc thus has a direct bearing on the complexity of the society involved; societies raising bitter manioc tend on the average to have a more extensive and complex network of social interaction than those relying mainly on sweet manioc and lacking storage facilities. In its simplest form this pattern of building an economic surplus may mean nothing more than the laying-up of a large supply of food to be consumed in a grand, inter-village fiesta. Of more interest to the archaeologist are the extensive networks of trade which were characteristic of the Amazon Basin and adjacent areas of Guiana. A high degree of craft specialization was typical, with one tribe manufacturing a surplus of canoes, and others concentrating on the production of grater boards, basketry, and pottery respectively. These commercial exchanges usually cut across major linguistic and tribal boundaries, and rested on the ability of the riverine groups to produce an excess quantity of foodstuffs. Manioc, in the form of flour and bread, was the crucial item of commerce in these systems and retained that place in Post-Columbian trade between Indian and mestizo populations.

There were other ways in which the food surplus made possible by manioc affected the social and political patterns of Tropical Forest peoples. It enabled warlike tribes such as the Mundurucú to keep armies, consisting of a large percentage of their adult male populations, in the field for a year or more, and to annihilate their enemies.

Another concomitant of manioc agriculture was so uniform among peoples of Tropical Forest Culture and so significant to the whole web of their social life that it deserves mention here. Manioc, either bitter or sweet, was the major ingredient from which beer was brewed, and beer was the most important lubricant for the larger patterns of interaction. The crucial mechanism by which one Tropical Forest village could achieve or maintain a position that would impress its neighbours was to give a fiesta which lasted longer, expended more beer, and unleashed more drunken brawls than any other fiesta in memory. The drunken brawls during these fiestas afforded a culturally sanctioned opportunity for discharging all the tensions and inter-personal aggression which had built up in the course of day-to-day living. In its form and functions the Tropical Forest fiesta pattern was not unlike that of the modern cocktail party, but it lasted far longer and, on the average, more crockery and heads got broken.

The uniformity of Tropical Forest fiesta patterns suggests that they are ancient in the area and that an early expansion of Tropical Forest peoples caused them to spread. The archaeological record tends to support this assumption. Some of the more primitive

Tropical Forest groups do their brewing in wooden troughs or old canoes, but those groups with any sophistication in material culture carry on the fermentation process in huge ceramic vessels. On surveying the average size of each of the functional classes of pottery used by the various surviving Tropical Forest groups, one is led to the conclusion that a vessel with a maximum diameter of more than 40 cm. is very likely to be a fermentation vessel. The presence of such large containers in an archaeological deposit can be taken as evidence that beer was present and that the whole fiesta pattern was in full swing.

Direct proof of the antiquity of manioc cultivation comes only from Coastal Peru and from Mesoamerica. Lanning concludes that sweet manioc was apparently absent in the ultimate, pre-ceramic agricultural villages but was a widespread cultigen among the earliest sites on the Coast having a developed ceramic tradition. Translated into absolute chronology this means that sweet manioc was widespread in Peru by 1000 to 1200 BC. It is clear that manioc was *not* developed on the Coast of Peru, but was introduced as a fully modified and efficient cultigen which had already reached its modern level of productivity. Bitter manioc never became important on the Coast of Peru, probably because maize was introduced at about the same time and offered a basis for building an economic surplus requiring less intensive labour.

In Mesoamerica the most important evidence on the early use of cultivated manioc as a food comes from the Tehuacán Basin in the Mexican State of Puebla. Here the human faeces from the various dry caves contained traces of manioc starch indicating that from Santa Maria times on (1000–200 BC), manioc was a significant though never dominant part of the diet. It is interesting that direct evidence of manioc in the Tehuacán Basin was confined to human faeces and that there were no stems, leaves, or peelings of root-stocks in the copious plant remains recovered from the bone-dry caves. One would expect such remains if manioc were being grown or processed there. The fact that much of the Tehuacán Basin is annually subjected to freezing temperatures makes it improbable that manioc was grown locally. It would appear that its inhabitants were receiving manioc in an already processed form. We can conclude that by 500 BC some lowland area adjacent to the Tehuacán Basin was growing and processing bitter manioc for the purposes of trade.

The indirect evidence bearing on the intensive use of bitter manioc is more widespread. Rancho Peludo in the extreme north-west of Venezuela is a crude ceramic complex with a limited range of decorative techniques. Griddles are common. A date of around 2700 BC has been claimed for this material, but there is some question as to the exact applicability of the relevant C14 assay. Rancho Peludo is the most primitive cultural complex in which bitter manioc griddles occur, and it may well turn out to be the oldest yet known.

Griddles and fire-dogs are a significant part of the Saladero complex which occupied the flood plain of the Lower Orinoco by 1000 BC. In the Barrancas complex which replaces the Saladero complex by 800 BC, griddles are far more common; also, huge urns with constricted necks are present, showing that beer was now an important part of the diet and ceremonial life. The earliest agricultural people to colonize the Antilles left the mainland of Venezuela before the time of Christ and had bitter manioc as their staple. In the flood plains of the major rivers in northern Colombia several of the earliest known ceramic complexes show a plethora of griddles, suggesting dependence on bitter manioc. The Malambo occupation on the Lower Magdalena probably started by 1100 BC, according to available C14 assays. The occupation on the Lower Sinú called Momíl Ia is not dated by C14, but the depth of cultural deposit at the Momíl site and the marked cultural difference between each of the four discrete occupations which make up the Momíl I midden suggest that Momíl Ia began well back in the second millennium BC.

Tropical Forest Culture

All the available evidence indicates that manioc is a very ancient crop in the tropical lowlands of the New World. The earliest testimony of its cultivation comes from the flood plains of the various major rivers in northern South America, where it would appear that during the second millennium BC bitter manioc was already the staple of a number of ethnic groups with markedly different ceramic traditions. It should be emphasized that by this time we are dealing with the most highly developed form of the cultigen and that there must have been a long period of prior cultivation when manioc was being modified from its wild ancestor into a highly productive crop. The new and copious information on plant domestication in Mesoamerica and the Middle East of the Old World suggests that it takes 3,000 to 4,000 years of selective propagation for a wild plant, viable without man's intervention but an inefficient food producer, to assume a form which is no longer viable without man's constant intervention but is a highly efficient food-producer. The modification of bitter manioc from its wild ancestor is extreme. If we should ever be lucky enough to find direct evidence on the beginnings of manioc cultivation, such evidence ought to date from around 5000 to 7000 BC.

The other important root crops of the Tropical Forest agricultural system included: the sweet potato; *Xanthosoma*; the New World yam called *cara*; *achira*; arrowroot; and *jíquima*. Available evidence suggests that all were brought under cultivation at a relatively early time in the humid lowlands to the east of the Andes. The high antiquity of both the sweet potato and *achira* is fully demonstrated, since both had been introduced to the Coast of Peru as fully developed cultigens by 2000 BC.

Two other major crops, the pineapple and the peach palm, were anciently developed as part of the Tropical Forest system of agriculture, and though not root crops, have been so modified by selection that they no longer set viable seed and must be propagated by cuttings. The peach palm is the more important from the dietary standpoint, and very early was spread throughout Central America. Botanical evidence indicates that the Ucayali Basin was the most likely point of domestication.

Of the seed crops which were certainly first domesticated in the Tropical Lowlands of South America, the peanut is the most important as a food. This aberrant legume has its only close relatives on the Brazilian Highlands and in other semi-arid regions stretching south-west to the lowland of north-western Argentina. It is clear that the peanut was domesticated within that zone. Its domestication and improvement is very ancient, since fully evolved cultivated strains were introduced into the South Coast of Peru well back in the second millennium BC. Interestingly enough they occur with the first ceramic complex known from the South Coast, Hacha, which has a number of peculiarities more reminiscent of the earliest Tropical Forest ceramics than of the other early pottery styles of Coastal and Highland Peru. Of all of the cultigens which are certainly an ancient part of the Tropical Forest pattern of agriculture, peanuts and the peach palm are the only foods which assay high in fats and high quality protein, and the peanut comes close to being the most dietetically desirable plant ever developed by man.

Other crops which were probably an ancient part of the Tropical Forest agricultural system include various chili peppers of the genus Capsicum, the large seeded Lima bean, the jack bean, the bottle gourd, cotton, and a wide range of fruit trees. The chili peppers and the Lima bean are of interest in that they were introduced into Coastal Peru as developed cultigens well before 2000 BC, again arguing strongly for the priority of developed agriculture in the tropical forest over developed agricultural systems on the Coast of Peru.

Maize, the various strains of the common bean *Phaseolus vulgaris,* and some squashes were probably first developed in Mesoamerica and were spread to South America at a later date. Most Tropical Forest groups received these crops before the time

Tropical Forest Culture

of Christ, but this Mexican pattern never reached the importance in the tropical forest that it had attained in Mesoamerica or the coast of Peru. Nowhere in the Amazon Basin does one find the multiplicity of maize varieties for specific culinary purposes so characteristic of both Mesoamerica and the Central Andes, and only in the tropical lowlands of northern Colombia can one trace the replacement of bitter manioc by maize as the basis for building up an economic surplus.

To understand the tremendous variety of plants utilized by the peoples of Tropical Forest Culture, one should have some idea of how they laid out their cultivated lands. The *chacras* are typically at a considerable distance from the house. These large, rectangular plots are planted in solid stands of one or two staples such as manioc, maize, or, more recently, cooking bananas. The area adjacent to the cleared courtyard of each house is also under intensive cultivation. The trees which partially shade the house are not a random assortment of tropical forest flora but are carefully selected, and in many cases transplanted, useful species. Invariably one finds the tree calabash, *Crescentia cujete*, source of containers, masks, and potting tools; one finds a bewildering array of fruit trees, including the *inga*, the cashew, the avocado, the papaya, and the *zapote*.

The cultivated land immediately adjacent to the house contains an equally diverse mixture of bushes also carefully selected for maximum utility. Here one finds the two most important dye plants: the dark reddish-brown *achiote, Bixa orellana*; and the nearly indelible blue-black paint, *Genipa americana*, which is important for face decoration. Also present are the various kinds of red peppers, the capsicums, important as condiments; and it is here that the large bushes of the perennial cotton, *Gossypium barbadense*, are grown.

Plate 64

Near ground level one finds a still more heterogeneous medley of small herbs and grass. Thirty or forty species may be represented each by only a plant or two. The plants in the herb gardens are carefully weeded, and each species has its own name and particular use. Many are used as perfumes, some for specialized medicinal purposes, others in the course of training for craft specialities, and still others for disciplinary functions. It is here, also, that one finds the fish poisons so important for a maximum utilization of the riverine resources of the Amazon Basin.

The peoples of Tropical Forest Culture were much given to the use of narcotic and hallucinogenic drugs. Some of these, such as the infusions derived from vines in the genus *Banisteriopsis* and the snuffs derived from trees in the genus *Piptadenia*, involved no attempt to bring the wild source under cultivation. Others, such as plants in the genus *Datura*, were in a state of semi-domestication. Coca, the source of cocaine was domesticated in the Upper Amazon, and large areas of the moist eastern slopes of the Andes are still devoted to its cultivation. It is noteworthy that both species of cultivated tobacco, which by the time of Columbus had spread even beyond the limits of food crop cultivation in the New World, had their probable origin in the Upper Amazon.

The distributional evidence suggests that there was no single point of origin for the Tropical Forest system of agriculture. Manioc and the sweet potato were most likely first domesticated north of the Amazon while the peanut was clearly first domesticated south of it. So it is better to postulate a series of widely dispersed populations, each experimenting with the food potential of a range of the local flora and each ultimately contributing one efficient cultigen or more to the pool of crops which ultimately became the Tropical Forest agricultural system. Such a model is similar to the model demonstrated by MacNeish for the origins of the Mesoamerican agricultural system.

TECHNOLOGICAL ASPECTS OF TROPICAL FOREST CULTURE

Many of the basic manufacturing processes and tool types are so uniform and so widespread among Tropical Forest groups that

Tropical Forest Culture

one suspects most material aspects of Tropical Forest Culture were developed very early and spread with the earliest waves of outward migration. It is worth reviewing the tools, processes, and range of materials used in order to remind ourselves how little of the total material culture is likely to be preserved in the wet, thoroughly leached middens of the Amazon Basin.

Both the bow and arrow and the *atlatl* were in use in the Upper Amazon Basin, but the bow and arrow (which is still used) was the more widespread weapon for hunting and for warfare. The bow, up to 2 metres long, was typically made of a single piece of palm wood. Arrow shafts were of cane in some instances with a carved wooden foreshaft. Projectile points for both spears and arrows were invariably of perishable material and their forms were highly standarized throughout the Tropical Forest zone. Besides the bow and arrow, the most formidable weapon was the *macana* or sword club. Made of heavy hardwood and most frequently furnished with two sharp cutting edges, these weapons were often beautifully decorated, and the men carried them to a fiesta as a part of their finery. Effective watercraft were the first prerequisite for an efficient exploitation of riverine resources and among all the tribes by the major waterways large, well made dugout canoes provided the typical means for fishing as well as affording the only mode for long distance transportation. Some of the marginal tribes along the smaller tributaries fashioned canoes from a single piece of shaped bark.

The tools used for grinding food were also largely impermanent. A cylindrical mortar of hardwood and a hardwood pestle was used for mashing various foodstuffs, while the rocker mortar was used for grinding harder grains such as maize. The stone rocker pestles, or *manos*, are occasionally preserved in archaeological sites but more frequently, after they had been broken, the fragments were used as whetstones until completely expended.

Plate 63

The wood-working tools used by the Tropical Forest peoples were of a simple nature and soon perished in the acid soils of their

The Upper Amazon

habitat. Heavier cutting and incising was done with the incisor of one of the large rodents hafted to a stick. Where more precision was necessary the lower jaw of a pirañha fish was used. Knives for various purposes were made of split toucan beaks, split peccary teeth, and ground bamboo. The latter were often employed for various forms of genital mutilation during puberty ceremonies.

We have made the assumption that cotton textiles were important in the tropical forest from a very early time, but the textiles themselves are perishable and no elements of the loom are likely to survive. The only direct evidence of an elaboration of the textile industry comes in the form of ceramic spindle whorls used in the production of the yarns.

Basketry was well developed in the Amazon Basin, with simple twills and various open, hexagonal weaves favoured. Palm leaves and split cane were the most frequently used materials, but direct evidence as to the ancient use of basketry and matting is rare and comes only in the form of impressions on the bottoms of pots and griddles.

The only artifacts besides ceramics which occur with any degree of frequency in Tropical Forest middens are stone axe-heads. Since the material for these, usually a volcanic rock such as andesite, had to be imported from a considerable distance outside the alluvial flood plains, axes were at a premium and were used right down to the nub through continual re-sharpening. Even the fragments were further employed as whetstones. The typical stone axe of the Upper Amazon Basin is that known as the T-shaped or 'Inca' axe. The butt is flat or concave and was fastened to the shaft of the axe handle. The two ears projecting laterally from the butt were used to bind the axe-head to the shaft. Within this general pattern there is considerable variation, and it is probable that a chronology of axe forms can be worked out when there is more material available. This form was transferred to cast bronze in late prehistoric times. It is certain

Fig. 37

Fig. 48

that the stone axes were used mainly for clearing agricultural land, and the presence of a reasonable number of axe fragments in a site is a good indication that agriculture was economically significant.

Of all the complex and specialized material culture which the Tropical Forest peoples had developed to cope with their difficult environment only a few axe fragments and a vast mass of smashed pottery remain. The archaeologist has been justly criticized for his preoccupation with pottery, but in the Amazon Basin the minutiae of ceramic style must carry the full burden of our attempts to study old population movements, old trade routes, and the boundaries of now extinct political units.

THE ORIGIN OF TROPICAL FOREST CULTURE

Ignoring the presently insoluble problem of the degree to which Old World root-crop agriculturalists may have influenced or triggered-off the development of the Tropical Forest cultural tradition in the New World, we will examine the more profitable question as to whether any known archaeological sites in South America cast light on the transition from hunting, gathering and/or shell-fish collecting to intensive root-crop agriculture. It has been suggested, or at least implied, that Tropical Forest Culture most likely evolved among the small communities of coastal shell-fish collectors who appeared along most of the favourable stretches of ocean shore in the immediate post-Pleistocene. Such groups have been called variously Archaic or Meso-Indian. It will be seen that the archaeological evidence to date does *not* favour such a derivation.

The entire eastern coast of Brazil from Recife to the border with Uruguay can be excluded as a possible hearth for Tropical Forest Culture. The whole pattern of Tropical Forest root-crop agriculture is late there and in most instances the spread of the pattern was the result of the expansion of the Tupí-speaking Tupinamba. Until the time of the first European contacts enclaves of non-agricultural peoples remained who subsisted by shell-fish collecting, hunting of small game and collecting such wild foods as palm nuts and Brazil nuts.

Until more archaeological work is carried out there, the Coast of Brazil from Recife to the mouth of the Amazon can offer no evidence relevant to our question. The coast of Brazilian, Dutch and French Guiana has yielded considerable evidence concerning the later development of Tropical Forest Culture but none concerning its origins. For north-western Guyana there is detailed documentation of the displacement of the peoples of the Archaic-type Alaka Culture by colonists with a fully developed Tropical Forest cultural pattern in the Barrancoid tradition. There is no doubt that the Tropical Forest intruders moved onto the Guiana Coast from the flood plain of the Lower Orinoco.

Cruxent and Rouse have proved conclusively that most of the Coast of Venezuela continued to be occupied by peoples of Archaic culture relying on fishing and shell-fish collecting and lacking ceramics long after the flood plain of the Orinoco had been occupied by peoples with developed Tropical Forest Culture and with several distinct ceramic and artistic traditions.

The broad expanse of alluvial land around Lake Maracaibo in north-western Venezuela is, from the ecological point of view, a plausible place to look for the beginning of Tropical Forest Culture, but the area is far from well known archaeologically. We have already mentioned that one of the earliest occurrences of bitter manioc griddles is in the Rancho Peludo Complex from slightly to the north of the Maracaibo Basin. It is a moot point whether the Maracaibo Basin should be considered a coastal or lacustrine environment: it certainly differs radically from the coasts that characterize Brazil, the Guianas, Colombia and most of Venezuela.

The Caribbean Coast of Colombia is particularly relevant here. The oldest securely dated pottery in the New World comes from the shell midden of Puerto Hormiga near Cartagena.

Though ceramic decoration is rare, what is present is sometimes elaborate and well executed. The technology suggests that the Puerto Hormiga ceramic complex (*c.* 3000 B C) is the result of the blending of two distinct traditions. In short, Puerto Hormiga ceramics do not appear to be close to the beginnings of pottery in South America. On the other hand the total picture which comes from a study of the refuse and non-ceramic tools at Puerto Hormiga suggests a typical Archaic-type economy with major dependence on shell-fish collecting, fishing, and hunting of small game in about that order of importance. There is no sign that agriculture contributed to the caloric intake of these peoples.

The sites of Canapote and Barlovento, also coastal shell middens in the same general area, show that the way of life of the Puerto Hormiga peoples continued essentially unmodified on the Caribbean Coast of Colombia until about 1000 B C in association with a remarkable array of technically competent and artistically imaginative ceramic styles.

At the same time that the Late Archaic cultures were flourishing on the Coast, the alluvial flood plains of the major rivers a short distance inland were occupied by peoples with a different economic pattern and with several distinctive ceramic traditions. From Bucarelia near Zambrano, about 150 km. up the Magdalena, there is a collection of pottery stylistically related to that of Puerto Hormiga but showing much more complex decoration and a wider range of vessel shapes. It is unfortunate that the available collection is highly selected for decorated pieces and that there is no information on the economic basis of the people involved. It is clear that the economy was not primarily based on collecting marine molluscs. I suspect that the Puerto Hormiga pottery is a pallid reflection of the more elaborate Bucarelia style rather than that the latter represents an inland extension of the style of the former, and that the Bucarelia Culture is a representative of developed Tropical Forest Culture, though perhaps without bitter manioc.

Somewhat later but still before 1000 B C we find the Malambo Culture on the alluvial flood plain of the Lower Magdalena and the Momíl Ia and Ib Cultures on that of the Lower Sinú. In both cases there are temporal overlaps between the Archaic Barlovento Culture on the Coast and the riverine-oriented complexes. For both Malambo and Momíl Ia-Ib there is clear evidence that shell-fish were not a significant part of the diet and that bread and flour produced from bitter manioc was the major staple in the economy. The ceramics of Momíl Ia, Ib are stylistically unlike the ceramics of Malambo and neither style could possibly have been derived from the ceramic continuum extending from Puerto Hormiga to Barlovento. All the available archaeological evidence argues strongly that the early Tropical Forest Cultures of Colombia were not directly derived from the late Archaic cultures of the Caribbean Coast.

The Pacific Coast of Colombia is the most difficult area for archaeological work in the New World. The findings of the Reichel-Dolmatoffs have pushed the sequence there back into the first millennium B C, but information on the crucial second and third millennium B C is lacking.

The Valdivia Complex of the Coast of Ecuador has given rise to much speculation in recent years. The early appearance of pottery showing an extensive and complex series of vessel forms and a wide range of well executed decorative techniques is an anomaly which cries out for explanation. Meggers, Evans, and Estrada would have us believe that Valdivia is a transplanted branch of an ancient Japanese ceramic tradition which was somewhat mangled during its long sea voyage, but I am not alone in finding this explanation dubious. I suggest that the possible antecedents of Valdivia are best understood in terms of the economic basis of the culture. It has been customary to equate Valdivia with such cultures of Archaic economy as Puerto Hormiga and Monagrillo in Panama. It is true that marine shell occurs in quantity in the Valdivia middens but the percentage

Tropical Forest Culture

which shell makes of the total volume of the midden is not high. In fact, Lanning has pointed out to me that there is less shell per unit volume of Valdivia midden than in the midden of any of the subsequent peoples inhabiting this stretch of the Ecuadorian Coast. There is thus the strong possibility that the economic basis of Valdivia was mainly agricultural. There is direct evidence that maize was a crop during the final phase of Valdivia Culture around 1300–1400 B C, but none as to what crops might have been present earlier. The distribution of Valdivia sites suggests that the economic orientation was not entirely marine. One of these sites is located a kilometre up-stream, a situation oriented not to marine resources but to an extensive stretch of self-irrigating bottom land which would have been excellent for agriculture.

Even the earliest pottery in the Valdivia tradition is sufficiently complex technologically and artistically to make it unlikely to be a local development on the Coast of Ecuador. My own alternative to a theory of Japanese origins is that Valdivia represents a branch of Tropical Forest Culture which was rather early extruded from the Amazon Basin and which settled in a locality that offered easily worked agricultural lands and, secondarily, fairly rich marine resources to make up the protein deficiency.

The Coast of Peru can be excluded as the area in which the Tropical Forest Agricultural pattern developed. The important plants all appear there relatively late and as fully evolved cultigens.

All this would seem to suggest that the origins of Tropical Forest Culture were continental rather than Coastal and that Tropical Forest Culture had reached a reasonably high state of efficiency by 3000 B C. The origins are to be sought in any of the extensive areas of riverine flood plain in the Amazon and northern South America. Lake basins with extensive alluvial fill, such as Valencia and Maracaibo in Venezuela, may also have made early contributions to this development.

CHAPTER IV

Languages of the Upper Amazon: Clues to Past Migrations and Ancient Demography

THE DISTRIBUTION of demonstrably related languages offers unequivocal evidence of past migrations. Unlike other domains of culture, such as technology or even art style, one's primary language is learned early and thoroughly and is not easily or willingly exchanged for other models offered by casual visitors. Wherever related languages are spread over wide areas of the earth's surface, we can be certain that this dispersal was achieved through the movement of fair-sized groups of speakers of these languages. In some instances a relatively small band of invaders will be able to impose its language on a larger number of conquered peoples. The spread of Spanish and Portuguese in Latin America frequently followed such a pattern. In other instances, and more frequently in ancient times, the spread of a language occurred through the replacement of an earlier population by numerically or militarily superior colonists. A classic instance of this was the almost total elimination of the Indian populations of North America by English- and French-speaking colonists.

By related languages we mean any group derived from a single parent language existing at an earlier point in time, in the way that the modern Romance languages are derived from Latin. Where the relationships are easily demonstrated through sound comparative methods, we may speak of a language family; and there is a strong implication that the languages involved have diverged over a relatively short span of time (in the case of the Romance languages slightly less than 2,000 years). Where the similarities among a group of languages are less numerous and less obvious, and where effective demonstration of relationship is facilitated by the comparison of several ancient parent languages, either known through preserved writings, as in the case of Latin, Classical Greek, and Sanskrit, or reconstructed, one may speak of a linguistic stock; there is the strong implication of a greater span of elapsed time from the point at which all the languages in a stock started to diverge (in the case of Indo-European between 4,000 and 5,000 years). Where full comparative studies have been made, and in cases where the parent languages of several stocks (the proto-languages) have been reconstructed, one may attempt to demonstrate ultimate historical relationships among several stocks, but such comparisons must rest on a vast body of previous scholarship. The taxonomic unit thus achieved is usually called a superstock.

The existence of a demonstrated linguistic family, stock, or superstock implies that at one time in the past the parent language was spoken by a single contiguous population confined to a circumscribed area. Where the daughter languages of the family or stock are found at a later date covering vast areas of the earth's surface, there are clear implications concerning past demographic and economic conditions. A dramatic increase in the area over which a language or related group of languages is spoken implies that there has been an equally dramatic increase in the population of those speaking it. Such population explosions are a good indication that the subsistence base supporting the population had become more efficacious. At any time subsequent to the initial peopling of a continent or particular ecological niche within a continent, the expansion of the languages of one family and the speakers of these languages must have been at the expense of the territorial holdings of other peoples in many cases speaking languages of other families. It can be assumed that the ability of a group to expand its territory at the expense of other groups depends on numerical, organizational, or military superiority. All three characteristics imply a secure and expanding economic base. In most instances the expanding groups will be

The Upper Amazon

selective about the nature of the territory which they colonize. Such preference, in terms of total ecological setting, will give strong evidence as to the nature of the subsistence economy.

Fig. 4

The pattern of distribution of languages within a particular linguistic family may also give clues as to the means of transportation favoured by the people and most used in their colonial ventures. If the distribution is lateral along the major rivers or includes islands well separated from the mainland, one can assume that watercraft were well developed and the preferred form of long distance transportation.

The linguistic map of South America is distinguished by the large number of distinct languages spoken at the time of the first European contact and the large number of languages whose relationship to other speech communities has not yet been established. It seems best to concentrate attention on a few of the linguistic families and linguistic stocks where the evidence for relationship is clear cut and has been presented in an orderly fashion. The zone of greatest linguistic diversity in South America is the Upper Amazon Basin along the eastern foothills of the Andes; and it was precisely this complex juxtaposition of discrete ethnic and linguistic units which led Steward to speak of 'a series of migratory waves that had spent their force against the barrier of the Andes'.

THE ARAWAKAN STOCK

Languages of the Arawakan stock had a far greater geographical range in South America than those of any other stock or family. To the north, Arawakan languages were dominant on the Greater Antilles and extended to the Bahamas off the east coast of Florida. To the south, Arawakan-speaking groups spread down into the Gran Chaco. They likewise extended nearly the full width of the South American continent, from near the mouth of the Amazon and the Upper Xingú River in the east to the Upper Peruvian Montaña and the Titicaca Basin in the west.

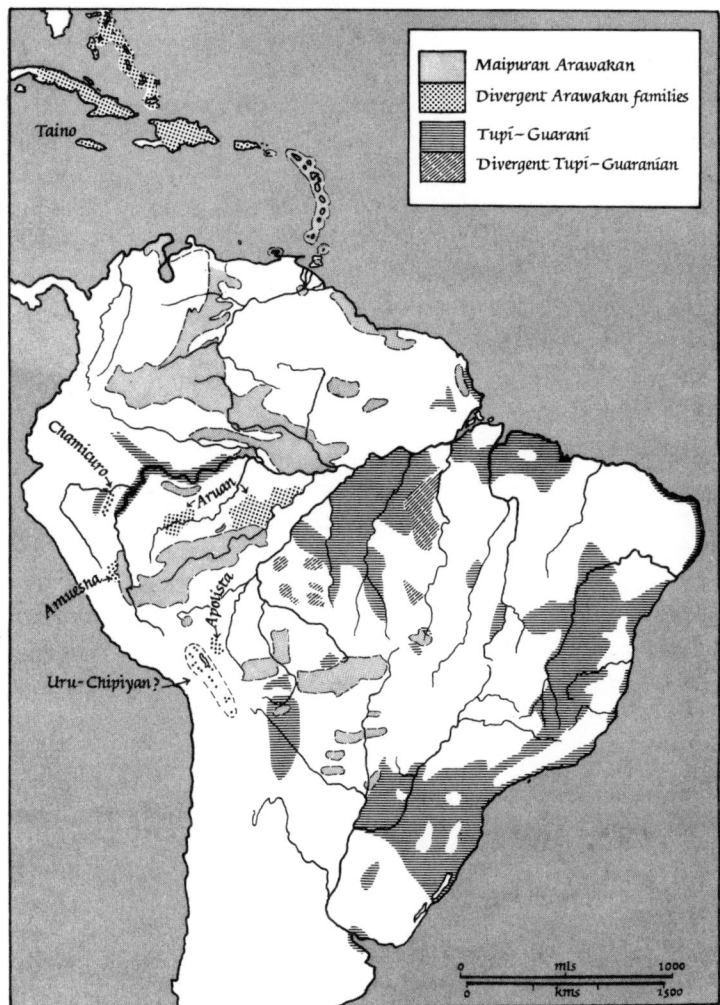

Fig. 4 The approximate distribution of Macro-Arawakan and Macro-Tupi-Guaranian languages at the time of the first European contacts. In terms of breadth of distribution and numbers of speakers these two were by far the most important linguistic stocks in Lowland South America. For both stocks the more divergent and more anciently distributed languages are differentiated from the more obviously related languages of the major branch: Maipuran from Macro-Arawakan, and Tupi-Guaranian proper from Tupi-Guaranian

The Upper Amazon

The relatedness of the various far-flung Arawakan languages was recognized very early by the Jesuit missionaries, when vocabularies collected from the Maipure on the Upper Río Orinoco were compared with those collected from the Mojos on the Llanos de Mojos in Bolivia. It was the North American linguist Brinton who first recognized that the Indian languages of the Greater Antilles were related to the already recognized Arawakan family and who expanded the family into something which should be considered a stock. A thorough analysis of the Arawakan languages was subsequently undertaken by Noble.

Fig. 4

As analyzed by Noble, the Aarawakan stock contains seven distantly related branches or families which all started to diverge from their proto-language at about the same time. Using the dating method of lexico-statistics, Noble suggests that this split in Proto-Arawakan took place between 4,500 and 5,000 years ago. Six of these seven divergent branches of Arawakan were represented at contact times by one or more than one closely related language in restricted areas: Taino on the Greater Antilles and the Bahamas; Chamicuro on the Río Samiria in the Montaña of eastern Peru; the various languages of Aruan in the Upper Basins of the Juruá and Purús in western Brazil; Amuesha on the head-waters of the Alto Pachitea and Palcazú in the Montaña of eastern Peru; Apolista in a small pocket on an upper tributary of the Bení in the Bolivian Montaña; and Uru-Chipaya in various small pockets in the Titicaca Basin. (There is still great disagreement among linguists as to the classification of Uru-Chipaya.) The seventh branch, Maipuran, is represented by a tremendous array of languages. Noble suggests that Proto-Maipuran began to disperse around 2,500 years ago. The two lexico-statistical dates of 4,500 to 5,000 years ago for the initial separation of Proto-Arawakan and 2,500 for the initial break-up of Proto-Maipuran into its various constituent languages cannot be taken as absolute values, but they do give a useful kind of indication as to the time span involved in these two waves of expansion. It will be noted that the more divergent families occur in a great arc around the western edge of the Amazon Basin and to the north of it on the Greater Antilles, while the Maipuran languages occupy a more central position. In several instances there is evidence indicating that the more divergent Arawakan groups were pushed or are being pushed into their marginal position by the expansion of the Maipuran peoples. Noble has accepted the frequently proposed suggestion that the homeland of Proto-Maipuran immediately before its dispersal was on the Upper Orinoco. But he has offered the more original hypothesis that the homeland of Proto-Arawakan, 4,000–5,000 years ago, was between the head-waters of the Ucayali and the Madre de Dios. Considered in terms of ecology, demography, and means of dispersal, Noble's suggested hearth seems unlikely, and I fail to understand the force of his argument in terms of the linguistic data.

I will now indicate some of the difficulties inherent in Noble's model of Arawakan dispersal and present an alternative model which seems to me more plausible. At the time of first European contact all Arawakan-speakers, with the exception of the questionable Uru-Chipaya were intensively agricultural, following the Tropical Forest pattern of root-crop cultivation. There is strong reason to believe that this was the economic pattern of the speakers of the proto-language at the time when they started their outward migrations, and that it underlay the population explosion forcing the outward migrations. The mountain chain between the head-waters of the Ucayali and the Madre de Dios was not a favourable area for Tropical Forest agriculture, or for any other early form of agriculture; a build-up of population pressures there is highly improbable. The distribution of Arawakan-speakers argues that canoes were the major means of dispersal. The whole core block of Maipuran-speakers is oriented along the network of waterways made up by the Upper Amazon, the Negro, the Casiquiare Canal, and the Orinoco, and it is clear that the Taino did not reach their final home by walking on water. The area pin-pointed by Noble is one of the least likely regions for the development of water transport since all the streams are rapid and rocky.

Let us see if it is not possible to arrive at the pattern of Arawakan distribution by assuming a more uniform and ecologically rational model of population expansion. Let us assume that around 3000 B C the speakers of Proto-Arawakan were concentrated on the flood plain of the Central Amazon near the present-day city of Manuas; that developed Tropical Forest agriculture was leading to increased populations which were putting a progressively greater pressure on the limited expanses of alluvial land in the Amazon flood plain; and that to relieve these population pressures daughter colonial groups started to move out, looking for other available areas of alluvial bottom lands. These colonists would have travelled by canoe and moved out along all available waterways where further alluvial land might be encountered. The subsequent course of events may be envisaged as follows. Some groups moved up the Madeira occupying alluvial lands and gradually expanding towards the Andes until ultimately the eastern slopes of the range were reached and further progress was blocked; one group remained in the Andean foothills and became the Apolista, possibly another such group was pushed all the way out of the Amazon Basin and became the Uru-Chipaya. Other groups moved up the Amazon until pressures forced them up the Juruá and Purús. Gradually they were pushed up-stream towards the head-waters of these rivers and in time became the several groups speaking Aruan languages. Still others colonized progressively further up the Amazon and in due course moved into the valley of its major tributary, the Ucayali, finding large areas of alluvial land to exploit there. Further pressures from down-stream forced these groups up the Ucayali and its tributary the Pachitea until ultimately they were pinned against the eastern flank of the Andes, becoming the

Languages of the Upper Amazon

modern Amuesha. Another group proceeded a short distance up the Marañón and then up its southern tributary the Samiria to become the Chamicuro. Others moved up the Negro and finding only restricted areas of alluvial land there moved on along the Casiquiare Canal and down the Orinoco where large expanses of fine alluvial lands were encountered in the middle and lower stretches of the river. These peoples occupied the Lower Orinoco for a long time until pressure from further groups moving down the Orinoco forced them onto the Coast of Venezuela and ultimately out into the Antilles, where they became the Taino encountered by Columbus.

Let us assume, too, that back on the Central Amazon flood plain patterns of food production and food utilization meanwhile continued to increase in efficiency so that even greater population pressures began to build up. Between 1000 and 500 B C further waves of migration of peoples speaking Proto-Maipuran moved out along all the routes followed by the earlier colonists: up the Madeira; up the Juruá and Purús; up the Ucayali; up the Japurá; up the Negro and down the Orinoco. This later wave of migration penetrated further into the alluvial lands of the Llanos de Mojos and even into the drier alluvial land of the Gran Chaco. Once this later wave of colonists had moved down the Orinoco and displaced the ancestors of the Taino, it fanned out along both the Venezuelan and Guiana coasts moving by coastwise canoe travel. There were even migrations down-stream along the Amazon, a direction not attempted by the earlier waves. One branch moved to the mouth of the Amazon and hence into Brazilian Guiana, while another moved up the major southern tributary of the Amazon, the Xingú, to occupy the small patch of alluvial land in its upper watershed.

Various stages of the process can be mapped. It assumes relatively continuous population pressures, relatively constant rates of migration, and the search for a single kind of ecological niche, good alluvial soils. The reader may decide whether the

Fig. 5

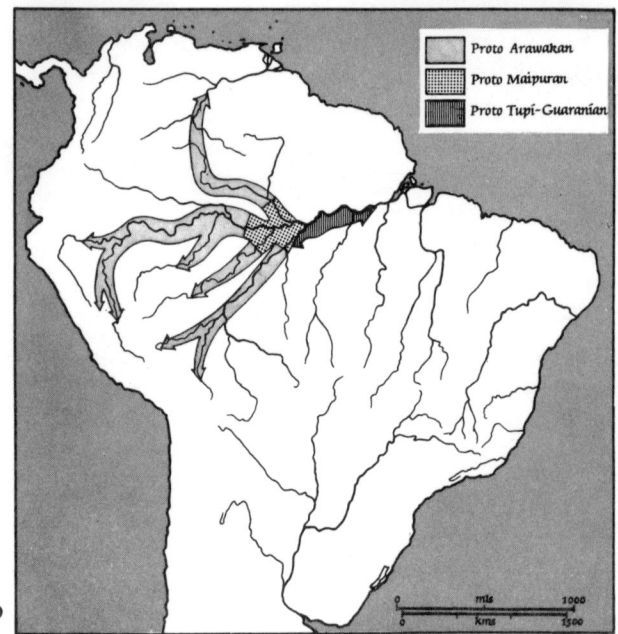

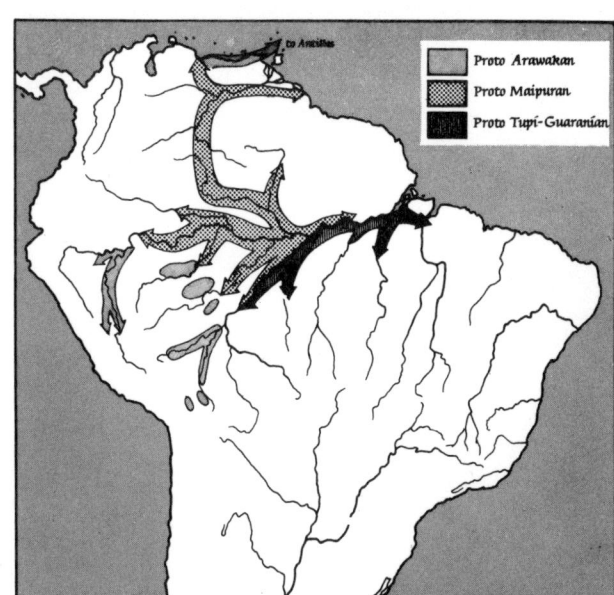

Fig. 5 Maps showing various stages of the model of population dispersal which would best account for the final distribution of Macro-Arawakan; a 3000 BC; b 2000 BC; c 500 BC; d AD 500

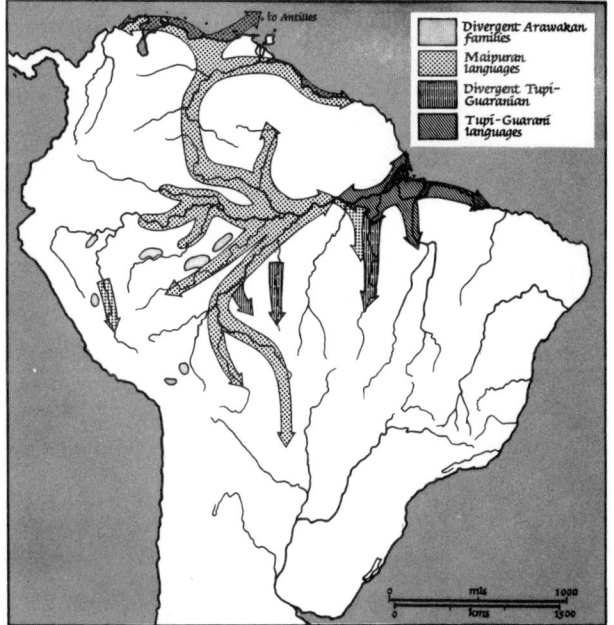

The Upper Amazon

available archaeological data as set out in later chapters supports or conflicts with this model of population dispersal suggested by linguistic data.

TUPÍ-GUARANÍAN

Fig. 4

Next to Arawakan, Tupí-Guaraníian is the most widely distributed linguistic stock in South America. At the time of first European contact, speakers of Tupí-Guaraníian languages were very numerous and expanding rapidly at the expense of neighbouring groups. Though the number of speakers has declined tremendously in historic times, the languages have greatly influenced the vocabulary of Brazilian Portuguese and Guaraní retains status as one of the two official languages of Paraguay.

As Arawakan was the dominant stock of the Upper Amazon Basin so Tupí-Guaraníian was the dominant stock of the Lower Amazon Basin, especially along the river's southern shore. Unfortunately we do not have detailed comparative studies of the various branches of Tupí-Guaraníian and there have been no attempts at a reconstruction of the proto-language, but Arion Rodrigues has made rough estimates of degree of relatedness among Tupí-Guaraníian languages on the basis of shared vocabulary.

Noble has demonstrated that Proto-Arawakan shares an appreciable amount of its core vocabulary with the proto-language of the Tupí-Guaraníian stock. It is thus probable that Proto-Arawakan and Proto-Tupí-Guaraníian are related, and certain that they were at least in close proximity at a time immediately prior to their dispersal. Given these facts I would locate the home of the Proto-Tupí-Guaraníian speech community on the south bank of the Amazon slightly down-stream from the mouth of the Río Madeira. Given the same economic base and the same kind of population pressures as were operating on Proto-Arawakan, it is easy to see how the ultimate distribution of Macro-Tupí-Guaraníán was achieved by contact times. The expanding Arawakans blocked movement up the main stream of the Amazon but colonial groups very early moved up the Madeira and its two eastern tributaries, the Aripuana and the Parana, ultimately coming to rest in small pockets of alluvial land at the foot of the Serra dos Parecis and accounting for five of the six divergent families of the stock. Other colonial groups moved down-stream along the south shore of the Amazon, one group moving early up-stream along the Xingú in search of alluvial lands and became the ancestors of the Yurunan family. Immediately before its dispersal the proto-language of Tupí-Guaraníán proper was located near the Mouth of the Amazon. All the languages in this family are closely related and much of their expansion took place in late times. Indeed much of the expansion of Tupí-Guaraníán proper was taking place under the observation of the first European explorers and, we have detailed accounts of the war patterns which permitted these peoples to override and exterminate their less numerous and less well organized neighbours. Only one branch of the Tupí-Guaraníán family penetrated far into the Upper Amazon Basin, that containing Cocama, Cocamilla, and Omagua.

Fig. 5

PANOAN AND ITS AFFINITIES

Panoan is a relatively small linguistic family in terms of the number of constituent languages and in terms of the geographical range of its speakers. The diversity among Panoan languages is not great, certainly less than that of the Maipuran family of Arawakan, suggesting that the dispersal of the Panoan-speakers from the original hearth of Proto-Panoan has been a relatively recent development. In spite of its moderate size the Panoan family is of particular interest to the present study. During the last few hundred years it has been a dominant linguistic family in the Ucayali Basin, the region of the Upper Amazon for which we have the most detailed archaeological information.

The Upper Amazon

Fig. 6

The groups that are universally conceded to be Panoan form a large semicircle with its north-eastern end on the south shore of the Upper Amazon in Brazil and its south-eastern end near the junction of the Guaporé and Madre de Díos. The western-most part of this arc runs through the Ucayali Basin at the foot of the Peruvian Andes. The northern half of the arc is continuous but the southern half is broken into two discrete areas by a block of Arawakan-speakers and again further to the south and east by the speakers of a small group of related languages, the Tacanan family. Most recent studies have indicated that the Tacanan family is closely related to the Panoan family and that both derived from a single proto-language of no great time depth. It is thus possible to speak of a Macro-Panoan stock containing the Panoan and Tacanan families.

There is less agreement as to the relationship of Macro-Panoan with any other families or stocks in South America. Some scholars have postulated a close relationship between Macro-Panoan and Macro-Guaycuruan, the most important and widespread linguistic stock of the Gran Chaco. The reality of Macro-Guaycuruan has not been systematically demonstrated, though it is regarded as probable by some scholars. Another scholar who has done intensive work in comparative Panoan and who has also done work on Aymara and Quechua, suggests that the proto-language ancestral to both Aymara and Quechua and the proto-language for Macro-Panoan derived from a still earlier proto-language at about 2000 B C. There is no inherent contradiction between these two theories of Macro-Panoan relationship and if either is correct, then it is almost certain that the homeland of Proto-Panoan was in the southern part of its present range since the initial homelands of Quechua languages and the total range of Guaycuruan are both to the south of the Central Ucayali Basin. The Panoans of the Ucayali Basin and of the rivers Juruá and Purús are thus relatively late migrants from the south. We will return to this point when we consider the

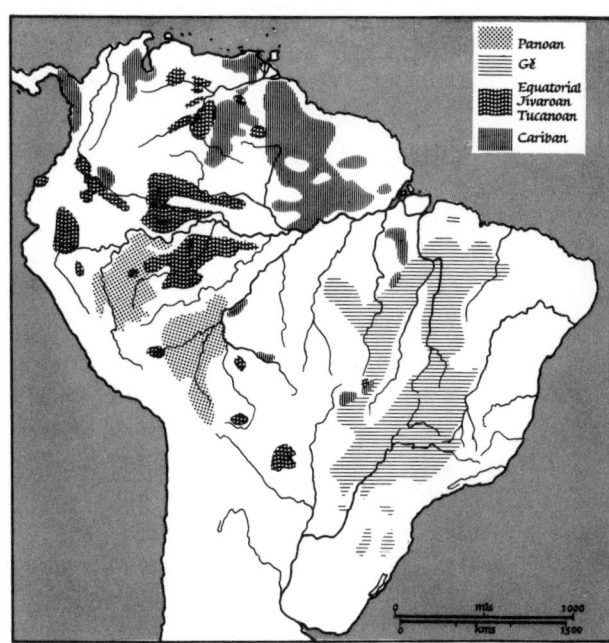

Fig. 6 Distribution of the other major linguistic stocks in and around the Amazon Basin

archaeological evidence relating to the arrival of the Panoans in the Ucayali Basin.

Unlike the distribution of Arawakan and Tupí-Guaraníán, the major axis of Panoan distribution is neither riverine nor coastal: it extends across the upper watersheds of several major rivers, the Madre de Díos, the Purús, the Juruá and the Ucayali. The total distribution suggests that the major part of Panoan expansion was on foot rather than by watercraft, an impression strengthened by the fact that many Panoan groups have poorly developed watercraft or lack them completely.

GĚ AND CARIBAN

There are two other large linguistic families whose territory adjoins or extends into the lowlands of the Amazon Basin. These are Gě and Cariban. The Gě languages form a nearly solid block dominating the drier sections of the Brazilian High-

Fig. 6

lands. They are highly distinctive when compared to the languages of Tropical Forest peoples. The cultural patterns and economic systems of the Gě-speaking groups show a considerable internal uniformity and contrast sharply with those of the Tropical Forest peoples. It is likely that the Gě-speakers have held their present homeland for a long time, and improbable that their ancestors were responsible for any of the prehistoric remains to be discussed.

At contact times the largest continuous block of Cariban languages was centred on the Guiana Highlands, but there were outliers as far away as the southern edge of the Amazon Basin and various parts of northern Colombia. Much of the north-westward expansion of Cariban languages was very late and some of these migrations were noted by the first Europeans. The study of Cariban linguistics presents certain difficulties which are the direct result of the patterns of territorial acquisition used by the Caribs. These warfare patterns, to be discussed in a later section, resulted in mixed languages, which present difficulties to the linguistic taxonomists. In some cases such a Chocó, on the Pacific Coast of Colombia, the language is clearly Cariban though there is a very large admixture of Chibchan elements. In other cases such as Island Carib, the language of the Lesser Antilles which is now also spoken along the Caribbean Coast of Central America, the Carib residue is so slight that the language can be classified as typically Maipuran.

Within the Upper Amazon, as defined in this book, there are only three enclaves of Cariban language. Two of these, Arara, along the Central Madeira, and Palmella on the Guaporé between Bolivia and Brazil were small in extent and number of speakers. The Carijona who held much of the Mesa de Para-doas at the eastern foot of the Colombian Andes were most extensive and numerous.

The weight of historical and linguistic evidence suggests that the ancient home of Proto-Cariban was on or adjacent to the

Languages of the Upper Amazon

Guiana Highlands possibly along the north shore of the Lower Amazon. The archaeological evidence is examined later.

EQUATORIAL

There remains in the arc around the western edge of the Upper Amazon Basin and on into the forest and savannah regions of the Upper Orinoco a bewildering array of isolated languages and small language families, which do not show obvious relationships either to each other or to any of the major linguistic stocks. Only two of these families, Catukinan in the Juruá Basin and Tucanoan with a discontinuous distribution in eastern Peru and eastern Colombia have even moderate geographical spread, but some of the geographically restricted languages such as Jívaro and Shirixana still retain large numbers of native speakers.

In his comprehensive classification of South American Indian languages Greenberg suggests that most of these small isolated languages belong in a super-stock which he has designated Equatorial. Arawakan and Tupí-Guaraníjan are stocks within the super-stock Equatorial, and Greenberg's arrangement might indicate that all the branches of Equatorial diverged from a single proto-language about a thousand years earlier than the proto-language which produced Arawakan and Tupí-Guaraníjan. I would again suggest that the location of this proto-language was on the Central Amazon near the junction of the Amazon and the Negro. If we assume that at 3500 to 3000 B C the proto-languages for the various divergent stocks of Equatorial were adjacent to Proto-Arawakan and Proto-Tupí-Guaraníjan but slightly up-stream from them on the Amazon, the Maderia, and the Negro, then the contact distribution of these languages is completely explicable in terms of the population explosions of Arawakans and Tupí-Guaraníjans. These divergent groups were simply pushed up-stream or off the major streams into their present marginal and generally undesirable locations by the expansion of their more numerous and more powerful neighbours.

Fig. 6

CHAPTER V

The Early Tropical Forest Cultures of the Upper Amazon

THOUGH ARCHAEOLOGICAL research is relatively recent in the Upper Amazon, it is clear on the basis of work already accomplished that large sedentary communities and complex and varied ceramics are at least as old in the tropical forests of the Amazon Basin as they are in the Highland or on the Coast of Peru.

EARLY TUTISHCAINYO

The oldest clear-cut evidence for human occupation in the Upper Amazon Basin comes from several points along the bluff of old alluvium near the northern end of Yarinacocha, a large ox-bow lake north-west of the Peruvian city of Pucallpa. Here an easily recognizable style of pottery has been recovered from the lowest levels of several excavations. Much of this pottery is highly weathered, indicating that it has been re-deposited by sheet erosion or the action of the river. Undisturbed refuse has been encountered in appreciable quantity only at two locations, and of these the Tutishcainyo site, UCA-6, is the larger and has yielded the most information.

The Tutishcainyo site covers a knoll of old alluvium about half a kilometre back from Yarinacocha. Once, about 1,800 years ago, the Aguatía, a large western tributary of the Ucayali, ran adjacent to the hill and cut away much of the cultural deposit. It is certain that the Early Tutishcainyo midden here has been considerably eroded so that the full extent of the ancient settlement cannot be determined and it is difficult to estimate the area or population of that community. The depth and density of the midden suggest that the settlement endured for a century or two and that the population was in the hundreds rather than in the tens.

Rather than an indication of low population density, the rarity of *known* Early Tutishcainyo sites is clearly the result of the destructive powers of the Ucayali and its tributaries, and of the difficulties of site-survey in the tropical forest.

The cultural materials surviving from the Early Tutishcainyo settlements consist almost entirely of pottery. Luckily this pottery is distinctive both as to the shapes and the decorative techniques and patterns. The several standardized forms are characterized by sharp ridges between the various segments of the vessel. Such highly inflected forms offer a number of technological difficulties for their successful execution, and it is clear that the Early Tutishcainyo ceramics were far beyond the fumbling beginnings of the potter's art.

The most common vessel form was a large, open-mouthed pot with a broad, labial flange and markedly concave sides. Most frequently a broader flange adorned the angle between its side and bottom. The size and form of this vessel are compatible with use as a cooking pot. Also common were small vessels with inward-sloping sides and sharp basal angles. There are several reasons for thinking that these functioned as drinking cups for gruel and beer. A broad, open bowl with short but markedly concave sides would have served well as a plate for solid foods. These three forms make up more than two-thirds of Early Tutishcainyo pottery, but a number of other highly standardized shape-categories do occur.

Fig. 7 a–c

Fig. 7 c

Fig. 7 h

Fig. 7 f, g

Of these rarer forms the double-spout-and-bridge bottle is most noteworthy. To shape this requires considerable skill and it is difficult to interpret the form on purely functional grounds. Nonetheless, it is widespread in Pre-Columbian South America. This bottle appears in the earliest ceramic complex on the South Coast of Peru, and remains the most impressive form for most of the history of that area. The double-spout-and-bridge bottle was

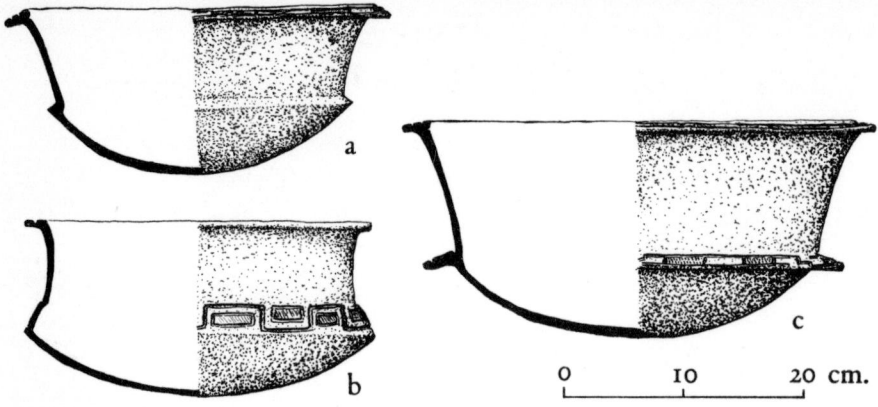

Fig. 7 Typical Early Tutishcainyo vessel shapes and zoned incised decoration. The forms indicated in a–c, f–g comprise over 80 per cent of all ceramics made. The relatively rare, large urns, i, were probably used in the brewing of masato *(manioc beer)*

also an integral part of the elaborately modelled Barrancas ceramics of the flood plain of the Lower Orinoco, where spouts were usually in the form of human heads. The form occurs in a number of early ceramic complexes of Colombia. So distinctive is the double-spout-and-bridge bottle that it seems probable that all the above-mentioned examples are somehow historically related.

Almost every pot made by the Early Tutishcainyo peoples carried some decoration. The most common embellishment consisted of alternate zones of textured and untextured surface delimited by broad, U-shaped incisions. The texturing might consist of fine-line hatching or cross hatching, of rows of punctations, or of short tally-like lines. The designs were mostly arranged in a geometric pattern and tended to be rectilinear, but one popular motif involved a curvilinear scroll.

Fig. 7 f

Fig. 8

Figural representations were extremely rare. The single example found so far is of considerable interest. It is a cat-head incised on the end of an oval bowl, and is one of the oldest feline

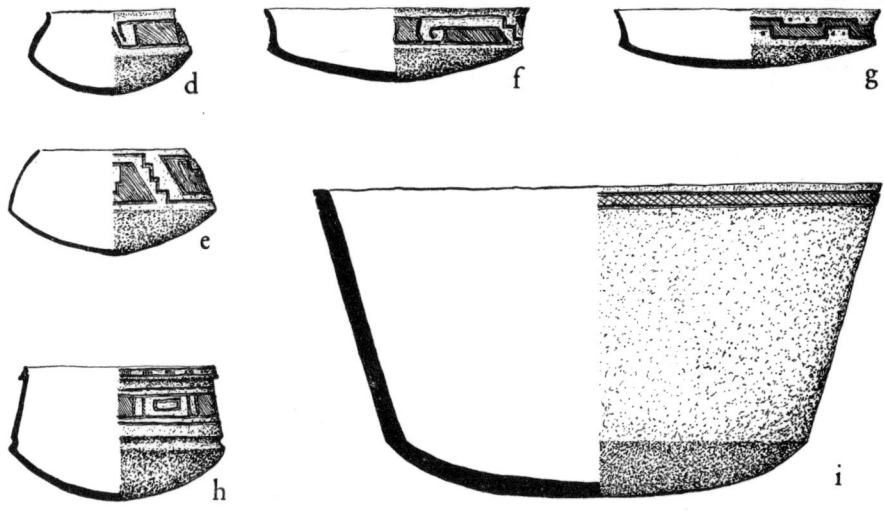

representations in the New World, far pre-dating the obsessive depiction of jaguars in the Chavín Horizon art of Peru.

The surfaces of most of the ceramics are eroded, but in a number of instances it was clear that the textured areas carried a red paint applied after the pot was fired. Very similar post-fired painting or crusting occurs early at the site of Kotosh in the Huánuco Basin, and one suspects that the post-fired crusting so typical of the Paracas potters of the South Coast of Peru was technologically identical and historically related.

Early Tutishcainyo shows most of the characteristics of Tropical Forest Culture. The settlement just at the edge of the old alluvium was clearly oriented to the resources of the riverine environment and was probably then adjacent to an active river channel or old ox-bow lake, now completely destroyed by later shifts in the river.

It is impossible to give a full inventory of the foods consumed, but materials included in the paste of the pottery give some evidence concerning subsistence. More than ten per cent of the pottery recovered was tempered with crushed shells of large freshwater molluscs, and it is probable that the meat of these creatures was not discarded. Microscopic examination of the paste of all of the sherds from the Tutishcainyo site revealed a number of fragments of pottery containing fish bones and fish scales as accidental inclusions. Fish were clearly an important source of food.

Direct evidence is lacking as to the quantity and nature of the vegetable foods consumed, but the amount of pottery in the midden and the considerable variety and high standardization of vessel shape all argue for a cuisine in which vegetable foods were varied and important.

As noted above, one of the common forms can best be interpreted as a cup for unfermented gruels or fermented beers. A very few rim sherds indicate that large urns were a part of the Early Tutishcainyo ceramic repertory, and wherever vessels of this size and form have survived until recently in tropical South America, they serve as brewing vats. The presence of manioc beer is thus strongly suggested, and there is in turn the indication of root-crop agriculture. On the other hand the highly specific forms associated with processing bitter manioc are absent.

Evidence concerning the dwellings of the Early Tutishcainyo peoples is meagre. A few post-holes have been noted but excavations have been too limited to expose full ground plans. All that can be said is that the supports were widely separated. These post-holes were dug into an irregular ground surface—evidence that the actual house floors were of cane or wood supported well above the ground. The Early Tutishcainyo middens contain quantities of partially fired clay fragments some of which bear clear impressions of woven cane and pole construction. Such remains indicate that the houses were tightly closed with walls of wattle-and-daub construction. The Indians of the Amazon Basin knew of two responses to the clouds of mosquitos typical of the area. One was to have a tightly shut house which was deliberately filled with smoke every evening: the other was to use

Fig. 7 h
Fig. 7 i

The Early Tropical Forest Cultures

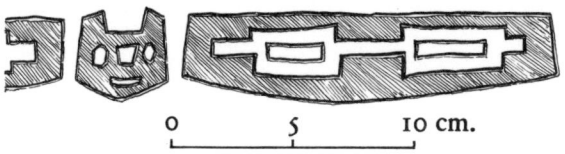

Fig. 8 Zoned incised design from a low, oval bowl, Early Tutishcainyo Complex. The cat-head is possibly the earliest appearance of this motif in Peruvian art.

woven mosquito bars or sleeping garments. It would appear that the Early Tutishcainyo people used the former.

The presence of ground stone axes in Early Tutishcainyo middens is further argument for the presence of agriculture. Other types of stone tools were absent, indicating that the hunting equipment was fashioned of perishable materials as among the recent Tropical Forest peoples.

A detailed study of the similarities between the earliest ceramics at Kotosh and Early Tutishcainyo pottery permit us to extrapolate from the well-dated sequence in the Huánuco Basin, and on this basis a segment of time between 2000 and 1600 BC for Early Tutishcainyo occupations seems most likely.

LATE TUTISHCAINYO

Late Tutishcainyo derived from Early Tutishcainyo, but the ceramic style shows considerable stylistic change, suggesting that at least 450 years separated them. The largest sample of Late Tutishcainyo materials again comes from the Tutishcainyo site, UCA-6. Here the 60 cm. of Early Tutishcainyo midden are buried by up to 50 cm. of Late Tutishcainyo refuse. Both stylistic and stratigraphic evidence argue that the site was deserted for a long time between these two occupations. The taste in vessel forms and ornamentation has changed. Incised decoration is executed with less care, and closely spaced, fine-line hatching has almost disappeared. Though incision declined as a decorative

Fig. 9

The Upper Amazon

Fig. 9 j

Fig. 9 a, b, d, h

technique, the Late Tutishcainyo pottery was by no means decadent. More extensive use was made of modelling and appliqué, and the ware was hard and better fired. Double-spout-and-bridge bottles continued, and the spouts were formed with considerable skill. Most characteristic of Late Tutishcainyo was the use of nicking on the rims, basal angles, and other salient ridges of the vessels.

There is nothing to suggest a modification in subsistence pattern or settlement size, though one group of pottery in the Late Tutishcainyo midden does throw light on the extent of long-distance trade. Fully five per cent of the pottery recovered was of a ware which could not have been manufactured in the immediate area. Not only was the clay chemically distinct from that of typical Late Tutishcainyo pottery, but the tempering material was fresh, unrolled crystals from extruded volcanic rock. The source of this pottery must have been well away from the Ucayali flood plain at a considerable distance from the Tutishcainyo site. The exotic pottery carried a sharply angular, narrow-line incision different from the typical Late Tutishcainyo style. The trade ware also showed zones of red paint applied before the vessel was fired, the first evidence of slip painting in the area.

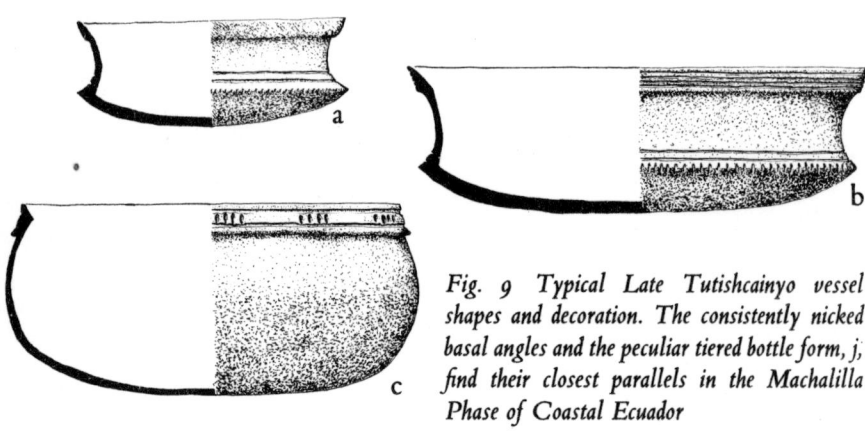

Fig. 9 Typical Late Tutishcainyo vessel shapes and decoration. The consistently nicked basal angles and the peculiar tiered bottle form, j, find their closest parallels in the Machalilla Phase of Coastal Ecuador

The Early Tropical Forest Cultures

That such a significant proportion of the ceramics used by the Late Tutishcainyo people was imported from a considerable distance, suggests that these people were able to amass a substantial economic surplus for the purpose of trade. It also points to the patterns of specialized manufacturing among various ethnic groups, and the concomitant necessity for long-distance trade, so characteristic of recent Tropical Forest groups, having already started at this early period.

There is other, less tangible, evidence of widespread trade and the exchange of ideas at this time. The Machalilla culture on the coast of Ecuador follows the Valdivia culture in that area. A number of the features which distinguish Machalilla ceramics are also found in Late Tutishcainyo. The same shallow, carinated bowl was present both in Late Tutishcainyo and Machalilla and sometimes bore nearly identical decorations. A highly specific form of nicking on carinations, rims, and other salient ridges was also characteristic of the pottery of both peoples. The style of angular, fine-line incision typical of the exotic pottery traded to the Late Tutishcainyo people is strikingly paralleled by the incision characteristic of the Machalilla type, Ayangue Incised. The stirrup-spout bottles of Machalilla appear to have derived from a

Fig. 9 g, h

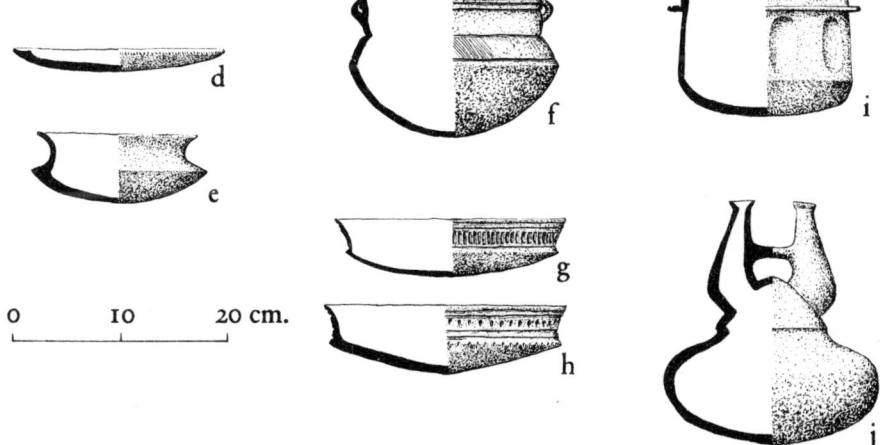

form of double-spout-and-bridge bottle typical of Late Tutishcainyo.

At the moment I am not suggesting direct influence from Late Tutishcainyo on Machalilla or vice versa. The situation was clearly more complicated than that, for the people at the unknown source of the volcanic-tempered pottery also shared in this exchange of ideas. I am suggesting that at this time there was little difference in cultural level between the Upper Amazon and the Coast of Ecuador and Peru and that there were no major barriers to trade and the free exchange of ideas between these two areas. In whichever direction the influences were moving, the closeness of the similarities between Late Tutishcainyo and Machalilla suggests that the radiocarbon dates for the Ecuadorian culture, between 1000 and 1200 BC, are more or less applicable to the culture in the Peruvian selva.

SHAKIMU

Shakimu ceramics were discovered in 1956. A deep excavation in the Shipibo village of San Francisco de Yarinacocha, UCA-2, encountered a midden containing Shakimu materials overlying a deposit containing Late Tutishcainyo ceramics, and buried under a deep and rich refuse layer of the later Hupa-iya culture. In 1964 Shakimu materials were recovered in abundance from Jose's Hill, UCA-34, a large site immediately to the northwest of the Tutishcainyo site, and in lesser quantity from the lowest levels of the Cumancaya site, UCA-22, about 100 kilometres up the Ucayali from Pucallpa.

The Shakimu materials from the 1956 excavations were so different from the Late Tutishcainyo ceramics that it was a moot point whether Shakimu represented an intrusion of new peoples into the Central Ucayali Valley or a highly modified outgrowth of Late Tutishcainyo separated from it by a considerable span of time. The materials from Jose's Hill definitely settled this question. It is clear that these represent an earlier manifestation of the

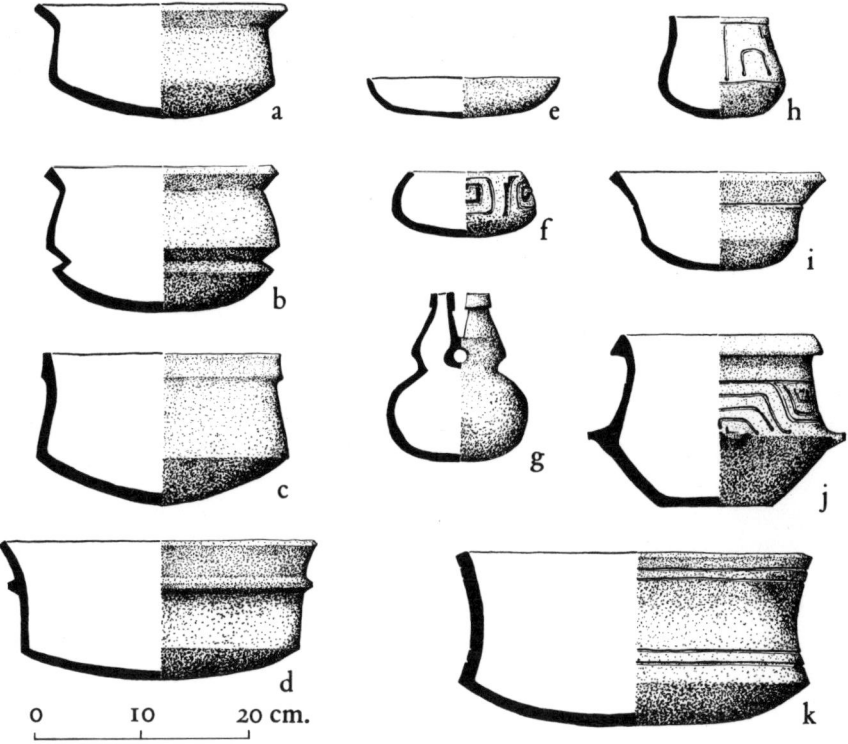

Fig. 10 Typical Early Shakimu vessel forms and decoration. Plain surfaces, a–e, g; incised, h–k; excised, f

Shakimu style and have been designated Early Shakimu. Most of the content of Early Shakimu culture was the result of gradual development out of Late Tutishcainyo, while a minority of cultural traits represent influence from outside the Ucayali Basin. In fact Early Shakimu is readily divisible into two distinct styles. The majority of vessels are plain with well-smoothed surfaces, or are decorated with very simple incised designs. In this group of pottery both the shapes and the design motifs are derived from Late Tutishcainyo, though the modifications through time have been considerable.

Fig. 10 a–d, g–k

93

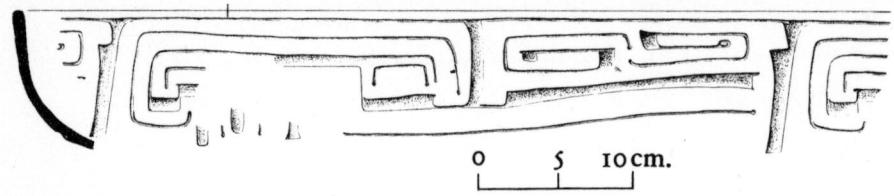

Fig. 11 Unrolled design from large, Early Shakimu bowl with excised decoration and heavy, highly burnished, dark red slip applied over the excised design.

Fig. 10 f
Plates 9, 12
Fig. 11

Fig. 11

The other group of pottery has complex excised designs frequently covered with a lustrous, red slip after the vessel had been carved, but before it was fired. These designs are largely confined to vessel shapes that are foreign to the Tutishcainyo tradition, the most important being three forms of flat-bottomed, open bowls. The inspiration for these vessels came from the Central Andes. In both the Highlands and the Coast of Peru, vessels of this form are associated with the Chavín art style and frequently carry fragments of Chavín iconography as their design motifs. It even seems possible that some of the design elements in Early Shakimu represent attempts at Chavín iconography by artists who only partially understood it.

Early Shakimu, then, represents a people still in the Tutishcainyo cultural tradition but strongly influenced by the spread of decorative techniques, vessel shapes, and iconography which is known as the Chavín Horizon. There has been considerable speculation about the political and religious institutions which underlay the spread of these forms, but no satisfactory answer has been found. Whatever the nature of these influences, they were felt well out into the Amazon Basin. As was the case in several areas of the Central Andes such as the Ica Valley, the Chavín style did not supplant the local style but was added to it and modified it. The radiocarbon date of $650 \text{ BC} \pm 200$ (Y-1543), on the Early Shakimu materials from Jose's Hill fits well with these suggestions of alignment with the Chavín Horizon in the Central Andes.

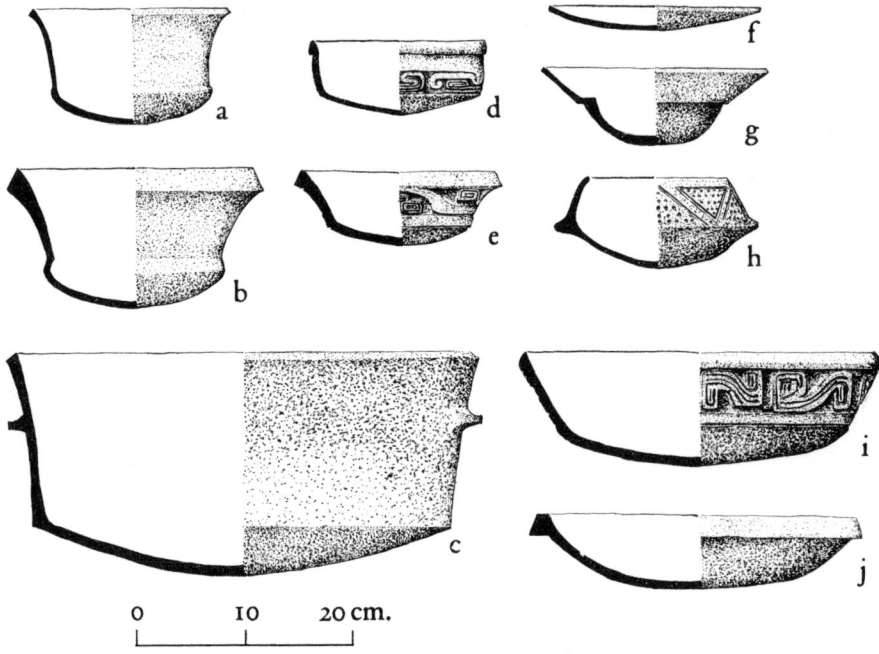

Fig. 12 Typical Late Shakimu vessels: a, b, f, g, j are characterized by highly burnished surfaces; d, e, i, by excised designs; h shows a rare example of zoned punctation; large urns, c, have plain, poorly smoothed surfaces

In Late Shakimu the two stylistic traditions had merged completely. Excised decoration became more common and was applied indiscriminately to almost all vessel forms. The slipped surfaces of the plain ware were polished to a brilliant sheen. All traces of Chavín influence had now disappeared.

THE ALTO PACHITEA

To date, our most extensive archaeological information on human occupation of the more humid *ceja* zone comes from the Río Nazaratequi at the point where it breaks out of Cerro del Sal. The elevation here is between 300 and 400 metres.

The Upper Amazon

At the time of the first Spanish contact nearly the whole of the Upper Pachitea Basin was occupied by the Amuesha, speaking one of the most divergent branches of Arawakan.

The excavations of William Allen are our source of information on the archaeology of the Alto Pachitea. On the basis of field work conducted in 1964, substantiated by further work in 1968, he has documented a long sequence of occupations extending from 1600 or 1700 BC to recent times. Excavations at numerous sites along the Nazaratequi, Neguachi and Pichis have shown the stratigraphic superposition of the several cultural complexes. The most complete stratigraphic column comes from deep cuts made at Casa de la Tía, PAC-14, and the following comments are based on materials from that site.

The earlier half of the cultural sequence in the Alto Pachitea consists of three complexes, all clearly in the same ceramic tradition and showing a progressively greater degree of artistic complexity. From early to late they are Cobichaniqui, Pangotsi, and Nazaratequi.

The Cobichaniqui complex is defined on the basis of 67 sherds recovered from the lowest levels at the Casa de la Tía site. There are three C14 assays from these levels, 1637 BC $\pm$ 95 (P-992), 1778 BC $\pm$ 65 (P-991), and 1418 BC $\pm$ 77 (P-990), indicating a date for the Cobichaniqui material in excess of 1500 BC.

The number of Cobichaniqui sherds recovered per unit volume of midden was small. Either pottery was rare during these times or, as is more likely, the deposit excavated was peripheral to the centre of the Cobichaniqui settlement. The most obvious technological features of Cobichaniqui pottery are an abundant fine sand temper, which in some instances was combined with crushed shell; and highly polished, slipped surfaces. It would appear that the potter had four distinct colours of slip to choose from, black, brown, tan and buff. There was no instance of these different coloured washes being used to paint designs but

The Early Tropical Forest Cultures

sometimes the exterior and interior of the vessel were slipped different colours. Brown was the most frequently used; black was next in popularity. Aside from the highly polished surfaces, there is no decoration on the small sample of Cobichaniqui pottery which has been studied so far. Only two vessel shapes are indicated in the sample but a larger number of sherds would almost certainly show greater range. The two shapes would have served for food vessels and/or drinking cups. The presence of a few thicker sherds with coarser temper suggests that the Cobichaniqui people had cooking pots.

Fig. 13

Until more Cobichaniqui villages have been excavated it will be impossible to flesh out our picture of these people. All that is certain is that between 1500 and 2000 BC there were people on the Alto Pachitea already making pottery far removed from the earliest experiments in ceramics.

The Pangotsi complex is represented by 355 sherds concentrated between 69 and 107 cm. deep in Cut D at Casa de la Tía, and in the lowest levels of Cut A. Copious Pangotsi material has also been noted at other sites on the Nazaratequi, and it appears that the people responsible for the Pangotsi complex already represented a large and widespread population. A C14 assay from the level containing the greatest concentration of Pangotsi materials yielded a date of 1275 BC $\pm$ 68 (P-993).

Pangotsi originated as a gradual evolution out of Cobichaniqui, but the development seems not to have taken place at the Casa de la Tía site. The most obvious distinction between Cobichaniqui and Pangotsi pottery is in tempering material. The two groups do not overlap in this respect. The coarse sand temper projecting

Fig. 13 The only vessel forms demonstrable for the Cobichaniqui Complex, the oldest known ceramics on the Alto Pachitea.

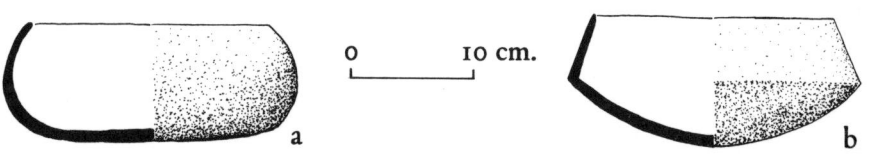

The Upper Amazon

from the surfaces of Pangotsi ceramics contrasts sharply with the fine sand temper of Cobichaniqui. A thick slip of fine clay was applied to mask irregularities. Four distinct slips were available to the potter: chocolate brown, light brown, black, and red. The slipped surfaces were well polished. Again there were examples with the interior painted one colour and the exterior painted another, but there were no painted designs. A red paint probably applied after firing can be noted in the incised lines of some of the better executed pieces.

Fig. 14 a, f, g

A small percentage of Pangotsi pottery was decorated with well executed incised lines. Most of the designs were simple, consisting of nested rectangles, although there were a few involved curvilinear scrolls. Excision is sometimes combined with incision to produce more complicated layouts. Rows of punctations occur below some rims; vertical strap-handles, horizontal lugs, and even crude *adornos* are present.

Fig. 14 c
Plate 15

Fig. 14 a, d, f, g
Fig. 14 e, h

A wide range of vessel shapes is indicated by the sample. The two shapes present in Cobichaniqui are continued. The finest surfaces and most carefully executed decoration are found on the small serving vessels. There is now abundant evidence for cooking pots of a coarser utility ware.

The Nazaratequi complex is present at many sites in the Alto Pachitea, and the refuse deposits are typically large with a high content of ceramic material. In Cut D at Casa de la Tía, Nazaratequi materials are concentrated between a depth of 25 and 68 cm. Cut D alone produced over 7,000 sherds of the Nazaratequi complex. All evidence suggests that settlements contained several hundred people and were of long duration. A high population density is indicated.

A date of 500–600 B C seems probable for the beginning of the Nazaratequi occupation. There are two C_{14} assays on charcoal from complexes which are demonstrably later than Nazaratequi and which indicate that the Nazaratequi domination of the Alto Pachitea could not have survived beyond A D 400.

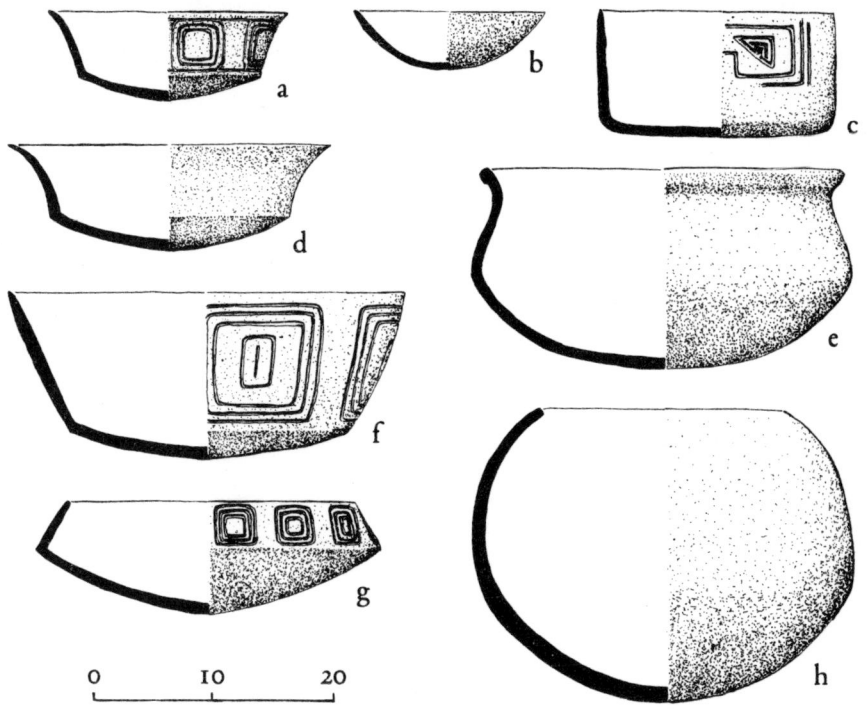

Fig. 14 Typical Pangotsi vessel forms. The broad line, incised designs, a, f, g, and the excised designs, c, are relatively rare

The Nazaratequi ceramic style is an outgrowth of Pangotsi. Profuse sand tempering continued to be the norm, but there was a considerable variation in the size of grain used. Fine sand was typical of the decorated serving ware, while very coarse sand was standard for the large utility vessels. The irregular surface of the sandy paste was again covered with a polished slip. Three colours were used: a brown slip considered appropriate for the utility ware; a black slip for the serving vessels; and a red slip used only on restricted zones bounded by incision.

The tradition of beautifully finished and decorated serving vessels continued, and the number of form categories increased.

Fig. 15 a–f
Fig. 15 g–i

Fig. 15 a–f

The Upper Amazon

Plate 17

Zoned red painting was frequent, and a thick red paint put on after firing was often used to fill the incisions and punctations on these vessels. The nested-rectangle motifs of Pangotsi continued, but typically they had evolved into more complex rectilinear designs. There is a great use of step motifs and zigzag lines, and the complex incised designs combined with three different colour schemes of zoned painting, black and red, brown and red, and brown and black, attest an advanced artistic tradition.

Fig. 15 d
Plate 17

The Nazaratequi ceramics offer a wide array of forms from which some important functional interpretations can be drawn. The *comal* is a clear indication that bitter manioc was now a staple. Containers for the transport and storage of water were now standardized. Very large urns could only have been required for

Fig. 15 g
Fig. 15 h
Fig. 15 i

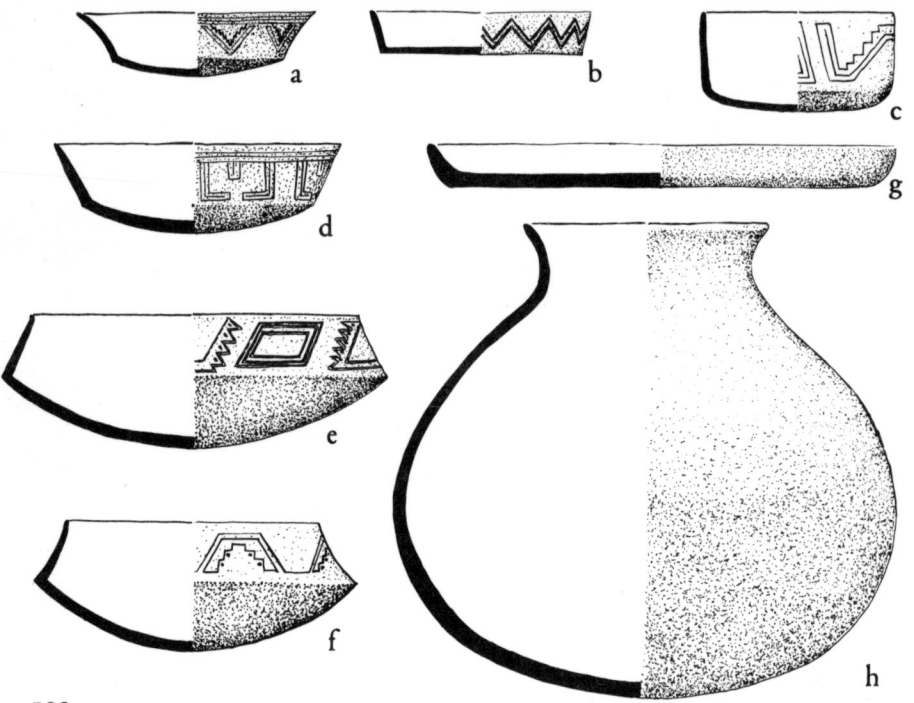

The Early Tropical Forest Cultures

the preparation of vast quantities of beer, and it appears that the Tropical Forest pattern of fiestas was already in full swing on the Alto Pachitea.

We can also infer that the participants in these fiestas carefully painted their bodies and faces in honour of the occasion. A cylindrical roller stamp of fired clay with a carved design was recovered from the Nazaratequi midden. Such stamps are still widely used in tropical South America to apply paint to the face and body. They are also a very ancient trait in Mesoamerica, in Coastal Peru, and in the Lowland of Colombia and Ecuador. Their sporadic archaeological distribution is probably due to the fact that the material used was more frequently carved wood than ceramics, and they are thus not preserved.

Plate 16

Fig. 51

Fig. 15 Nazaratequi vessel forms. Zoned red slipping and post-firing red fill of incisions and punctuations were frequent additions to the incised decoration. Incised decoration was typical on vessels with a black slip while utility ware was finished with a brown slip. The presence of comals, g, *makes it highly probable that bitter manioc was being processed for bread and flour*

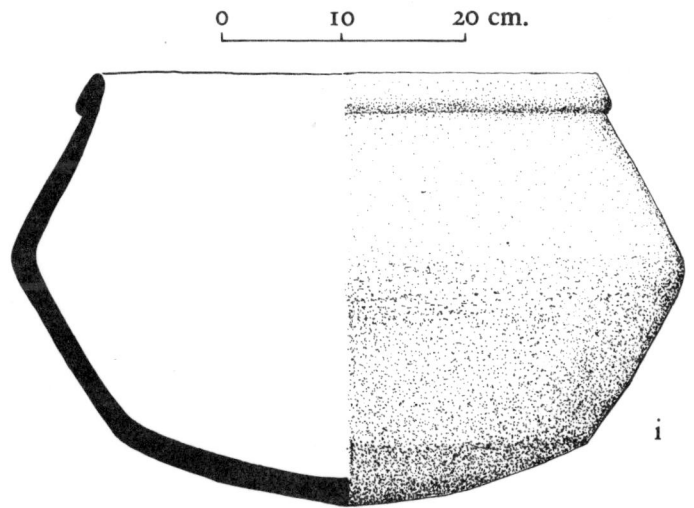

The Upper Amazon

The evident prosperity and high level of culture of the Nazaratequi peoples was terminated by the invasion of peoples of a completely different cultural tradition.

The cultural development from Cobichaniqui to Nazaratequi forms a continuum which can well be designated the Nazaratequi tradition. It is clear that much of the time span occupied by this continuous cultural development in the Alto Pachitea overlaps that involved in the long continuous evolution from Early Tutishcainyo to Late Shakimu on the Central Ucayali. Though there are certain generalized similarities between the Tutishcainyo tradition and the Nazaratequi tradition, especially in the carefully shaped and nicely decorated food bowls, it is impossible to derive the former directly from any known member of the Nazaratequi tradition or vice versa. The latter is consistently simpler and lacks many of the more complex features of the Tutishcainyo tradition such as basal flanges, labial flanges, zoned texturing, and double-spout-and-bridge bottles.

THE CAVE OF THE OWLS

The Cave of the Owls, a huge solution cavern also in the *ceja* zone near Tingo María, has produced a very early ceramic style. The cave is one of the largest known rookeries of the Oil Bird, *Steatornis*, and one suspects that the archaeological remains resulted from the Indians' long-term exploitation of the young birds as a source of oil. It is too damp to be a pleasant place to live in.

The archaeological materials come from a mixture of guano and palm husks which has been much churned by recent guano-mining operations. Two distinct styles of pottery have been recovered from the cave, and though clear-cut stratigraphy is lacking they are clearly of different age.

For the moment our interest is entirely on the thin, hard pottery which has been designated Cave of the Owls Fine Ware. This closely resembles the ceramics of the Kotosh tradition in the

The Early Tropical Forest Cultures

Huánuco Basin and the ceramics of the Tutishcainyo tradition on the Central Ucayali. Besides its highly polished, slipped surfaces, Cave of the Owls Fine Ware is characterized by carefully executed, zoned, fine-line hatched incision. The textured areas were frequently treated with a red paint applied after firing. In execution the zoned hatching closely parallels that of the earliest member of the Kotosh tradition, Kotosh Waira-jirca. Two fine-ware sherds from the Cave of the Owls are identical to Kotosh Waira-jirca types and were more probably manufactured near Huánuco rather than near Tingo María. Cave of the Owls Fine Ware differs from Kotosh Waira-jirca pottery mainly in its greater emphasis on modelling and appliqué, its more frequent use of handles, and in its range of vessel shapes. The only common vessel form represented in Cave of the Owls Fine Ware also occurs in Late Tutishcainyo.

Plates 13, 14

Fig. 9 f

The style is of greatest importance for it indicates that still a third area of the tropical lowlands of Peru was occupied well back in the second millennium BC. It also offers evidence as to the proper chronological alignment between the Central Ucayali sequence and the Huánuco Basin sequence, suggesting at least some temporal overlap between Late Tutishcainyo and Kotosh Waira-jirca.

THE HUANUCO BASIN

All the early settlements in the Huánuco Basin are located on the arid slopes immediately adjacent to the fertile, self-irrigating flood plain. The settlement pattern is oriented to the flood plains, and to their agricultural potential. It would appear that even in these early times the people were unwilling to waste good agricultural land for dwelling-sites.

Plate 19

Large, deep mounds are common around the edge of the flood plain for its total length. They are made up of a series of super-imposed occupation levels. From a very early time the towns had buildings of masonry, and the mounds consist mainly of the rubble of house and temple walls which were partially demolished and levelled off before each rebuilding. The structure of these occupation mounds more closely resembles that of the tells of the Tigris-Euphrates Valley than that of most New World sites.

In terms of the origins of New World agriculture the Huánuco Basin and other basins of similar characteristics, such as the Cochabamba Basin of Bolivia, are of particular interest. In his stimulating discussion of agricultural origins Carl O. Sauer postulated that the complex of crops adapted to the cold climates of the Central Andean Highlands was developed from the Tropical Forest pattern of agriculture. He suggested that Tropical Forest farmers gradually penetrated the basins of the eastern slope of the Andes, first occupying those of intermediate elevation and climate, and experimenting with crops such as potatoes, *oca*, and *ulluco* which will tolerate cool to cold growing conditions. Since the Huánuco Basin presents in actuality the ecological setting which Sauer discussed as a hypothetical possibility, the long record of agricultural occupation in the basin is of greatest significance.

The importance of the site of Kotosh to the culture history of Peru was first recognized by the great Peruvian archaeologist Julio C. Tello, who accurately assessed some of its chronological implications without the benefit of excavations. Since 1960 Kotosh has been the scene of three sessions of intensive excavation by a team of Japanese archaeologists headed by Seiichi Izumi.

During the 1960 excavations, the only session on which we have full publication, extensive samples were obtained from the eight uppermost construction levels of Kotosh, and a pit of limited extent penetrated into the ninth and tenth construction levels. It was in the tenth construction level, Level J, that the remarkable ceremonial structure, The Temple of the Crossed Hands, was discovered. Unlike many of the later structures at Kotosh which were partially razed to provide a level base for subsequent construction, the Temple of the Crossed Hands was

The Early Tropical Forest Cultures

carefully filled with cobbles to provide a platform for a later shrine. Considering its great antiquity, the temple shows many features of architectural sophistication. The relief sculpture of crossed hands modelled in clay is the oldest architectural use of sculpture known in the New World. The central sanctuary shares a number of features with Chuquitanta, one of the largest early temple structures on the Coast of Peru, dating from the late Preceramic.

Plate 18

During subsequent sessions of excavations the whole of the Temple of the Crossed Hands has been cleared and several still deeper levels have been exposed.

Such materials as were recovered from Levels I and J during the 1960 excavations gave no evidence that the inhabitants made and used pottery, and subsequent excavations have fully confirmed the preceramic nature of the lower construction levels. There is limited evidence concerning the economy of the earliest inhabitants of Kotosh. As already noted, the location of the site suggests an agricultural base, and the massive constructions in Levels H and I, as well as in still more ancient levels, argues strongly for a flourishing agricultural system.

The occurrence of cameloid bones as a sacrificial offering in one of the wall niches of the Temple of the Crossed Hands is of great interest. It is probable that the bones are those of the llama and thus an indication of animal domestication and a flourishing pastoral economy. The use of the llama as a sacrificial animal is a typical cultural pattern in the Central Andes; even today most ceremonies of propitiation, divination, curing, and black magic must be sanctified by the sacrifice of a llama. A common food source in the preceramic levels was the domesticated guinea pig.

Plate 18

In contrast to the lack of pottery in Levels I and J, Levels G and H produced quantities of sherds representing the varied and elaborate ceramic industry designated Kotosh Waira-jirca. Carbon from these levels is dated at 1850 ± 110 B C. The earliest preceramic occupations here must date well back into the third millennium B C.

The Upper Amazon

The pottery of Kotosh Waira-jirca is remarkably complex in its range of decorative techniques. This complexity and the high level of technical competence suggests that the ceramic industry did not develop *de novo* in the Huánuco Basin. The nature of Waira-jirca ceramics strongly suggests that the style results from the fusing of two completely distinct ceramic traditions with separate histories. This ceramic heterogeneity might suggest that during the Waira-jirca period the Huánuco Basin was drawing in populations from widely separated parts of Peru.

One of these traditions is part of what Lanning has designated Chira, the earliest pottery on the north-central Coast of Peru. The utility vessels in this tradition, thin and well fired, show a restricted range of shapes. A large globular cooking pot with no external modification around the mouth, but with an internal thickening of the rim giving a comma-shaped rim profile, is by far the most common. This form can occur with either a conical or an evenly rounded bottom. Much of the Coastal pottery in this utility-ware tradition is without decoration. In Kotosh Waira-jirca some of the cooking pots are plain, but many carry well-executed decorations consisting of a shallow incision which grades into linear pattern burnishing. The range of designs executed in shallow incision is small. A semicircle is the germinal motif, and these are arranged either pendent on the rim or in an arcade design immediately below the rim.

The other ceramic tradition which contributed to Kotosh Waira-jirca contained a wide range of sharply carinated vessels. Waira-jirca carinated vessels seldom have decorated labial flanges and never show the decorated basal flanges which are so typical of Early Tutishcainyo, but if one makes these subtractions, almost every one of the Waira-jirca carinated forms has a close parallel in the range of vessels typical of Early Tutishcainyo. The two cultures also share double-spout-and-bridge bottles of very similar form with short, squat spouts and a high, steeply arched bridge which greatly exceeds the height of the spouts.

Fig. 7

The Early Tropical Forest Cultures

The decoration on the carinated vessels in the Waira-jirca tradition consists of carefully executed, fine-line hatching used in zones delimited by broad-line incision. Technically, Early Tutishcainyo zoned hatching and that of Waira-jirca are almost indistinguishable, and in some instances the design motifs and layouts are almost identical. Typical Wira-jirca zoned hatching was covered with a paint applied after firing, which was probably resin-based. In short, all the smaller, better made, and more carefully decorated Waira-jirca vessels derive from a ceramic tradition very much like and very closely related to Early Tutishcainyo, a Tropical Forest ceramic tradition. It would be difficult to derive the non-Andean part of the Waira-jirca ceramics *directly* from Early Tutishcainyo. Given the evidence, one would postulate a collateral relative of Early Tutishcainyo located on the broad flood plain of the Huallaga whose valley broadens immediately down-stream from the city of Tingo María, and suggest that this riverine culture could have contributed the Tropical Forest part of the Waira-jirca ceramics. The poorly known Cave of the Owls Fine Ware discussed above would appear to be a slightly later, direct descendant of such a culture.

The evidence from Kotosh strongly supports Sauer's contention that peoples of Tropical Forest Culture penetrated deeply into the middle-altitude basins along the eastern slope of the Andes and contributed significantly to the evolution of Central Andean civilization.

THE BEND OF THE MARAÑON

Fingers of tropical forest extend up the deep valleys between the ranges of the Andes. The furthest penetration of the *selva* into the mountains is along the Valley of the Marañón above the Pongo de Maseriche. It is drier here than in the Amazon Basin proper, but the cover is continuous forest rather than the scattered thorn of the Huánuco Basin. Various western tributaries of the Marañón lead up to low passes in the Peruvian and Ecuadorian Andes and

Plate 20

The Upper Amazon

the distance from *selva* to the Pacific Coast of northern Peru or to the Guayas Basin is small. From earliest times this should have been a major avenue for travel and commerce between the Coast and the Amazon Basin. Our knowledge of this crucial area comes from the work of the Peruvian archaeologist, Pedro Rojas Ponce. Most interesting is the site of Huayurco, west of the bend of the Marañón at the junction of its tributaries, the Chinchipe and Tabaconas. The excavations of Rojas indicate at least a two-fold stratigraphy. The upper level of Huayurco produced a range of late pottery including corrugated ware similar to that of the Cumancaya complex on the Central Ucayali. The lower stratum contained quantities of broken stone bowls, potsherds, and several burials with an impressive quantity of grave goods. One of the burials had a necklace of nicely worked marine-shell beads. Trumpets of marine conch shells also occurred as grave offerings. Several complete stone bowls, some with polished plain surfaces, others with excised scroll designs, were found in association with the burials. The excised scroll designs are similar to those of Early Shakimu. The workmanship on the stone bowls was of a high order, and a wide range of lithic materials was used. Noteworthy is a small bowl of veined onyx with walls ground so thin as to be translucent, showing the veining to advantage. A number of stone bowls were furnished with *adornos*. The most remarkable of these, representing the head of a male howler monkey in the act of vocalizing, shows a fine command of technique as well as careful observation of the subject.

The quantity of fragmentary and unfinished stone bowls from Huayurco indicates that it was an important manufacturing centre. It is clear that the people of Huayurco were engaged in lively trade with Coastal Peru, since bowls similar to those of Huayurco have been found in a range of late Preceramic and Initial Period sites. A careful study of lithic materials may enable us to trace the area over which Huayurco bowls were traded.

The Early Tropical Forest Cultures

The pottery from the lower stratum of the Huayurco site serves to date this occupation in relation to the sequences of the near-by Highlands. Much is burnished black ware of a kind widespread during and slightly before the Chavín Horizon. The most spectacular example is a graceful bottle which would be equally at home at Chavín de Huantar or in Kotosh Kotosh or Kotosh Chavín levels of the Huánuco Basin site. Some of the pottery from the lower level is different in style with vertical ribs of appliqué and punctate decoration strongly reminiscent of the appliqué work in Late Tutishcainyo.

Plate 22

Plate 24

ECUADOR

Yasuní, the oldest ceramic complex encountered by Evans and Meggers during their survey of the Río Napo, dates only to 50 BC ± 90 (SI-300). The pottery is in abominable condition and has lost most of its surfaces. A few sherds carry traces of crude zoned hatching, but the total range of shapes present in Yasuní does not suggest close affinities with the Tutishcainyo tradition, and there are definite indications of Barrancoid influence from the Central Amazon.

From further to the south in the Ecuadorian Montaña there are other collections of probably early date. Bushnell has published sherds from Macas, including carinated vessels and a double-spout-and-bridge bottle strongly reminiscent of Late Tutishcainyo. Harner, in the course of his ethnographic work among the Jívaro, made several test excavations, exposing deep cultural deposits. The ceramics have never been studied in detail, but it is clear that several components are represented. Some of the sherds exhibit zoned lustre painting similar to that of the Chorrera Phase in the Guayas Basin. Other sherds show vessel shapes and decoration very similar to Late Tutishcainyo. A third group of large coarse sherds, which are frequently of the corrugated variety, relates to the much later Cumancaya complex on the Central Ucayali.

The Upper Amazon

THE MORE DISTANT CULTURAL RELATIONSHIPS OF THE EARLY TROPICAL FOREST CULTURES OF THE UPPER AMAZON

In discussing distant relationships between ceramic complexes I shall proceed on the assumption that the most reliable indications of historical relationship are to be found in the sharing of a similar set of vessel shapes. As suggested above, the total set of vessels made by a group can tell us a lot about the basic economy. The set of shapes is also intimately related to the ceremony and etiquette of offering and consuming food. Basic modes of food preparation and serving and the vessel shapes that they require are likely to be more stable over long periods of time than the modes of surface treatment and decorative motifs. This proposition can be proved repeatedly in the Central Andes and also holds for the Tutishcainyo tradition.

Working on the assumption that sets of vessel shapes are the most important indication of distant historical relationships (a view not shared by some anthropologists), I regard as highly significant the similarities in serving vessels shared by most of the ceramic complexes discussed so far. All have nicely finished, in most cases attractively decorated, bowls with round bases, markedly concave sides and a sharp ridge at the juncture of side and bottom of the vessel. It is also interesting that the most common or only form of bottle among many of these complexes is a double-spout-and-bridge type.

In northern South America there are a number of ceramic complexes which also emphasize finely made and carefully decorated serving bowls with round bases, concave sides and marked carinations at the boundary between the two zones. These are most common in Venezuela on the flood plains of the Lower Orinoco, on the Coast, and on out into the Antilles. The basic set of vessel forms and a tendency to red and white painted decoration is common to all of these complexes, and there is no doubt that a valid historical relationship exists among all of them; the ceramic tradition embracing them has been designated

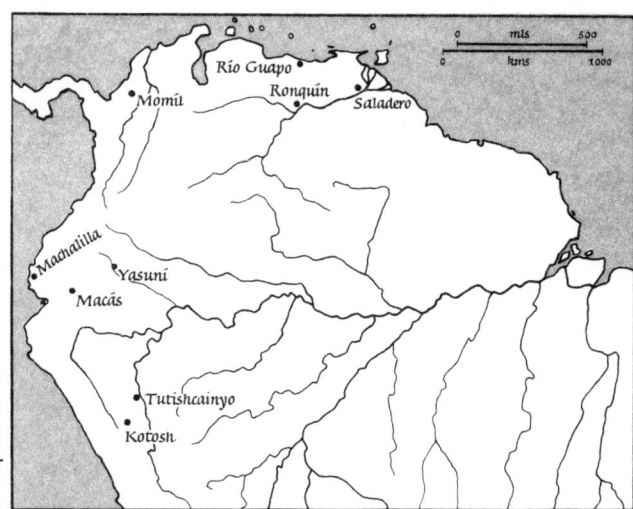

Fig. 16 *The distribution of early ceramic complexes having a range of vessel shapes similar to that of Early Tutishcainyo*

Saladoid by Cruxent and Rouse after the best known of these complexes, Saladero, on the Lower Orinoco. Saladero gives a minimum age of 1000 B C. The carinated vessel forms of Saladero lack either labial or basal flanges, and in this respect more closely resemble the simpler set of shapes of the Nazaratequi tradition than the elaborated forms of the Tutishcainyo tradition. A marked fondness for decorative additions to vessel rims is noticeable in the Antillian Saladoid materials, in the early coastal complex, Río Guapo, and in the very lowest levels of the Ronquín site on the flood plain of the Middle Orinoco. All three diverge from Saladero in this respect and resemble the Tutishcainyo tradition. Antillian Saladoid and Río Guapo show zoned, fine-line cross hatching very like that of Early Tutishcainyo in both technique and decorative effect; while the painted and zoned incised scroll designs typical of the lowest levels of the Ronquín site are very like the scroll designs common on Early Tutishcainyo serving bowls.

Fig. 7 f

Given the network of waterways connecting the Amazon and Orinoco Basins, I cannot believe that the cultural similarities

The Upper Amazon

between the early Tropical Forest Cultures of the Upper Amazon and the Saladoid tradition of Venezuela are fortuitous. The ceramic evidence suggests to me that all these ceramic traditions converge to a single ceramic complex and a single homeland at some point 1,500 to 1,000 years earlier than the earliest known representatives. The shared simplicity of the Saladero complex and the Nazaratequi tradition on the one hand, and the closely similar elaborations of Antillian Saladoid, Río Guapo, Lowest Ronquín, and the Tutishcainyo tradition on the other, together suggest that it was a question of two waves of migration rather than one. The bearers of Saladero and the Nazaratequi tradition moved out earlier than the ancestors of those responsible for the more fully elaborated ceramics.

Fig. 16

The distribution of these complexes around the whole periphery of the Upper Amazon Basin suggests that this homeland is to be sought in the Central Amazon near the confluence of the Upper Amazon, the Negro and the Madeira. The ceramic evidence points to a pattern of population movement similar to that indicated by the distribution of the more divergent branches of Arawakan. It is of greatest interest that the Antillian Saladoid ceramics can be attributed without reasonable doubt to the speakers of Proto-Taino, the northernmost of the non-Maipuran Arawakan families, while there is every reason to believe that the Nazaratequi tradition was the work of the speakers of Proto-Amuesha.

No trace of these carinated ceramics has appeared on the Lower Amazon, suggesting that there were no down-stream migrations at this time. Though now known to be very early, Ananatuba, the oldest culture on Marajó at the mouth of the Amazon, is completely distinct from any of the ceramic complexes we have been discussing, and the use of zoned cross hatching in Ananatuba resembles neither Early Tutishcainyo nor Río Guapo in technique and design layout.

CHAPTER VI
The Barrancoid Peoples and their Migrations

CERAMICS of the Barrancoid tradition have a remarkably widespread distribution in South America, and follow such a consistent stylistic patterning that they are easily recognizable wherever they occur. It was the obvious similarities between the Hupa-iya ceramics of the Ucayali Basin and the Los Barrancos ceramics of the Lower Orinoco that first started me thinking about the problem of population movements in the tropical lowlands of South America.

NORTHERN BARRANCOID

The Barrancoid or Modelled-Incised tradition was first recognized on the flood plain of the Lower Orinoco, and the most copiously illustrated representatives of the tradition are still in Venezuela and Guyana. The first agricultural settlers on the alluvial flood plain of the Lower Orinoco were the people making pottery of the Saladero Style discussed in the last chapter. By 700 to 800 B C the Saladero population had been displaced by a wave of immigrants making pottery of a completely different aspect. It would appear that the newcomers were more numerous than the Saladero peoples and had a different pattern of settlement. While the garbage of the Saladero peoples was concentrated in mounds of limited extent, the intruders, making pottery of the Barrancas Style, left their refuse in a thick continuous sheet covering huge areas of the river bank. The Barrancas middens contain a tremendous amount of pottery, and most of the vessels were attractively decorated. Broad-line incision on smoothed to polished surfaces was combined with appliqué and the modelling of the sides of the vessels into high relief. Most commonly the

The Upper Amazon

Fig. 17 a appliqué was geometric, just domes or pellets used to emphasize key points of a design; but not infrequently modelling and appliqué were combined to turn the whole vessel into an anthropomorphic or zoomorphic effigy.

When not seeking to be representational, Barrancas designs are relatively simple, consisting of widely spaced lines arranged in evenly flowing curves and spirals. Frequently the only decoration will be two parallel lines on the upper surface of a broad labial flange, rather like the flanges on Early Tutishcainyo vessels. These parallel lines are frequently interrupted at the *Fig. 17 a* quadrants of the vessel by appliqué pellets. Double-spout-and-bridge bottles usually have anthropomorphic spouts.

The griddles used for making manioc bread and flour are a prominent part of the ceramic refuse along with thick sherds from huge fermentation urns. The size and duration of the Barrancas settlements as well as the aesthetic elaboration of the pottery attest a secure economic basis and the complex patterns of social and political controls necessary to make such large communities stable.

Once the Barrancas peoples had settled on the rich alluvial lands of the Lower Orinoco, they continued to flourish for more than 1,000 years. The ceramic style gradually evolved as the incised lines became more closely spaced, and design layouts more complex. The use of small appliqué pellets with central punctations increased, and the simply decorated, continuous labial flanges of Barrancas changed into asymmetrical, dis-*Fig. 17 e, f* continuous rim-lugs with intricate designs. This later segment of the stylistic continuum is designated Los Barrancos.

The taking-over of the Lower Orinoco was by no means the limit of the territorial acquisitiveness of the Barrancoid peoples. Before the Barrancas style had started to evolve into Los Barrancas colonies were budding-off from the settlements on the Lower Orinoco. One wave moved east along the Guiana Coast *Fig. 17 c, d* becoming the Early Mabaruma Phase of north-western Guyana.

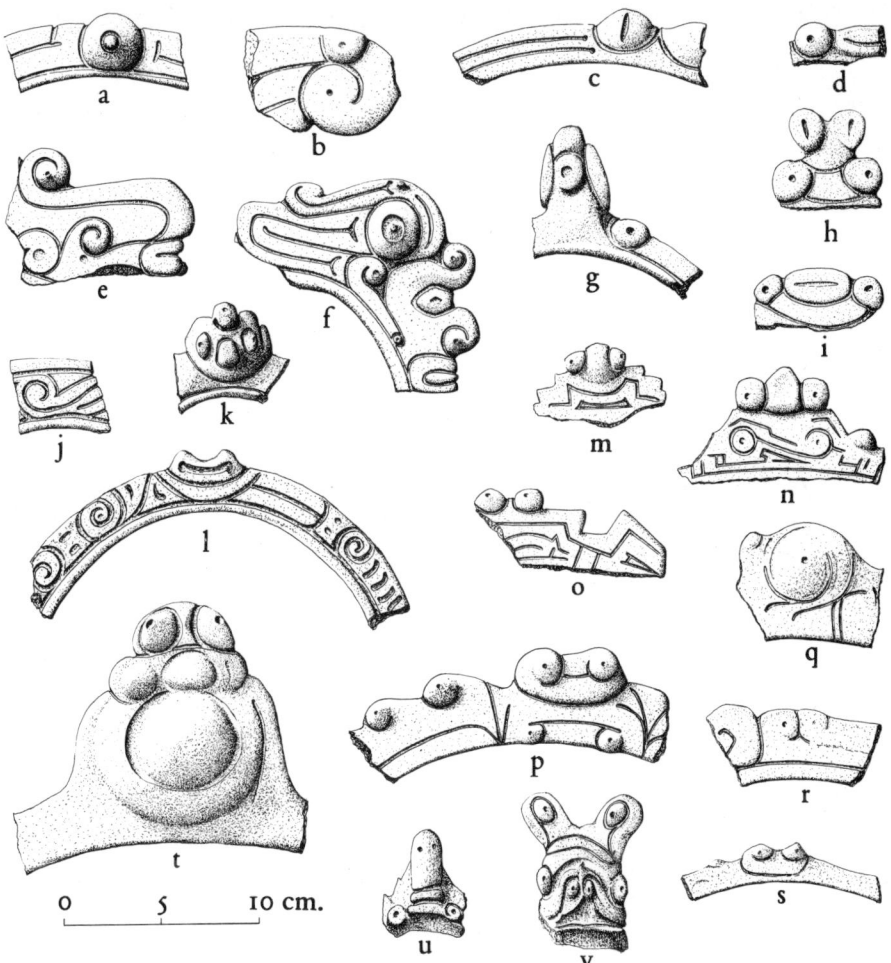

Fig. 17 Sherds in the Barrancoid Tradition from Venezuela, Guyana, and the Amazon Basin; all showing a combination of modelling and broad-line incision. Barrancas Style, Saladero Site, Lower Orinoco, Venezuela, a–b; Los Barrancos Style, vicinity of Barrancas, Lower Orinoco, Venezuela, e–f; Early Mabaruma Phase, Northwestern Guyana, c–d; El Palito Style, El Palito Site Coastal Venezuela, g–i; Santarém, mouth of the Río Tapajós, Lower Amazon, j–l; Oriximiná, mouth of Río Trombetas, Central Amazon, m–o; Site of Mangueira, Río Japurá, Upper Amazon Basin, p; Site of Mangueiras (possibly the same site as Mangueira), Río Japurá, Upper Amazon Basin, q–s; Manacapurú, mainstream of Upper Amazon, t; Site of Mamiá, near Coarí on mainstream of Upper Amazon, u–v

The Upper Amazon

Fig. 17 g–i

To the west, people with a ceramic complex derived from Barrancas spread to the Coast at El Palito where particularly large middens with high sherd content are found. El Palito preserved more of the elaboration of Barrancas than does Early Mabaruma, and anthropomorphic double-spout-and-bridge bottles are common. Somewhat later a Barrancoid ceramic style was spread into Trinidad. This last expansion more closely resembles Los Barrancos than Barrancas. The migration routes and distribution pattern of the Antillian, Venezuelan and Guianan Barrancoid peoples makes it almost certain that they were the invaders who introduced Maipuran Arawak into these areas.

It is clear, then, that the Barrancoid peoples appeared as intruders on the Lower Orinoco and that their cultural tradition did not evolve there. Barrancas is the oldest style within the northern branch of the Barrancoid tradition and is ancestral to all the others in Venezuela, the Guianas and the Antilles. In order to determine whence the Barrancas invasion entered the Lower Orinoco and from what ceramic tradition the Barrancas complex derived, one must search for complexes which are specifically similar to Barrancas, not complexes which show a generalized similarity to the later members of the Barrancoid tradition.

It is clear that the Guiana Coast and the Antilles can be eliminated immediately. It appears to me that a derivation from the west either along the Caribbean Coast or along the Venezuelan Andes is equally unlikely. One should remember that a migration of ceramic-using, agricultural people along the Caribbean Coast of Venezuela is extremely unlikely since during this time the coast of Venezuela continued to be occupied by peoples of Archaic economy, lacking ceramics.

Since north, east, and west are excluded as possible sources for the Barrancas people, we must look to the south and conclude that the bearers of the Barrancas style came down the Orinoco

The Barrancoid People and their Migrations

and had their ultimate origins in the Upper Orinoco, Río Negro or Amazon Basin.

HUPA-IYA

Around 200 B C a new group of people appeared on the Central Ucayali displacing the previous inhabitants. These invaders brought with them a Barrancoid ceramic style which has been designated Hupa-iya. There can be no doubt that the Hupa-iya people were intruders since their ceramic style shows no continuities with the previous, Late Shakimu, pottery style. There is a new range of vessel shapes. The designs and the organization of the decorative fields are totally different.

The Hupa-iya invasion was from down-stream and ultimately from the Central Amazon. The Highlands of Peru, Ecuador, and Colombia are sufficiently well known for them to be excluded as possible hearths for a Barrancoid style. Though several hundred years later, the appearance of the Hupa-iya peoples on the Central Ucayali is a demographic phenomenon identical to the push of the Barrancas peoples into the Lower Orinoco.

The Barrancoid characteristics of the Hupa-iya Complex can be summarized briefly. The most common vessel shapes are hemispherical to slightly constricted bowls with evenly curving, convex exteriors. Usually these bowls are furnished with broad, horizontal lugs immediately below the rim. The lugs are decorated on their upper surface with a combination of incision and appliqué pellets, and resemble closely the lugs in Los Barrancos, though the Hupa-iya examples are less elaborate. The decorative field covers the bottom of the bowl and is delimited by a horizontal line about 2 cm. below the rim.

Fig. 18 a–d

Fig. 18 b

Fig. 18 a–c

The broad-line incision of Hupa-iya is organized into simple scroll designs typical of other Barrancoid complexes. The decorated, vertical loop handles common in Hupa-iya are also an invariable feature of Barrancoid complexes from Barrancas on. The modification of vessels into zoomorphic forms, the use of

Plate 28

Fig. 18 j

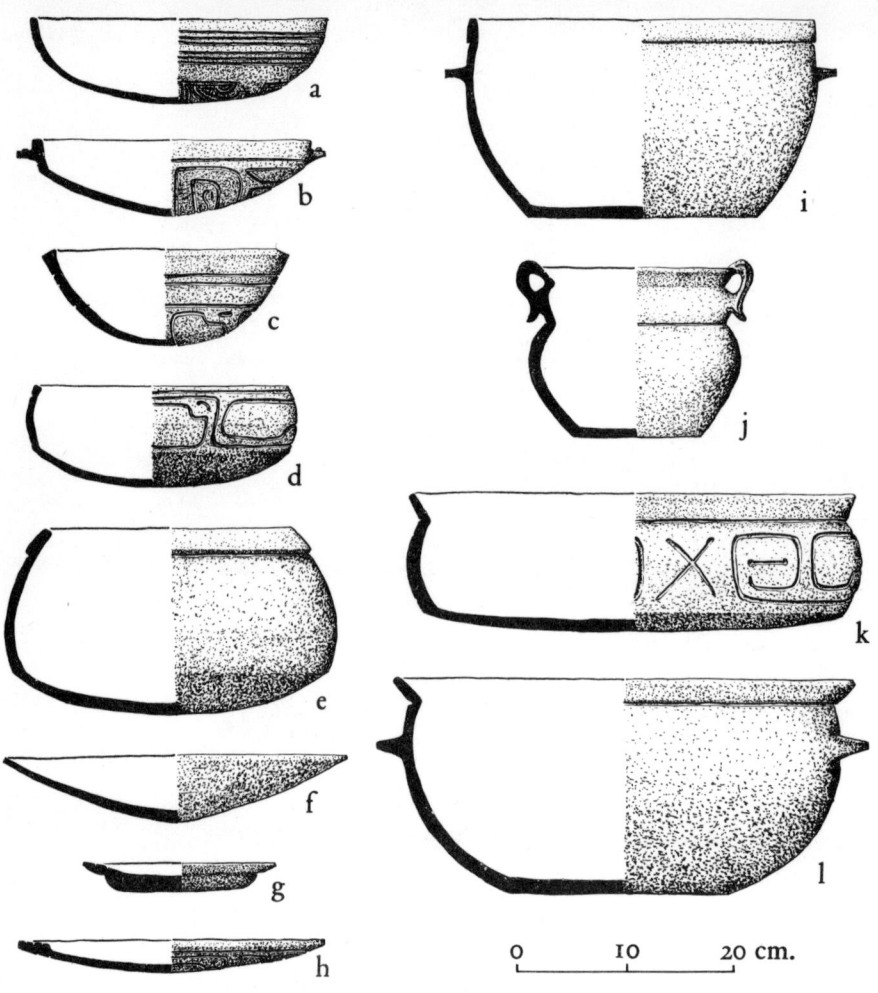

Fig. 18 Vessel shapes and broad-line incised decoration typical of the Hupa-iya Complex

Plate 30

strips of appliqué to indicate the limbs of birds and animals and the affixing of zoomorphic *adornos* to the rims of bowls all occur in Hupa-iya, and are by no means rare. Well over fifty per cent of all Hupa-iya pottery carried some form of incised or modelled and incised adornment.

The Barrancoid People and their Migrations

The frequency of the buck-pot form suggests that bitter manioc was the staple and was being processed for bread and flour. Small to medium-sized circular platters appear to have served as comals.

Fig. 18 k, l

Fig. 18 g, h

There is little evidence for the size, physical layout, or population density of the towns of the earlier Tropical Forest peoples on the Central Ucayali, since the remaining middens are eroded to fragments of their original extent. For the Hupa-iya occupation more information is available. At the Hupa-iya site, UCA-2, a mantle of dense midden extends for 600 m. along the edge of the bluff and frequently reaches a depth of 70 cm. Using observations of the modern Shipibo community which covers part of the same area and the volume of midden it is producing, it is estimated that the Hupa-iya midden implies a community of 500 to 1,000 people lasting for a couple of hundred years.

Though we have no house plans, certain assumptions can be made about Hupa-iya architecture. The tremendous volume of daub characteristic of middens of the Tutishcainyo tradition is absent from Hupa-iya refuse. Its disappearance suggests a switch to unwalled houses with earthen floors, rather like the houses of the modern Shipibo.

Quantities of carefully made ceramic spindle whorls appear for the first time. These objects provide the most complete examples of Hupa-iya designs, and indicate a flourishing textile industry. It seems possible that much of the cotton cloth produced was used as a protection against mosquitos, either in the form of the mosquito bar or the thick, loosely woven, outer garment, the *cushma*, which is essentially a portable mosquito bar. The evidence of the spindle whorls suggests that *cushmas* and possibly even fixed mosquito bars made their appearance on the Central Ucayali, permitting the shift to the more comfortable and more healthful open houses.

Plate 29

Plate 59

The prosperous and dense Hupa-iya occupation on the Central Ucayali was abruptly terminated by the invasion of the

The Upper Amazon

people making Yarinacocha-style pottery. It is doubtful if the contacts between the two ethnic groups were amicable. By AD 100 Barrancoid peoples had been eliminated from the Central Ucayali.

BARRANCOID STYLES OF THE CENTRAL AMAZON

The circumstances surrounding the Barrancas migration into the Lower Orinoco and the Hupa-iya migration into the Central Ucayali suggest that both migrations originated in the Central Amazon Basin, and it is there that we should look for the origins of the Barrancoid style. At present no securely dated styles of a sufficient age to be picked as the source of Barrancas are known, but several styles of blatantly Barrancoid affinities do exist in the Central Amazon, and the recent work of Hilbert has provided dates for some of them.

The Jauarí site on the Lower Amazon flood plain is known from a small collection of sherds. *Adornos* and decorated lugs very like those of Hupa-iya occur, and vessel shapes at Jauarí appear to be basically of Barrancoid type.

Fig. 17 j–l

Many sites near the mouth of the Río Tapajóz, which produce the proto-historic Santarém-style ceramics in quantity, also yield lesser amounts of a very different style which must be earlier. The earlier pottery shows inward-facing rim *adornos*, widely spaced broad-line incision, and simple scroll motifs all of which are emphatically Barrancoid.

Fig. 17 m–o

Up-stream from Santarém, around the mouth of the Trombetas and the Jamunda, there is another cluster of large, deep sites which yield quantities of a highly distinctive style known as Kondurí. Some of the sites producing Kondurí-style pottery also produce lesser amounts of a second style, Estilo-Globular, which in its modelling, its use of appliqué, and its incised scroll designs is typically Barrancoid.

The Itacoatiara style has been recovered at a number of sites from Itacoatiara up-stream to Manaus. As defined by Hilbert

The Barrancoid People and their Migrations

it is a rather heterogeneous collection of pottery, some of which is obviously very late. Most of the Itacoatiara material, however, shows classic Barrancoid *adornos*, Barrancoid vessel forms, and Barrancoid scroll design, though with an overlay of a distinctive style of fine-line incision. The two C_{14} assays relating to Itacoatiara materials are compatible with the obvious Barrancoid affinities of that style, 95 BC $\pm$ 150 and AD 86 $\pm$ 58 (P-372).

The region around Manacapurú, on the Upper Amazon a short way above Manaus, has produced several pottery styles. The polychrome Guarita materials will be discussed later, but other materials show incised labial flanges and complex *adornos* of a Barrancoid form. The stratigraphic excavations of Hilbert at the Manacapurú site demonstrated that the more typically Barrancoid features occur toward the bottom of the midden. There is a date of AD 425 $\pm$ 58 (P-406) for the upper levels.

The site of Mangueiras on the Río Japurá has yielded quantities of pottery of a style known as Japurá. The modelled-incised decoration on some of the bowls is classically Barrancoid, but as will be emphasized in a later chapter, the painted decoration is already evolving in the direction of the Polychrome tradition. The date of AD 635 $\pm$ 59 (P-588) fits nicely with the transitional position of the style between the Barrancoid tradition and the Polychrome tradition.

Fig. 17 p–s

The widespread distribution of Barrancoid styles along the Upper, Central and Lower Amazon is established beyond doubt, and it is almost certain that the linkage connecting Amazonian and Orinoco Barrancoid styles was along the Río Negro and the Casiquiare canal. The Barrancas-like ceramics from the Cotua site on the Upper Orinoco are evidence that this route was used.

NARANJAL AND THE MODERN CAMPA

The sudden disappearance of the Hupa-iya communities from the Central Ucayali Basin raises the question of the fate of those

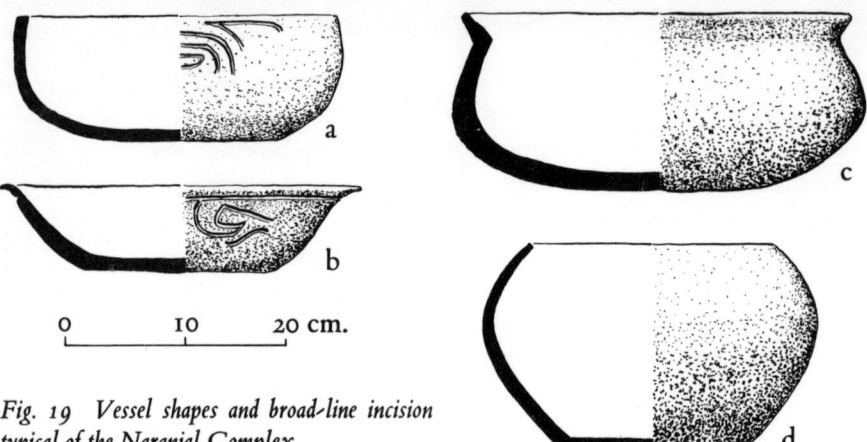

Fig. 19 Vessel shapes and broad-line incision typical of the Naranjal Complex

once-numerous people. Information on the sequence in the Alto Pachitea, and in the Huallaga valley is sufficiently complete, so that these two regions can be excluded as the refuge areas into which the Hupa-iya people were driven. If the Hupa-iya people had retreated up the mainstream of the Ucayali, they might ultimately have arrived in the valley of the Lower Urubamba, the valley of the Lower Apurimac, or in the Chanchamayo, the fertile basin drained by the Perené. Nothing is known of the archaeology of the first two areas, but some site-surveying has been done in the Chanchamayo. Two very different ceramic complexes were noted around the towns of San Ramón and La Mercéd. One of these, a very rough, grit-tempered ware, was found on sites high above the floor of the valley. The other group of ceramics was found on the fertile alluvial deposits immediately above the river.

The Naranjal site, PER-7, covers an area of about 700 m. by 400 m.; the whole being densely strewn with sherds.

Much of the pottery is plain; a few sherds show the kind of scraped or corrugated surfaces which are typical of the Cumancaya complex. The most common form of decoration was an indifferently executed, broad-line incision with design organization similar to that of Hupa-iya. There is a small amount of

The Barrancoid People and their Migrations

appliqué decoration in the form of strips and pellets. The vessels usually decorated are hemispherical bowls, while the buck-pot form is typical of the utility ware.

Fig. 19 a–b
Fig. 19 c

We can be reasonably certain that the Naranjal ceramics are the product of the historic Campa. At the time of the first Spanish contact, the Chanchamayo Basin was occupied by this large and widespread ethnic group. In the seventeenth century the very populous Campa communities were resettled around a chain of Franciscan missions. Early in the eighteenth century the Campa rebelled, and organized under the Messianic leader, Juan Santos Atahualpa, completely expelled the Spanish from the Chanchamayo. The Campa continued to hold the Chanchamayo until the 1870's when Peruvian colonists started to push them back into the hills, and again regained control of this rich agricultural area. Naranjal ceramics are by far the most common style in the Chanchamayo, and the site, PER-7, was probably at one time the location of a Franciscan mission. T-shaped stone axes with flaring bits, of a form typical of other areas recently dominated by the Campa, characterize Naranjal culture.

The broad-line incised decoration of Naranjal strongly suggests that the fifteenth- to nineteenth-century style is directly derived from Hupa-iya through 1,500 years of gradual simplification. The entire previous discussion supports the assumption that it was the ancestors of the modern Campa who brought the Barrancoid Hupa-iya culture into the Ucayali Basin. As was the case in the Orinoco, the most logical candidates for the purveyors of Barrancoid style were the Maipuran Arawak, Campa being a typical Maipuran language.

EASTERN BOLIVIA AND THE UPPER XINGÚ

It is unlikely that any of the ceramic styles at present known from the Lowlands of Bolivia date from earlier than A D 600 to 700. The two earliest of these complexes, that from the site of Chimay on the Río Bení and that from the lower stratum of Mound

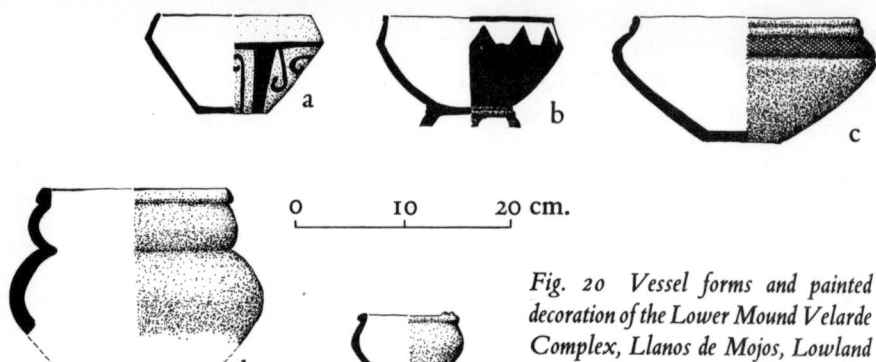

Fig. 20 *Vessel forms and painted decoration of the Lower Mound Velarde Complex, Llanos de Mojos, Lowland Bolivia*

Fig. 20 d, e

Velarde on the Río Mamoré, share a number of features which suggests that they are related to one another, and that both are ultimately derived from the Barrancoid tradition.

Chimay was a very large town which left refuse extending as a continuous mantle 20 cm. thick for 300 m. along the river bank. The midden is now buried under a metre of sterile alluvial deposit laid down in the 1,200 years or so since the town was abandoned. These sterile deposits give a clear indication of the rapid aggregation of the eastern Bolivian lowlands and are an adequate explanation of our ignorance of really early sites. The Chimay site was exposed only in the river bank.

Modelling and incision are the only forms of decoration on Chimay ceramics, and frequently take the form of inward-facing *adornos*, representing animals. The use of circular, appliqué pellets is particularly suggestive of a Barrancoid derivation for the style. The vessel forms are similar to those of the later Barrancoid styles but typically are furnished with four short feet, a trait not otherwise known in Barrancoid styles.

In his early excavation at Mound Velarde, Nordenskiöld demonstrated the existence of two distinct, superimposed strata of midden with different cultural content. The complex from the lower level, usually referred to as Lower Velarde, shows a wide range of vessel forms, some of which are particularly suggestive of Barrancoid. Lower Velarde shares tetrapodal supports and

124

Fig. 21 Sherds of the Lower Mound Velarde Complex showing the two major traditions of decoration, painting and modelled-incised decoration usually in the form of inwardly facing adornos. A pestle of fired clay is depicted in i

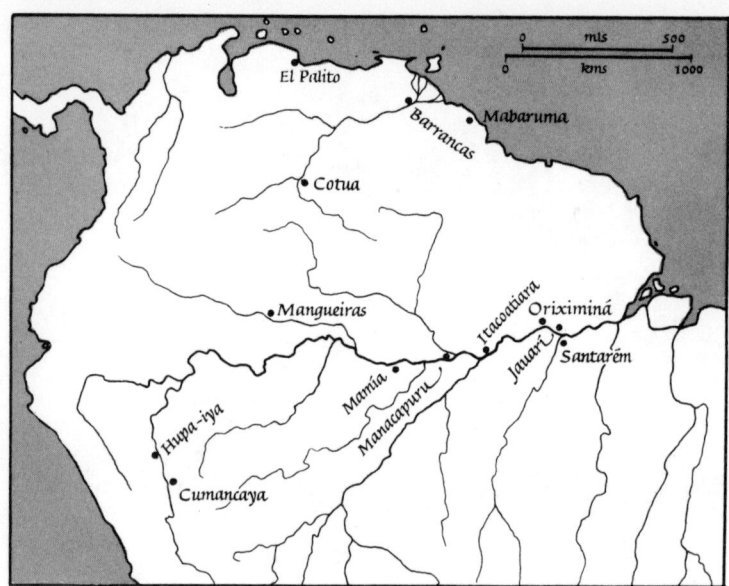

Fig. 22 Distribution of sites producing ceramics clearly in the Barrancoid tradition

inwardly-facing anthropomorphic and zoomorphic modelled-incised *adornos* with Chimay, but in addition shows a wide range of bichrome and polychrome painting.

Fig. 21 b, e
Fig. 21 f–h

The lip lugs and the modelled incised *adornos* could well have evolved from Barrancoid antecedents, but the painted style is clearly derived from the eastern slope of the Andes. We now know that a ceramic tradition emphasizing scroll motifs developed on the slopes of the Bolivian Andes long before the spread of the Tiahuanaco style. The painted motifs of Lower

Fig. 21 a–d

Velarde relate to the Yampara style which is mixed with Tiahuanaco motifs at Misque. The Andean sources for the non-Barrancoid part of Lower Velarde style suggests a dating of AD 600–700.

Tributaries of the Upper Xingú in the Brazilian Highland drain a small pocket of alluvial land which supports a number of groups of Tropical Forest Culture who until recently were

The Barrancoid People and their Migrations

little modified by contact with western civilization. Though speaking diverse languages, some Maipuran, some Tupían, some Cariban, and some a tongue probably related to Gě, these tribelets share a common material culture and intermarry. The kind of inter-village trade and craft specialization so typical of Tropical Forest Culture is well developed here, and it is the Maipuran-speakers who do the potting. Most characteristic of these modern Maipuran ceramics are large, squat buck pots and bowls in the form of animal effigies with modelled-incised inward-facing *adornos* for heads. The nature of the modern ceramic style of the Upper Xingú, brought into the area by Maipuran-speakers, suggests an ultimate derivation from the Barrancoid tradition on the Central Amazon.

SUMMARY

The distribution of ceramic styles which are clearly in the Barrancoid tradition is extensive. The dating and distribution of these styles suggests that they originated on the Central Amazon or perhaps on the network of waterways connecting the Río Negro and the Río Orinoco; their spread took place mainly during the first millennium B C. Linguistic evidence suggests that the Maipuran languages of the Arawakan stock were spreading out of this same area on this time level. Both in Venezuela and in Eastern Peru there is reasonably good evidence that the Barrancoid styles were introduced by invasions of peoples speaking Maipuran languages, and it is assumed that most of the groups of Maipuran-speaking colonists took with them ceramic styles in the Barrancoid tradition. Even if this assumption is correct, we should not expect that all of the Maipuran-speaking groups would still be making Barrancoid-style pottery at the time of the first Spanish contact. In the two millennia following the Maipuran expansion many groups would have adopted the styles of their neighbours or so modified their own style as to make a Barrancoid derivation no longer evident.

Fig. 22

CHAPTER VII

Displaced Persons

EVIDENCE FOR hunting/gathering peoples in the Amazon Basin preceding the expansion of Tropical Forest agriculturalists is meagre. Its dense forests are not favourable to peoples oriented towards hunting. The earliest waves of expansion of Tropical Forest peoples may well have met with little resistance from the small scattered groups living there; frequently they settled previously uninhabited land.

Even later waves of Tropical Forest expansion, as represented by the Tutishcainyo tradition in the Ucayali Basin and the Barrancoid tradition in the Orinoco, were able to push the previous owners of the fertile alluvial bottom lands further from the centres of population pressures and into lands not previously occupied by farmers. The Saladoid people of the Orinoco were driven, first onto the Coast of Venezuela and ultimately into the Antilles. The people of the Nazaratequi tradition were forced up-stream along the Pachitea and onto the reasonably good farmlands of the Andean foot-hills. If the Alto Pachitea can be taken as a typical stretch of Andean foot-hills, we must conclude that these areas were generally and intensively occupied by 1000 BC. By the beginning of our era the more attractive farm lands of the Amazon Basin were all under cultivation.

As population pressures continued to build up in the Central Amazon, and with the previously available safety valves fully pre-empted, further displacement of peoples was of necessity onto the broad expanses of relatively infertile old alluvium away from the major rivers. Here agricultural productivity was much lower. Fishing was non-productive; and dependence on hunting, to make up the protein deficiency in the starchy root-crop diet, necessitated smaller, more dispersed, and more mobile settlements. Detailed studies of groups inhabiting this zone today indicate

Displaced Persons

that it is the quick depletion of game resources rather than the exhaustion of soils which enforces a semi-nomadic way of existence.

Groups pushed even temporarily onto the uplands of old alluvium could be expected to lose the more complex aspects of their social and religious life, and there would be far less time for non-functional embellishments of ceramics. As the struggle to retain or regain the limited stretches of flood plain grew more acute, outright warfare became the normal condition between adjacent societies. A great expenditure of time and energy was directed towards war by both the 'have-nots' on the uplands and the 'haves' on the flood plains. The battle was not entirely one-sided since the more mobile forest people could maintain incessant guerrilla raids on their sedentary enemies, and could retreat into the almost limitless expanse of jungle if pursued by their more numerous and better organized opponents. Several cultures known from the Central Ucayali and from the Alto Pachitea appear to show the degrading effects of a temporary displacement and a state of continuing and unresolved warfare.

YARINACOCHA

The Hupa-iya peoples of the Central Ucayali were displaced by a group making pottery of a style called Yarinacocha. The largest Yarinacocha community known is Jose's Hill, UCA-34, where a continuous mantle of Yarinacocha midden, up to 30 cm. deep, covers an area at least 175 m. in diameter. The Yarinacocha refuse overlies a thin layer of Hupa-iya refuse, which in turn caps the rich midden whose ceramic content permitted the definition of Early Shakimu (see page 93). A date of AD 90 ± 110 (N-313) relates to the Yarinacocha occupation here.

After the artistic mastery and technical control of Hupa-iya ceramics, Yarinacocha pottery represents a tremendous retrograde step. The pottery is thick, and tempered with coarsely ground crushed sherds. The thin wash of clay spread over the surface

Fig. 23

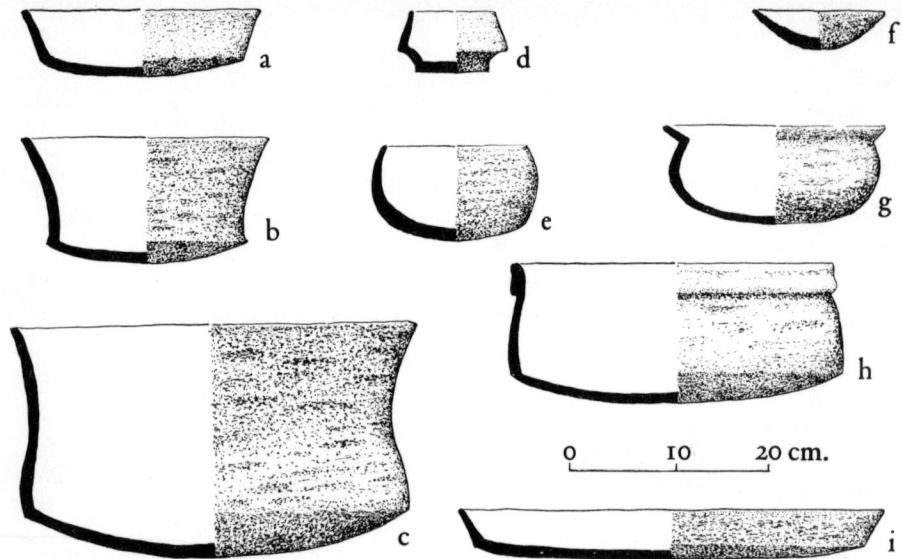

Fig. 23   Vessels typical of the Yarinacocha Complex. An orange-hued, floated finish over poorly smoothed, irregular surfaces is typical. The form of comal depicted in i is still in use in the Vaupes region of Eastern Colombia

Plate 31

Fig. 23 a–c, h

Fig. 23 i

with a wet rag does not mask the many irregularities left on the surface of the vessels. Lopsided, randomly asymmetrical pots and rims which change profile from one part of the vessel to the other indicate that little care and pride were involved in the forming of Yarinacocha vessels and that standards of execution were lax. Some of the typical vessel shapes which can be ascertained recall those of Late Shakimu, but whereas that pottery was carefully slipped, highly polished, and beautifully decorated, no such care was lavished on the similar Yarinacocha forms. Only occasional examples of an all-over red slip and a few sherds showing illegible traces of red and white or black, red, and white painted designs relieve the utilitarian monotony of the style.

The large clay griddles with raised rims are an entirely new vessel form in the Central Ucayali Basin and indicate the importance of bitter manioc.

Displaced Persons

Given the vast areas of terra incognita still existing in the Upper Amazon Basin one cannot rule out the possibility that the Yarinacocha complex represents an intrusion of peoples from outside the Central Ucayali Basin. I think it more probable that these people represent the culturally degraded descendants of the Late Shakimu peoples who had been pushed off the flood plain by the Hupa-iya invaders. A two- or three-hundred-year banishment on the uplands of old alluvium would have accounted for the complete deterioration of ceramic technology and art style. Ultimately these people were able to fight their way back onto the flood plain and displace their ancient enemies, but they were not capable of bringing about an immediate resurgence of the ceramic arts.

PACACOCHA

The people of the Yarinacocha culture were unable to hold on to their segment of the Ucayali flood plain for more than a few hundred years. By AD 400–500 another ethnic group with a different, but equally undistinguished ceramic complex, Pacacocha, had replaced them.

The Pacacocha people dominated the Central Ucayali Basin for about 400 years and during this period of time their ceramic tradition evolved through three phases: Pacacocha, Cashibocaño, and Nueva Esperanza. The vessel forms of Pacacocha are simple, with globular vessels predominating. The pottery is poorly fired and the surfaces are not well smoothed. Some of the pottery shows an all-over red slip, but there were no other kinds of decorative surface modification. The only decoration apart from this takes the form of inward-facing *adornos* so stylized and crudely executed that one cannot identify the species of animal intended. Griddles with low rims indicate that bitter manioc continued as the staple. Solid ceramic pot supports with a cylindrical body and flaring ends became common at this time, and these still remain in use in the Ucayali Basin. Large brewing

Fig. 24

Fig. 24 d

Fig. 24 f

Plate 68

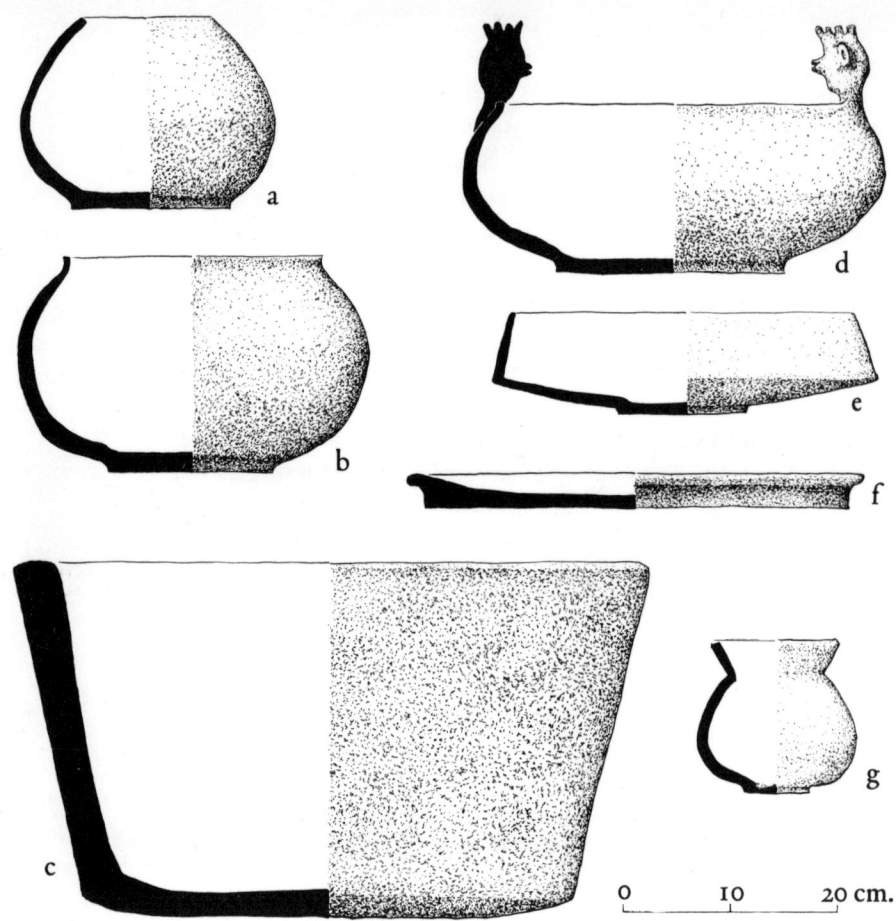

Fig. 24 Vessels typical of the Pacacocha Complex. Cursorily modelled adornos and a fairly fugitive all-over red slip are the only attempts at decoration. The large brewing urns, c, were also used for secondary urn burial

Fig. 24 c   urns were common and were used for secondary inhumation of disarticulated human skeletons.

The Cashibocaño complex differs from the Pacacocha complex chiefly in rim form and in the fairly frequent use of a single row of thumb-print corrugation immediately below the rim.

Displaced Persons

The Nueva Esperanza complex is known from a single site north-west of Yarinacocha. The pottery tends to be thinner and better-made than Pacacocha ware. *Adornos* continue in common use and clearly recognizable bat-heads are most characteristic. Scraped ware and all-over corrugated ware are now being made with some frequency and these traits appear to have spread from the Cumancaya people who were already occupying the southern part of the Central Ucayali Basin.

Fig. 25

The refuse of the Nueva Esperanza village forms a large circle over 100 m. in diameter. The central part of the circle shows almost no build-up of midden while there is a considerable depth of refuse around the periphery. Such a deposition pattern might result from a single large community house surrounded by a carefully swept plaza or more probably from a circular arrangement of smaller family houses facing onto a swept plaza. This latter type of village plan, typical of the Upper Xingú tribes and of the recent Gě and Bororo, is invariably a cognitive model of certain features of the social structure of the community. We have a date of AD 770 ± 105 (N-312) for the Nueva Esperanza community.

The inhabitants of Nueva Esperanza were ultimately displaced by the Cumancaya peoples moving in from the south. Their fate or relation to surviving tribes is unknown.

Fig. 25 The inward-facing, bat-head adornos *which are the most distinctive characteristic of the Nueva Esperanza Complex*

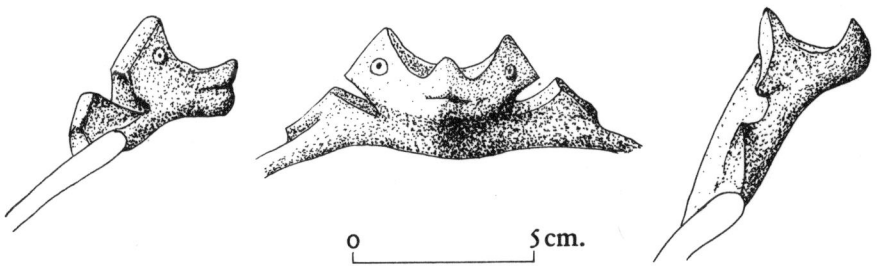

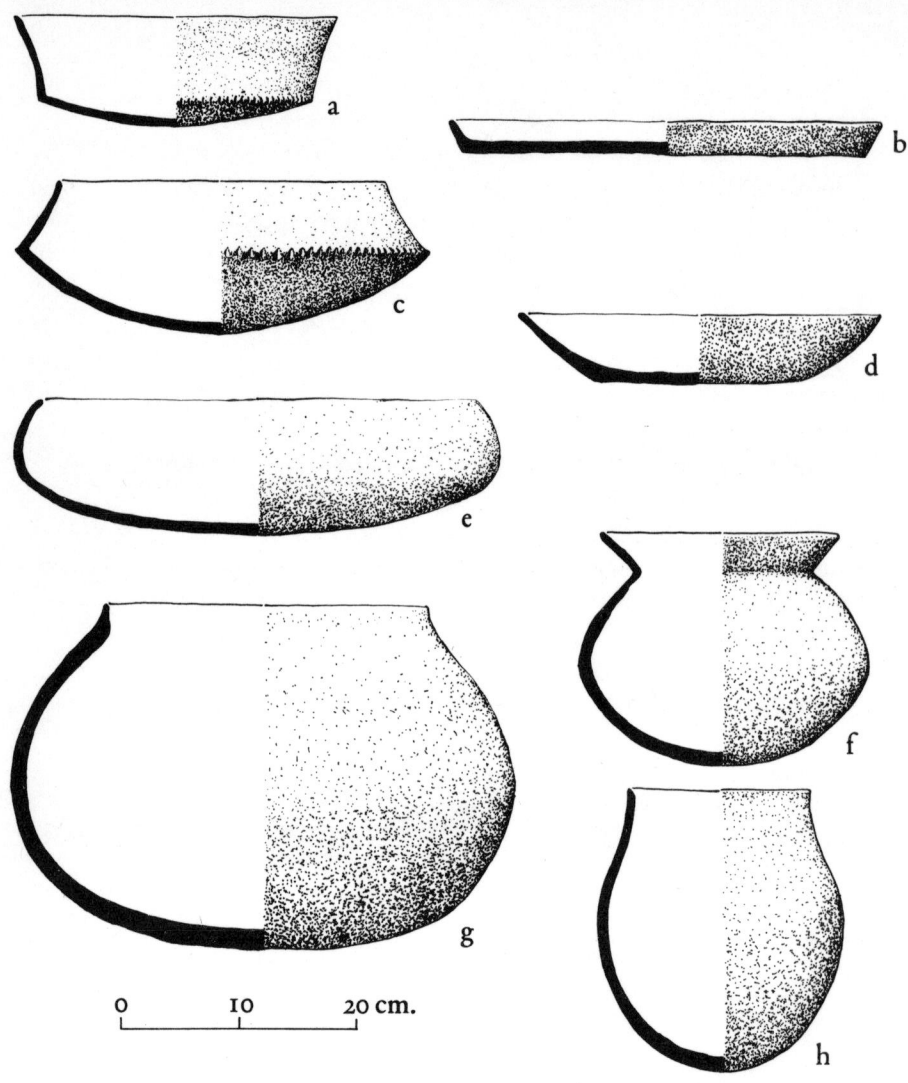

Fig. 26 Typical vessels of the Enoqui Complex. The comal, b, *was almost certainly used in the processing of bitter manioc, while the form,* e, *was probably used for parching maize kernels*

Displaced Persons
ENOQUI AND THE MODERN AMUESHA

We have already discussed the long and prosperous Nazaratequi occupation on the Alto Pachitea. The Nazaratequi domination of this area was temporarily ended by the invasion of the Naneini peoples about AD 650. Since the Naneini ceramics are very similar to those of Cumancaya, it is believed that the Naneini incursion was one branch of the wave of Panoan-speaking peoples who overran the whole Ucayali Basin at this time. Naneini domination of the Alto Pachitea was short-lived, and most of the sites in the area show as their latest component a refuse layer left by peoples of the Enoqui complex. There can be little doubt that the Enoqui people were descendants of the Nazaratequi. Most of the major categories of vessel-form survive, and the practice of using both red and black slips continues. The carinated forms are typically slipped black on the bottom and red on the sides. Incised decoration is now rare and very poorly executed; a more common form of embellishment is a simple notching of the ridge of carinated vessels. Manioc griddles are common, and a broad, slightly constricted bowl probably served for parching maize, indicating an increasing importance of that crop.

Fig. 26

Fig. 26 a, c

Fig. 26 a, c
Fig. 26 b

Fig. 26 e

Though the Enoqui complex represents a continuation of the Nazaratequi tradition, the decoration is far more primitive. It would appear that the invasion of the Panoan-speaking peoples exerted a permanently disruptive effect on the societies of the Alto Pachitea. The fact that the Enoqui complex is the most widespread and latest ceramic complex in the area occupied until very recently by the Amuesha, makes it probable that the Enoqui middens can be attributed to the proto-historic and historic Amuesha. It is important to bear in mind the continuity of the Nazaratequi tradition into the modern Amuesha in appraising ancient population movements in the Upper Amazon.

CHAPTER VIII

Further Invasions of the Ucayali Basin

DURING LATE prehistoric times the Central Ucayali Basin was swept by two further waves of migration. The earlier probably came from the south and brought with it the Cumancaya ceramic tradition. The last prehistoric invasion moved up the mainstream of the Amazon as the Tupí-speaking Cocama and Omagua conquered the territories which they held at the time of the first European contacts.

CUMANCAYA

There were at least two occupations earlier than Cumancaya on the 1,000 m. stretch of natural levee along the north-east shore of the ox-bow lake, Cumancaya; the first by people of Late Shakimu culture, and the second by people of Hupa-iya culture. In contrast to the profusion of sherds left by the huge Cumancaya settlement there, the limited 1964 excavations yielded few ceramics from these two earlier components.

Cumancaya ceramics are distinguished from previous pottery on the Central Ucayali by the variety of ways in which the surface was treated. The most common of these semi-decorative manufacturing techniques is corrugation. The successive coils of clay are pinched between the thumb and index finger so as to weld them to the growing vessel, and the evenly placed thumb-prints are left on the outer surface. About twenty per cent of Cumancaya pottery was finished in this way. As a variant of corrugation the coils of moist clay might be left intact on the outside of the pot, or scored with a sharp stick or the finger tip. This second type of corrugated surface was rare at the Cumancaya site, UCA-22, but becomes progressively more important in a variety of later styles of the Cumancaya tradition; it still continues in use among the modern Shipibo.

Fig. 27 e
Plates 35, 36

Fig. 52 g, h

Plate 75

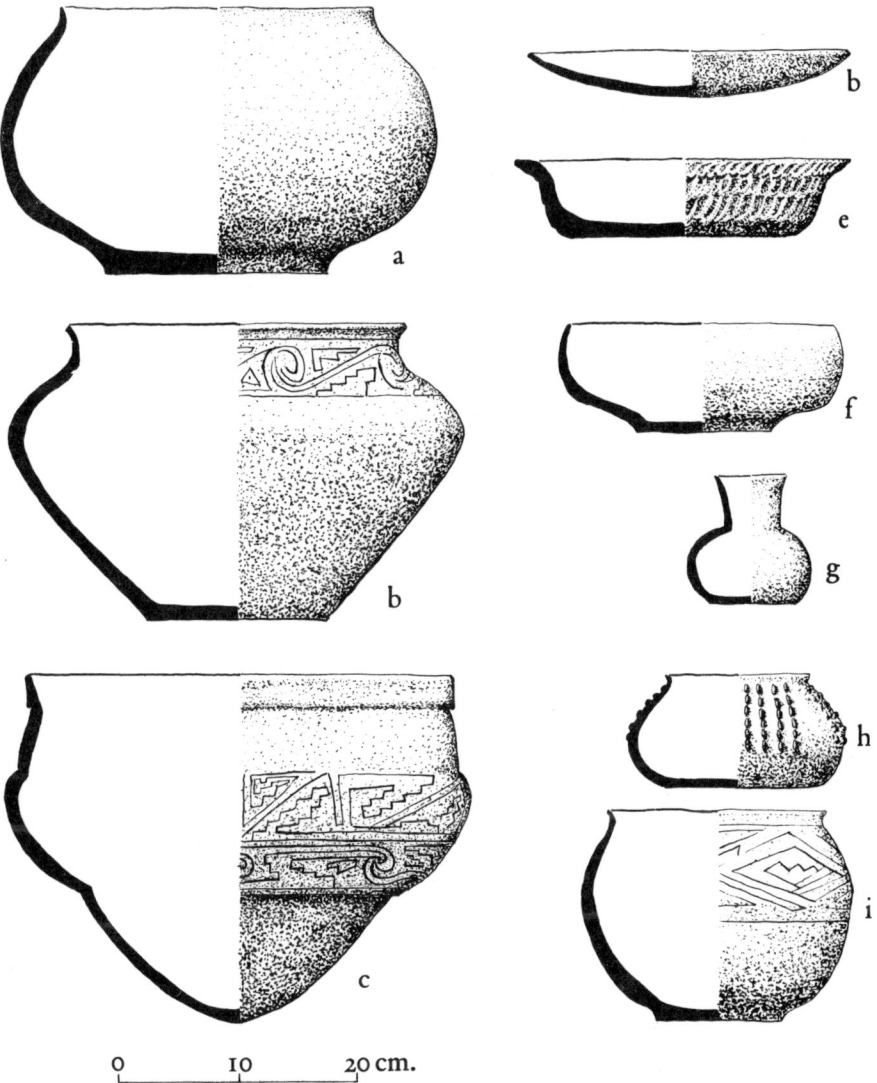

Fig. 27 Vessels of the Cumancaya Complex from UCA-22, the Cumancaya Site, and from the Cumancaya Complex burial at TAM-2, Caimito. Possibly all of the fine-line incised pottery, b, c, i, was zoned bichrome (red on buff), but most specimens have lost their surfaces. Corrugated ware, e, is common and occurs in a wide range of shapes

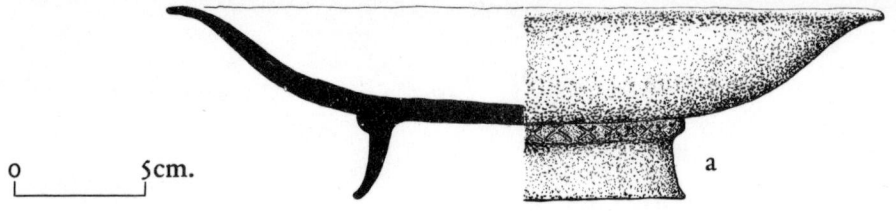

0 5cm. a

Plate 33

Plate 72

A second kind of textured surface is characterized by multiple, parallel striations. The surviving Isconahua make this kind of pottery, and the tool which they use for roughing the surface is the jagged edge of a split palm seed. It is probable that all the striated pottery in the Cumancaya tradition was made with the same kind of tool.

Fig. 28 a
Fig. 27 h

Appliqué decoration, usually in long strips with nicked edges, was typical, and occasionally one finds whole areas of a vessel covered with small appliqué pellets.

Fig. 27 b, c, i

Fig. 29

About ten per cent of Cumancaya pottery shows more complex and controlled decoration. Elaborate interlocking scroll and step-fret motifs were executed in fine-line incision. Sometimes the incised designs were on an otherwise plain surface, but more frequently this style of decoration was combined with zoned red painting. The frequency of the latter at the Cumancaya site itself is hard to determine since the surface of much of the pottery is badly eroded. At near-by Imaríacocha the grave of an important personage of Cumancaya society was excavated in 1964. The body was covered with several layers of deliberately smashed pottery, and the pottery from this grave was in a better state of preservation than that from the Cumancaya site. Well over half of the fine-line incised pottery here was also zone-painted. Charcoal from the bottom of the grave furnished a date of AD 810 ± 80 (Y-1545) which should be near the beginning of the Cumancaya occupation in the Central Ucayali.

Plate 32

Zoomorphic *adornos* occur on a small percentage of Cumancaya pots. Most are so highly stylized as to be reduced to a series of conical nubbs, but occasionally one finds a recognizable toad.

Fig. 28 Pedestal bowl, compotera, *from the Cumancaya Complex burial at TAM-2, Caimito. The exterior has incised appliqué while the interior, b, shows bichrome, geometric painting, dark brown on cream. The painted surface was protected by a coating of resin applied after firing, a practice still followed by the modern Shipibo and Conibo*

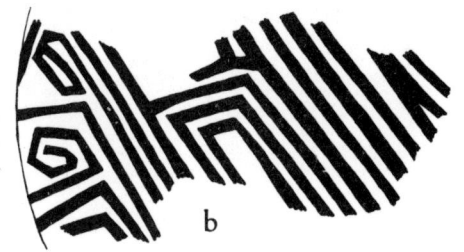

One sherd from the Cumancaya site shows faint traces of resist decoration in the form of polka-dots. Elegant pedestal bowls were made with the upper surface showing Chocolate-on-Cream painting quite different in style from the zoned red decoration. Some of the Chocolate-on-Cream sherds show traces of the resin glaze applied after firing, so typical of modern Shipibo-Conibo ceramics.

Ceramic colanders, presumably for straining fibre out of manioc beer, appear on the Central Ucayali at this time, while ceramic pestles, an important part of the Lower Velarde complex, also occur in Cumancaya.

The considerable discontinuity between Cumancaya pottery and any of the earlier ceramic traditions on the Central Ucayali suggests that the appearance of the Cumancaya ceramic style is the tangible manifestation of yet another wave of colonists moving into the area.

Fig. 28

Plate 39

Plate 39

Fig. 29 Typical decorated sherds from the Cumancaya burial at TAM-2, Caimito, showing interlocking scroll and step-motifs, in specimen a zoned red slipping is added to the incision

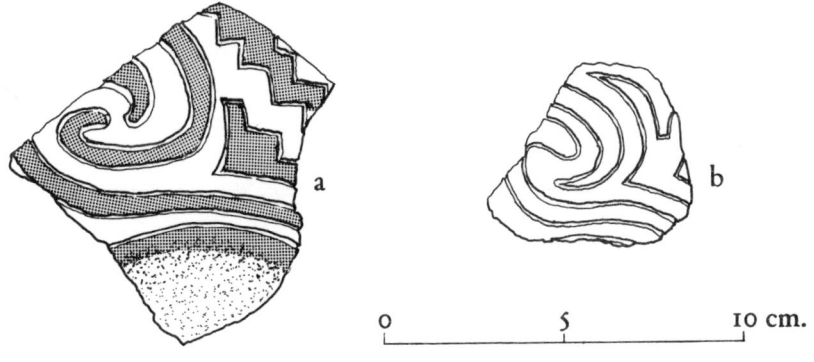

The Upper Amazon

A number of lines of evidence indicate that the Cumancaya peoples were the ancestors of the modern Panoan-speaking groups in the Ucayali Valley and the adjacent parts of the Juruá and Purús Basins. The dating of the Cumancaya invasion fits well with the relatively slight differentiation among the various northern Panoan languages.

It is easy to show how the ceramic industries of the surviving Panoan tribes in the Ucayali Basin could be derived from Cumancaya ceramics. The tribes on the uplands such as the Amahuaca, Remo, Mayoruna, and Cashibo, make little or no use of slip or painted decoration applied before firing. Though it varies from group to group, every form of surface treatment used by them for their utility wares has its equivalent in the Cumancaya complex, and all the functional categories used by these backwoods Panoans have antecedents in Cumancaya ceramics. Furthermore, the painted and woven designs of the Cashinahua, the backwoods Panoan group with the most developed art style, are similar to the motifs on the Cumancaya Chocolate-on-Cream style.

The ceramics of the riverine Panoans, the Shipibo and Conibo, are more elaborate and more divergent from Cumancaya, but a number of continuities are evident, none the less. All the decorative techniques applied to Shipibo-Conibo utility ware are found in Cumancaya. The right-angle step, the most productive Cumancaya motif, grows progressively smaller in later adherents of the Cumancaya tradition, and there is thus a complete continuity into the right-angle steps which are such a persistent part of modern Shipibo-Conibo art. Cumancaya lacks the black and red on white, and white on red painted decoration which is characteristic of modern Shipibo-Conibo ceramics, but the probable source of these stylistic elements will be noted in a later section.

It is less easy to come to a decision about the ultimate origins of the Cumancaya style, since similar ceramics have a particularly

Fig. 29 a

Fig. 53 a–c

Plate 61

Fig. 30 Painted designs of the modern Mbayá-Caduveo of the Southern Mato Grosso of Brazil. Specimen a is from a painted calfskin. The use of interlocking scrolls and interlocking step-fret motifs is strikingly similar to that of the Cumancaya Complex

wide range of distribution along the eastern slopes of the Andes. The designs of the Cumancaya zoned red ware are highly distinctive in their complex organization and their very limited vocabulary of motifs (almost exclusively step-frets and interlocking scrolls). One art style similar to Cumancaya is found in

Fig. 30

The Upper Amazon

Fig. 30

the pottery, face paintings, and hide paintings still being made by the Mbaya-Caduveo of the Brazilian Matto Grosso. The most striking similarities are seen by comparing Cumancaya designs with Caduveo hide paintings, which show more conservatism than the contemporary pottery. If the similarities between Cumancaya art and the art of the Mbaya-Caduveo are not just accidental, then the ancestors of the Cumancaya people must have been in contact with the ancestors of the Caduveo and other Guaycuruan tribes of the Gran Chaco around AD 300–400. prior to the movement of the Cumancaya peoples into the Ucayali Basin. Since I have suggested an east Bolivian hearth for Proto-Panoan on linguistic grounds, we might look to east Bolivia to see if there was a style which could have been ancestral both to Cumancaya and to the modern style of the Caduveo.

The Mojocoya Trichrome style is most common on the eastern slopes of the Bolivian Andes, specifically in the Department of Chuquisaca on the head-waters of the Río Pilcomayo. On the basis of work by Rydén and Walter it can be shown that Mojocoya Trichrome was flourishing before the spread of the Tiahuanaco style out of the Titicaca Basin, and so extended back into the AD 300–400 time range. It is characterized by designs

Fig. 31

built up of a limited range of motifs, almost entirely interlocking scrolls and step-frets. One should note that the Río Pilcomayo is the major river of the Gran Chaco and the main route connecting it with the eastern slope of the Andes, and remember that the Mbaya were anciently in a central location in the Gran Chaco and moved to Brazil only in historic times.

Even if we discount completely the stylistic similarities between Cumancaya and Mojocoya Trichrome, there are other reasons to look to east Bolivia for the source of the Cumancaya art style. Corrugated pottery is relatively common there. The Río Palacios

Fig. 32

complex described by Nordenskiöld not only has corrugation identical to that of Cumancaya but almost completely duplicates its range of vessel shapes. The peculiar inflection toward the

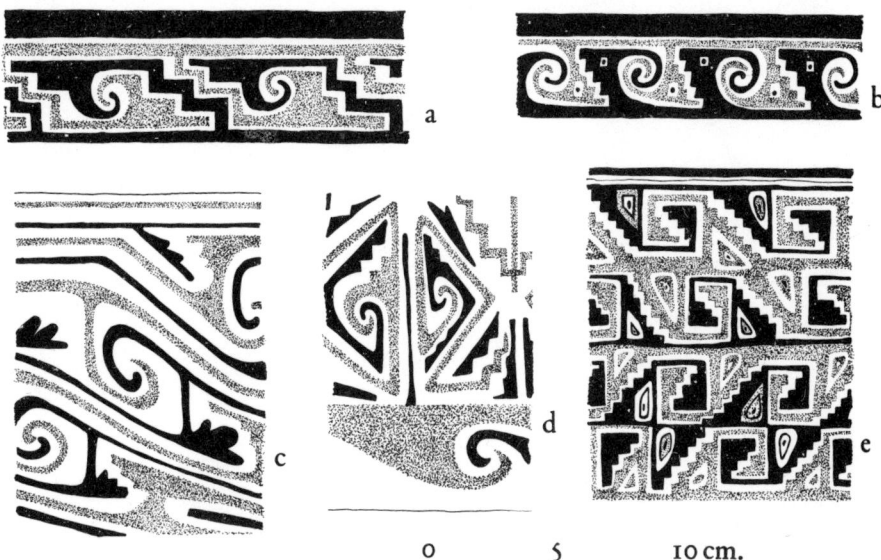

Fig. 31 Design layouts from Mojocoya Trichrome Style vessels, most common in the upper basin of the Pilcomayo River, Department of Chuquisaca, Bolivia. The colour scheme is typically black and dark red on a light red to orange slip. The organization of the designs shows parallels both to the Cumancaya Complex and the art style of the modern Mbayá-Caduveo

base of large Cumancaya urns is found in the Río Palacios materials, and in other ceramic styles even further to the south, including the Candelaria style of north-west Argentina. It does not, to my knowledge, occur north of the Ucayali Basin or in the Central or Northern Andes.

There are other styles in the Upper Amazon which are of about the same age as Cumancaya and share certain of its features. The Tivacundo Phase which Evans and Meggers have discovered on the Río Napo has zoned-red painting, in scroll designs which bear a resemblance to those of Cumancaya, and ceramic colanders are common. A date of AD 510 ± 70 (SI-330) has been obtained on these materials.

Dr Mejía has recently described some unusual ceramics from the Aspusana River which enters the Huallaga a short distance

Fig. 27 c
Plate 36

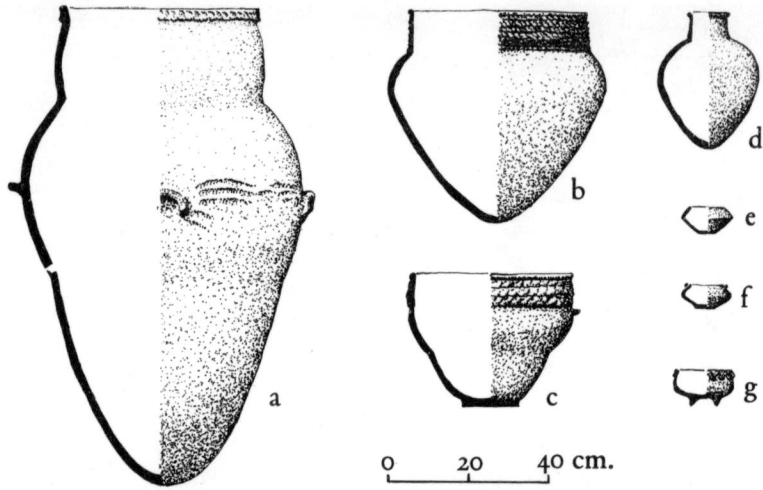

Fig. 32 Pottery from urn burials on the Río Palacios in the lowlands of South-eastern Bolivia. Specimens a, and d–g are from Site 1, Burial 1, specimens b, c, from Site 2, Burial 5. In form and technology these ceramics show a number of similarities to the Cumancaya complex and the modern ceramics of the Ucayali Panoans. In terms of the form categories shared by the Peruvian Panoan groups, b and c are quënti aní, *large cooking pots for making* masato, d *is a* chomo, *water jar, and* e *is a* quënpo, *drinking vessel*

below Tingo María. A nicely modelled head would seem to be related to the Moche or Recuay styles of the Central Andes, but the zoned, bichrome sherds have their closest stylistic parallels in Cumancaya though technologically they are far finer than any pottery in the Ucayali Basin.

The Naneini Complex on the Alto Pachitea is without antecedents in the pottery of the earlier Nazaratequi tradition and was introduced into the area by a group of invaders. We may postulate that these invaders spoke Panoan since Naneini pottery is clearly in the Cumancaya tradition showing the same vessel shapes, the same kinds of corrugated and scraped surfaces, and very similar bichrome designs. The date on Naneini materials is fully compatible with its close relationship with Cumancaya.

Further Invasions of the Ucayali Basin

The southern affinities of the Cumancaya tradition and its probable relationship to the spread of Panoan-speakers have already been stressed. It is only fair to point out that some of the characteristics of the Cumancaya tradition are widespread in northern South America. Corrugation and unobliterated coiling very similar to that of Cumancaya is typical of the later ceramics at the Colombian site of San Agustín, in the Guaribe complex of the Llanos de Orinoco in Venezuela, and in the Portacelli complex at the base of the Guajiro peninsula in Colombia. All of these materials probably date from between AD 800 and 1200. I am loath to suggest that Cumancaya culture *per se* or Panoan-speakers expanded along the full length of the Andean foothills as far as the Caribbean Sea. It would appear, however, that the extent of the cultural contacts along the Eastern Andean foothills was quite considerable towards the end of the first millennium AD.

CAIMITO, NAPO, AND THE POLYCHROME TRADITION

All the evidence suggests that Imaríacocha, the drowned valley of the Río Tamaya, had the densest concentration of Pre-Columbian population in the Central Ucayali Basin. The complicated shore line is well over 150 km. long and has not yet been thoroughly explored, but most areas of high ground facing onto the main axis of the lake are covered with a continuous mantle of midden 30 to 40 cm. deep. A population of several thousand may be inferred for the lake shore, and since it is the lake rather than the land which was the major avenue of travel, the Caimito occupation here can best be viewed as a large community facing onto an aquatic Main Street. The uniformity of ceramic remains from all of the lake-shore sites confirms the impression of a single homogeneous community. The two C_{14} dates fall in the fourteenth century, AD 1320 $\pm$ 60 (Y-1544) and AD 1375 $\pm$ 105 (N-310), but it is doubtful if they encompass the full length of this occupation.

Plate 5

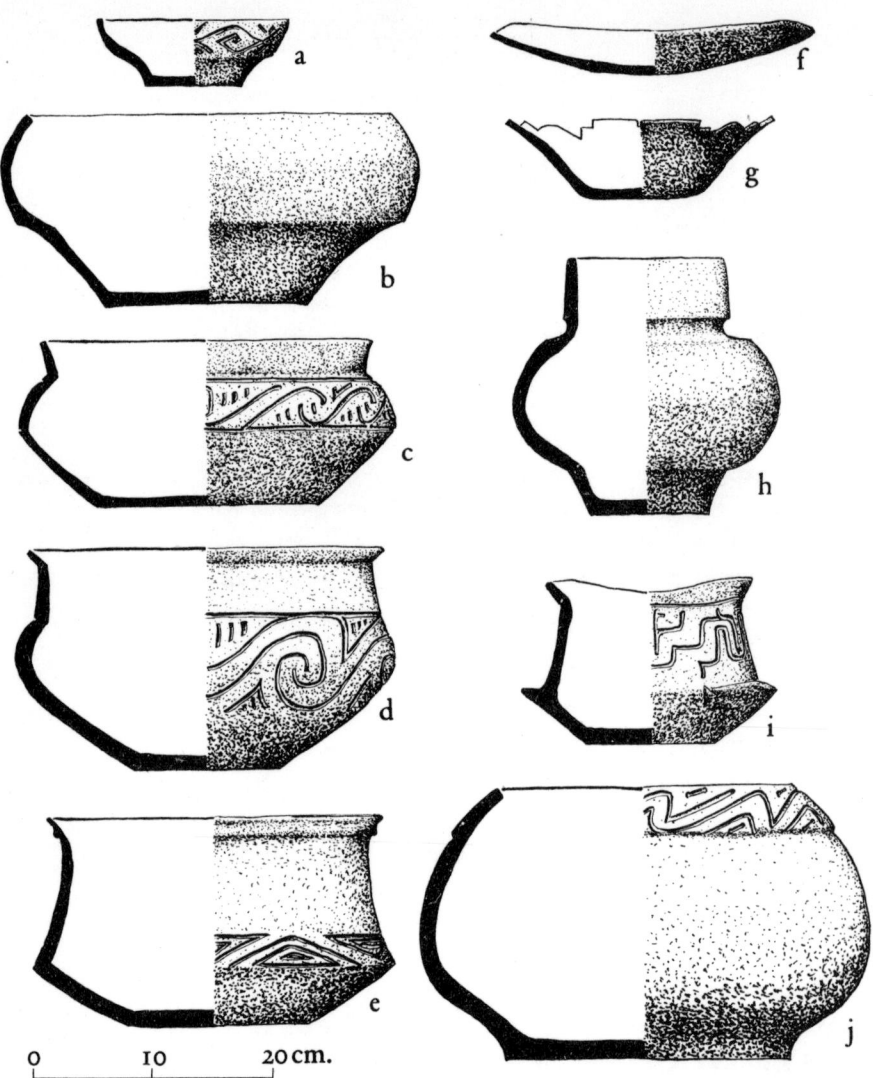

Fig. 33 The more common vessel forms of the Caimito Complex. All are from TAM-2, Caimito. The incised decoration is typically executed in a broad, shallow groove with markedly striated bottom, in a number of instances approaching the Double-line Incision typical of the Napo Phase in Ecuador. The forms illustrated in b *and* h *frequently carried black and red on white decoration, but no examples have yet been found with extensive areas of the design preserved. The vessel illustrated in* e *contained the charred palm kernels which have been dated at* AD 1320 ± 60: (Y-1544)*

Further Invasions of the Ucayali Basin

The Caimito ceramic style is exceptionally complex and varied. The large vocabulary of vessel shapes is only partially illustrated. Caimito vessels typically have a squarish rather than round horizontal cross-section.

Fig. 33

Incision, well controlled and showing a number of motifs, is the most readily observed form of decoration. Slipped surfaces have in most cases been removed by the annual alternation between extremely wet and extremely dry soil conditions, but a large number of sherds show faint traces of black and red on white, or white on red painted decorations. In a very few instances the complete design is preserved. The most elaborately decorated vessels were squarish plates or bowls. The designs on the interior of such vessels combined broad-line incision and the excision of small areas prior to the application of a white slip; fine-line incision through the white slip; and red and black painting over the white slip, in many cases filling the broad incised lines. Frequently appliqué is used to indicate the features of the human face. Other examples of Caimito sculpturing are less stylized.

Fig. 34
Fig. 33 f, g

Fig. 35
Plates 41, 42

Fig. 34 Unrolled design from the body of an anthropomorphic burial urn, Caimito Complex, TAM-2, Caimito. The body of the urn is cylindrical with limbs and genitals indicated in relief. The whole outer surface was covered with black on white painting. Collection of the Museo Nacional de Antropología y Arqueología, Pueblo Libre, Lima, Peru

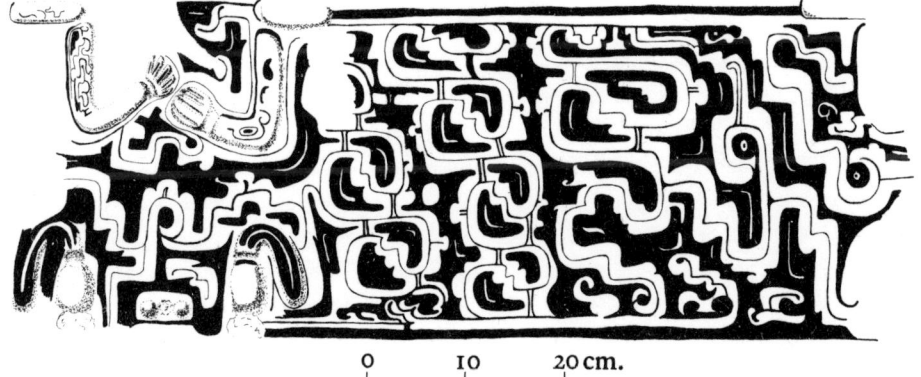

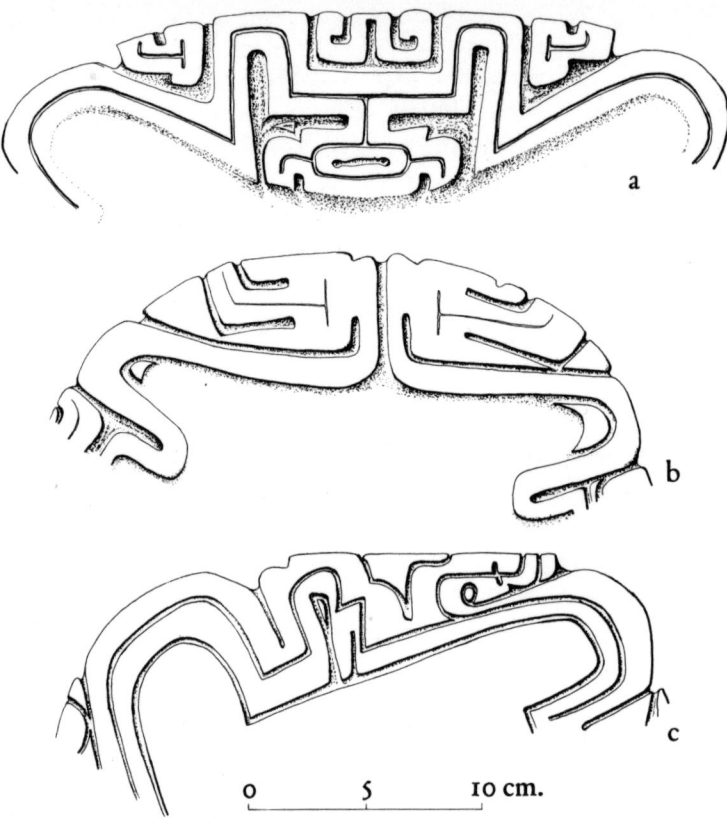

Fig. 35   Incised-excised designs from three squarish basins, Caimito Complex, TAM-2, Caimito. The incision was covered with white slip. Faint traces of black and red painting remain

Fig. 36 a

Fig. 36 b, c
Plate 43

Fig. 36 d

The sensitive modelling of the red-slipped, highly polished female figurine fragment from Caimito is unusual. Droll renderings of such prominent members of the local fauna as the anaconda and the turtle are fairly common as *adornos*. Small frog effigies were sometimes included as burial offerings, and there are examples in which the foot of a pedestal bowl took the form of a frog.

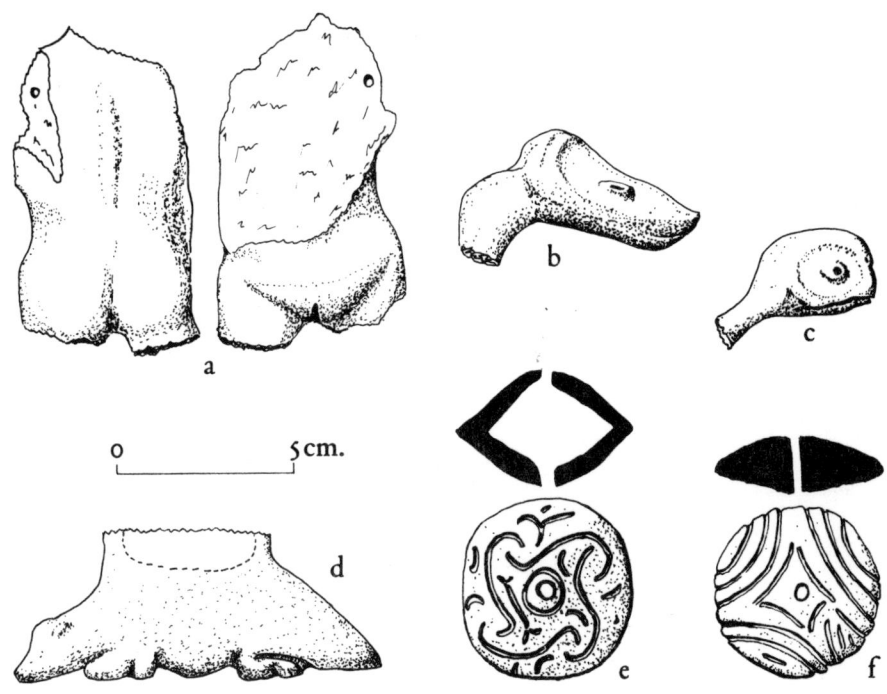

Fig. 36 Various ceramic objects of the Caimito Complex. The female figurine, a, is covered with a highly polished red slip except in the pubic triangle. Droll, modelled animal heads such as the anaconda, b, and the turtle, c, are common, but it has not yet been determined to what class of vessel they were attached. Hollow spindle whorls such as e are also typical of the Marajoara Phase at the Mouth of the Amazon. The frog effigy, d, is the base for a pedestal bowl. All except d are in the collection of the Robert H. Lowie Museum of Anthropology, University of California, Berkeley

Decorated spindle whorls are common, including hollow examples which have their closest parallels in the whorls of the Marajoara complex at the Mouth of the Amazon. Other unusual forms such as small, four-lobed bottles also find their nearest prototypes in Marajoara ceramics. The most common form of ground stone axe has a shape distinct from earlier T-shaped axes.

Fig. 36 e

Plate 44

Fig. 37

The Upper Amazon

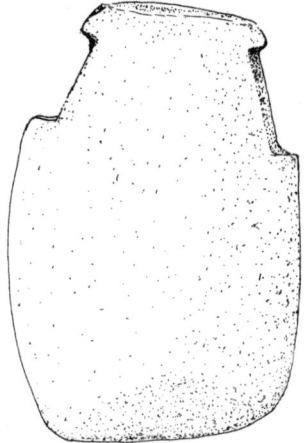

Fig. 37 Polished stone axe-head of andesite, from the Caimito Complex site, TAM-13, Junín Pablo

0 ⊢――――――――⊣ 5 cm.

The complexity and artistic merit of Caimito ceramics are notable, but even more remarkable than the style itself are the precise stylistic similarities which relate Caimito to a wide range of other styles from the Río Napo in Ecuador to the Río Gurupy on the Coast of Brazil, well to the east of the Mouth of the Amazon. All experts agree that these stylistic parallels indicate the closest historical connections. Thanks mainly to the recent work of Hilbert, we know of a number of styles along the Brazilian Amazon which belong to this tightly knit stylistic unit, best designated the Polychrome tradition.

The only point of disagreement remaining is the direction of the migrations which effected the wide dispersal of the Polychrome tradition. Meggers and Evans, as well as Hilbert, have argued for one or more down-stream migrations out of the Colombian Highlands. On the other hand, I have persistently held the view that Marajoara culture evolved within the tropical lowlands of South America and that the presence of styles in the Upper Amazon which are clearly related to Marajoara is due to an up-stream migration, and that the specific migrants involved were the ancestors of the historic Omagua and Cocama. The remainder of this chapter will attempt to evaluate the available evidence in terms of this basic disagreement.

It has seemed unnecessary to illustrate extensively the near-identity of Caimito ceramics and the ceramics of the Napo Phase on the Río Napo in eastern Ecuador. Recent publications by Meggers, and Evans and Meggers, have a wealth of accompanying illustrations of Napo materials. The Napo Phase sites resemble the Caimito sites on Imaríacocha in their large size. It is clear that populous communities were involved in both instances. The C14 assays relating to the Napo Phase are AD 1168 ± 53 (P-347) and AD 1179 ± 51 (P-269) from the Nueva Armenia site N-P-2, and AD 1480 ± 180 (SI-299) from Nuevo Rocafuerte N-P-3. Evans and Meggers prefer the two earlier dates and would discount the latter, arguing that since the first European explorer through the area, Orellana, found this stretch of the river deserted in 1542, the region could not have been densely occupied 60 years earlier. I myself believe that all three dates are correct and that the Napo Phase occupation of the Ecuadorian segment of the Río Napo and its tributaries, the Aguarico and Tiputini, lasted from about AD 1100 to 1700.

Fig. 38

We will first examine the stylistic and distributional evidence indicating that Caimito and Napo ceramics are, in fact, leavings of the ancestors of the historic Cocama and Omagua. Then we will consider evidence suggesting that the complex and historically specific tradition of black and red on white polychrome pottery—which includes Napo, Caimito and Marajoara and a large number of style in between—did, in fact, evolve *in situ* in the Central and Lower Amazon Basin.

It is clear on linguistic grounds alone that the Cocama and Omagua represent a late up-stream migration from the Central or Lower Amazon. All the other closely related Tupian languages are in that region. At the time of the first white contact, the Cocama dominated the lower half of the Ucayali and were numerous, aggressive, and politically unified. A slightly less

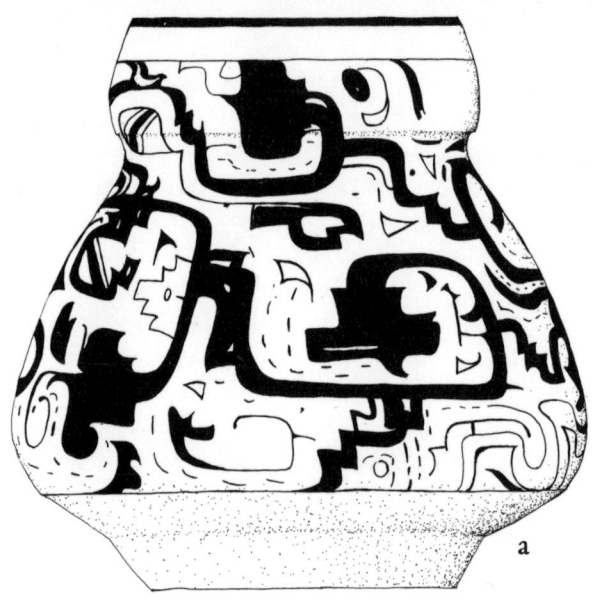

Fig. 38 Napo Phase burial urn, a, and three sherds from the late-eighteenth and early-nineteenth century Franciscan mission of Sarayacu. The sherds are almost certainly attributable to the Cocama. The scale refers to the sherds only, as the precise size of the urn is unknown. The sherds are black and red on white. The urn is predominantly black on white but there is probably red detail which cannot be

populous branch of the Cocama, the Cocamailla, were located on the lower Huallaga. During the same period the Omagua dominated the whole flood plain of the Amazon from the mouth of the Napo to the mouth of the Juruá, and all the earliest explorers comment on the great population density of the Omagua throughout that zone. According to Métraux:

'When first discovered, the *Omagua* were in full expansion. Annual war parties followed the innumerable water roads of the Amazon Basin and penetrated remote regions to raid villages or settle as independent tribelets. Early missionaries found Omagua colonies far up the Napo, Aguarico, and Quebeno Rivers. Aparia the Lesser, who is mentioned by Carvajal as a chief of

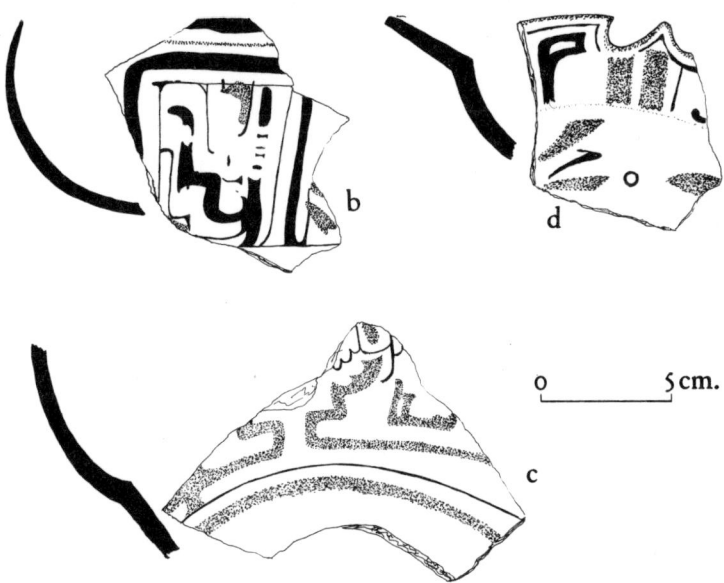

differentiated from black in the photograph available. The sherd, d, indicates that the elaborately decorated squarish basins, so characteristic of the Napo Phase and the Caimito Complex, were still in use in the nineteenth century when Sarayacu was flourishing. A comparison between b, d and plates 69, 70 makes the identification as Cocama likely

the Napo River, may well have been an Omagua chieftain. Like the *Cocama*, the *Omagua* seem to have deserved the name of "America's Phoenicians" given them by Hervás (1800–05).'

Thus, though the Ecuadorian part of the Napo was not occupied in 1542, when traversed by Orellana and his chronicler Carvajal, the lower Napo, in Peru, was dominated by the Omagua. The tributary Aguarico appears as rich in Napo Phase remains as the Napo itself. During most of the early historic period, the Aguarico was dominated by a branch of the Omagua, the Omagua-yeté, who remained independent of the Spanish.

The two-pronged migration pattern necessary to achieve the distribution of the Napo-Caimito stylistic tradition, along the

The Upper Amazon

Ucayali and along the Napo, coincides exactly with the two-pronged up-stream migrations of the Cocama and Omagua.

The earlier travellers through the territory of the Omagua commented enthusiastically on the beauty and complexity of Omagua pottery. There is simply no other late ceramic style known from the shores of the Upper Amazon of sufficient complexity to have so excited the admiration of the early European explorers. These early descriptions must relate to a variant of the Napo-Caimito style.

A direct comparison of Napo-Caimito styles with the pottery made by the historic and recent Cocama is strongly indicative of a direct continuity. Modern Cocama polychrome pottery differs from that of Napo or Caimito mainly in terms of a reduction in the number of shapes made. The larger and more complex vessel forms have been lost but some of the more distinctive forms, such as the elaborately decorated, squarish plate so typical of both Caimito and Napo, survived into the nineteenth century. This survival is indicated by one of the Cocama-style polychrome sherds recovered by Thomas Myers from the late eighteenth- and early nineteenth-century mission site of Sarayacu. The design layout of the other two Sarayacu sherds is very similar to that of the Napo and Caimito styles. Even more striking are Napo-Caimito survivals in Cocamilla pottery of the late nineteenth century, before the European-derived floral designs, now so common on Cocama pottery, made much impact on traditional Cocama style. Particularly noteworthy is the double-headed serpent motif on an illustrated bowl. This motif is also illustrated by Meggers on a large square plate of Napo style (*Ecuador* Plate 75). Contemporary Cocama pottery uses floral motifs, but these are organized according to the principles of design layout and modular band width basic to Napo and Caimito styles; and, as late as 1964, I saw pottery produced by the Cocama colony at Yarinacocha which had typical Napo motifs.

Fig. 38 d

Fig. 38 b, c

Plate 69

Plate 70

Since the Cocama and Omagua could only have arrived in their historical habitat as the result of massive and continuing up-stream migrations, we must look down-stream in the Amazon Basin for the origins of the Polychrome tradition which unites Napo and Caimito with a wide range of styles far to the east, in the Amazon Basin and beyond.

Hilbert has recently summarized what is known about the archaeology of the Central Amazon Basin, organizing his data in terms of the major waves of migration from the Andes into the tropical forest conjectured by Meggers and Evans; however, it is possible to demonstrate that the data from Hilbert's own excavations demolish rather than support the idea of multiple migrations out of the Andes.

Hilbert defines a number of ceramic phases which he places in the Polychrome horizon. While all these complexes clearly belong to a single stylistic tradition of considerable time depth, there are clearly two distinct sub-traditions represented in these Central Amazonian materials. One, exemplified by the Guarita, the Tefé and the Sao Joaquim Phases, is characterized by a simple range of vessel shapes, and a lack of anthropomorphic burial urns. The use of *cariapé* temper (siliceous ash) is typical. We might designate this group the Guarita sub-tradition within the Polychrome tradition. The other sub-tradition is best represented by the Pirapitanga Phase from near the Peru-Brazil border. It is also manifest in the materials collected from the long-famous site of Miracanguera and in collections from a number of other Central Amazonian sites producing anthropomorphic burial urns. To this second grouping I would insist on adding the Napo-like excised materials which Hilbert arbitrarily placed in the Itacoatiara 'Phase'. This second group is characterized by a more complex vocabulary of vessel shapes, squarish vessels, and anthropomorphic burial urns. Tempering is variable, in some instances *cariapé*, in other instances *cauxí* (the siliceous skeletons of fresh-water sponges). This second grouping is probably best designated the Miracanguera sub-tradition, by adopting the name of the site at which these materials were first recognized.

The similarities between the Guarita sub-tradition and the Napo-Caimito materials are vague. On the other hand those between Napo-Caimito and the Miracanguera sub-tradition are numerous and obvious. As might be expected, the Pirapitinga Phase, which is closest to both Napo and Caimito geographically, is also closest stylistically.

On the basis of Hilbert's published materials it is easy to demonstrate the origins of the Guarita sub-tradition. We have already seen that during the first five centuries A D, Barrancoid ceramic complexes were wide-spread in the Central Amazon. The most frequently decorated vessel form was a hemispherical bowl with a fairly broad labial flange, on the upper surface of which the decoration was usually concentrated. It was out of this Barrancoid heritage that the Guarita tradition evolved without major discontinuities and without major external influences. Hilbert's excavation at the Manacapurú site is most informative in this respect. From the bottom to the top of the 75 cm.-deep midden one notes a decrease in Barrancoid-style modelling, a decrease in Barrancoid-style broad-line incision, a gradual shift towards *cariapé* tempering, and the beginnings of black and red on white polychrome painting. But there are *no major shifts in the tradition of vessel shapes!* Guarita polychrome vessels, especially those from Manacapurú, typically have their polychrome decoration on the upper surface of broad labial flanges, and the spiral motifs of these early Guarita polychromes are classically Barrancoid in their organization. The top levels of the Manacapurú site date from the fifth century and it is clear that the transition from the Barrancoid Manacapurú phase to the Polychrome Guarita phase was already well under way.

The stratigraphy at the Caiambé site shows the same gradual transition from *cauxí* to *cariapé* tempering without major changes

Further Invasions of the Ucayali Basin

in either the vocabulary of vessel shape or the range of decorative techniques and motifs.

The stratigraphy at Manguieras, well up the Río Japurá, has already been mentioned. It showed a ceramic complex almost precisely between the Barrancoid tradition as classically defined and the Polychrome tradition as classically defined. Hilbert claims that Japurá is a ceramic tradition completely distinct from the other Central Amazonian styles representing a separate wave of migration from outside the Amazon Basin. This position is rendered untenable by the near-identity of vessel shapes noted when one compares Japurá pottery either with the Manacapurú-Guarita cultural continuum at the Manacapurú site or with that of Caiambé-Tefé at the Caiambé site. All three groups of pottery are clearly in the same tradition.

Hilbert's evidence indicates that all the crucial characteristics of the Guarita sub-tradition were present in the Central Amazon by AD 500 to 600 at the latest. The emergence of the Guarita tradition occurs as a gradual evolution out of the previous Barrancoid styles and there is no logical necessity for invoking a separate wave of migration.

The Miracanguera sub-tradition is clearly a development parallel to, rather than out of, the Guarita sub-tradition. The fact that its distinctive style of anthropomorphic burial urn has close affinities both with the Pacoval variant of the Marajoara style on Marajó, and with the very late Maracá style at the Mouth of the Amazon, suggests that it evolved at some point along the flood plain of the Lower Amazon. It was peoples bearing the Miracanguera sub-tradition who expanded into the Upper Amazon, spreading the Napo and Caimito styles and ultimately becoming the historic Omagua and Cocama.

We have seen that the archaeology of the Central Ucayali and the Río Napo conforms to the expected pattern of multiple upstream migrations from the Central Amazon. The other expectation inherent in our general model of population dynamics is

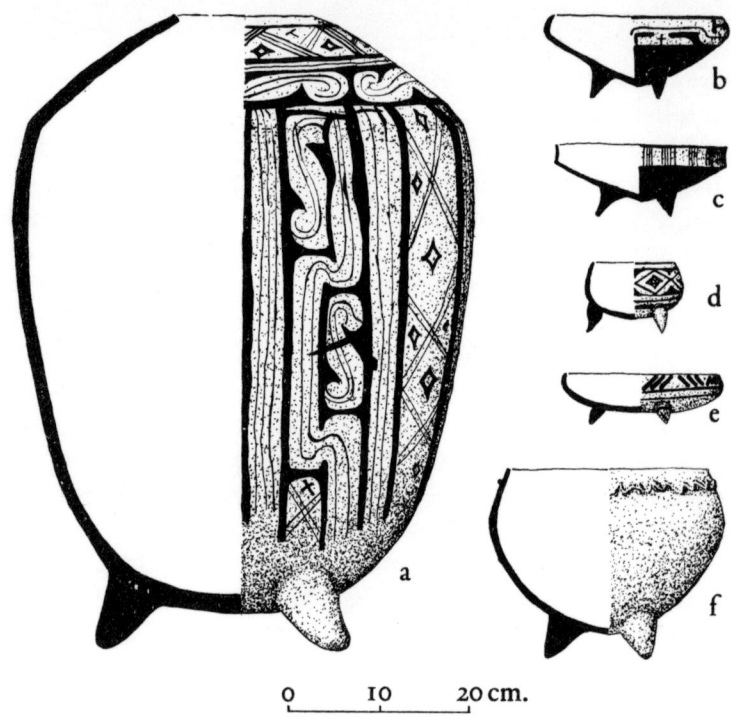

Fig. 39 Pottery from urn burials of the Upper Mound Velarde Complex, a–c, and the related ceramic complex of Mound Hernmarck, d–f, Llanos de Mojos, Lowland Bolivia. The colour scheme of the painted pieces is typically a very dark brown on a buff to cream surface. Red is sometimes added as a third colour. The emphasis on negative scroll designs and the juxtaposition of broad and narrow bands of dark pigment produce designs markedly similar to those of Napo and Caimito (compare with Fig. 35), though the vessel forms are completely different

that the flood plain of the Central Amazon has long been an area of dense population, indeed over-population; and that it was the source rather than the recipient of most of the major population movements. Such a demographic situation should have resulted in a continuous and gradually evolving cultural tradition. The gradual and continuous evolution of the Barrancoid ceramic

Further Invasions of the Ucayali Basin

tradition into that of Guarita fits the expectations perfectly. Intrusive cultural traditions, such as the Paredão and the Miracanguera style, enter late either from the north-east or from further down the mainstream of the Amazon.

We have concentrated on the up-stream movement of the Polychrome tradition along the Ucayali and Napo. Urns in the Miracanguera tradition are also found up the Juruá, up the Purús, and up the Madeira. There is even a ceramic style in the Llanos de Mojos which suggests that peoples with ceramics in the Polychrome tradition penetrated that area.

The vaguely Barrancoid ceramics from the lower level of Mound Velarde have been noted. The upper levels of that site and another major mound in the region, Mound Hernmark, are characterized by a completely different ceramic style which shows, as Howard first suggested, stylistic similarities to the various Polychrome tradition complexes. The colour scheme of Upper Velarde and Hernmark pottery, the extensive use of the open scroll motif, and the combination of broad and narrow painted bands all are strongly suggestive of Central Amazonian affinities. Whereas primary inhumation was characteristic of the lower levels of Velarde, secondary burial in elaborately painted urns was typical of Upper Velarde and Hernmark.

Fig. 39

Fig. 39 a

CHAPTER IX

Ridged Fields

THE CONTINUING EFFECTS of population pressures on the limited amounts of riverine flood plain within the Amazon Basin have been noted. As long as the Tropical Forest peoples made no effort to increase their agricultural efficiency or to expand artificially the amount of land suitable for their agricultural system, warfare and outward colonization were the only obvious solutions to the mounting population pressures. Warfare and outward colonization did continue at an ever-increasing pace until the time of the first European contacts, but well before 1500 the Tropical Forest Indians were also attacking this problem through a deliberate modification of their environment.

It was the annually flooded grasslands of tropical South America which were most extensively reclaimed for agricultural use. Our best evidence on the extent and nature of these artificial farm lands comes from the Llanos de Mojos.

Denevan has recorded a wide variety of the topographical features on the Llanos de Mojos which are beyond doubt artificial, and which could have served only as agricultural fields. He distinguishes three major divisions: large raised fields up to 300 m. long and up to 27 m. wide; ridged fields up to 300 m. long but not over 9 m. wide; drained fields separated by closely spaced ditches. Denevan has estimated that at the minimum there are 100,000 linear raised fields covering at least 15,000 acres, and suggests that several hundred thousand fields covering 50,000 acres is a far more probable total for the Llanos de Mojos.

The form of the longer drained fields and their relation to one another suggests the configuration of the parallel point-bar formations (see page 29) in the flood plains of the major rivers. As noted earlier, it is the tops of these natural ridges that were intensively farmed by the Tropical Forest groups. It appears that

Plate 45
Plate 46

Ridged Fields

the linear drained fields of the Llanos were a conscious and deliberate attempt to expand the ecological conditions present in the limited areas of riverine flood plains.

The agriculturally beneficial effects of the raised fields extend far beyond lifting the cultivated plants above the level of the annual flood. Though the soils of the Llanos de Mojos are young alluvium, they have a tendency to form clay pans, so that the soils of highest fertility are somewhat below the surface. The extensive digging of ditches and mounding-up of the resulting material would have brought the more fertile soils to the surface. The maintenance of these fields at maximum efficiency would require that the intervening ditches be cleaned periodically; and the muck from the bottom of the ditches, with its high organic content, would be dumped on top of the fields, acting as fertilizer. The ditches would serve to retain part of the water as the flood receded and so would ameliorate drought during the dry season.

Denevan estimates that this agricultural system supported a population of half a million on the Llanos de Mojos, which represents a far higher population density than has usually been estimated for the various areas of Pre-Columbian South America east of the Andes. It also represents a far higher population density than that supported in the Llanos de Mojos today.

The system of intensive agriculture present in the Llanos de Mojos demanded a large and continuing expenditure of labour and considerable co-ordination if it were to be effective. The societies involved must have been relatively complex, and the fragmentary early descriptions of groups, such as the Mojos, indicate very large socio-political units, hereditary rulers with considerable authority, and a professional priesthood. So far it has proved impossible to identify the builders of the raised fields with a particular archaeological complex.

There can be no question that the raised fields of the Llanos de Mojos are Pre-Columbian, but the exact date when such constructions were started can only be determined by far more

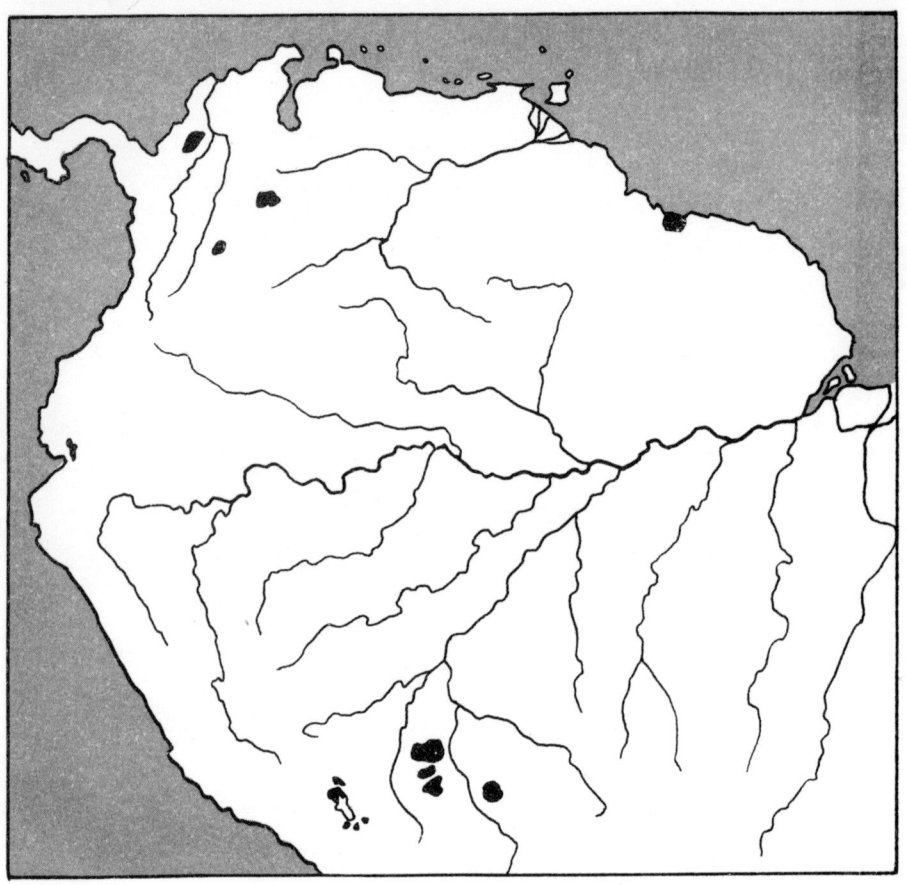

Fig. 40 Extent of raised agricultural fields in South America

intensive site survey and excavation than has been conducted until now. Similar earthworks have been identified in various other parts of South America. All are in periodically inundated lands and all were certainly used for agricultural purposes.

The extensive areas of drained fields in the Guayas Basin of Ecuador are probably associated with the Milagro culture, which post-dates AD 500. Milagro is characterized by numerous large habitation and burial mounds as well as by the raised fields.

Ridged Fields

Many aspects of Milagro culture besides the habitation mounds and the raised fields have more in common with cultures to the east of the Andes than with those of western Ecuador. Large burial urns are typical and, as Estrada noted some time ago, the peculiar style of appliqué decoration that characterizes Milagro resembles the Santarém and Kondurí styles of the Lower Amazon far more than it does other Ecuadorian styles.

The density of Milagro occupation gives a clear indication that the introduction of raised agricultural fields permitted a tremendous expansion of population in the Guayas Basin, and the distinctive nature of Milagro material culture suggests that at least a partial replacement of population was involved in the shift from Tejár to later Milagro. The possibility of deliberate colonization cannot be ruled out. Some group east of the Andes may have become aware of the potential of the Guayas swamp lands, if reclaimed through raised fields, and moved in, replacing the previous less dense population.

It appears that all the raised-field systems are derived from a common source, though as yet the area with the earliest examples cannot be specified. Once the pattern developed there is clear evidence that the amount of land under cultivation was greatly expanded. It is also certain that dependence on this relatively efficient agricultural system led to further population growth and a series of outward migrations in search of other localities where the system could be implemented.

CHAPTER X

The Carib Expansion out of the Amazon Basin

THE EXPANSION of the Caribs was progressing rapidly at the time of the first European contact and was thus fairly well described. Along the Guiana Coast, through much of the lowlands of Venezuela and Colombia, out through the Lesser Antilles, the social patterns of indigenous groups were being destroyed by Carib domination and conquest.

There is little reason for further speculation on the economic basis of the Carib population explosion, though in Surinam and in the San Jorge Valley in Colombia the Carib expansion may have related to the spread of the raised-field agricultural systems.

The cultural mechanisms which permitted the Caribs to dominate and destroy their neighbours are better understood. The Carib groups placed an unusually high value on interpersonal aggression, warfare as the route to prestige, and being a 'real man', all of which traits are found in surviving Carib social groups.

The expansion of the Carib followed a distinctive pattern. Whole villages or lineages did not invade the territory of the enemy. Rather it was raiding parties of young men who attacked the neighbouring peoples. All adult males of the conquered villages were barbecued and eaten while the more desirable women were taken as wives.

As a result of this kind of partial ethnic replacement, not all aspects of Carib culture would have been disseminated with uniformity and full understanding. If it is correct to assume that art style and ceramic technology were feminine domains, it would be predictable that these patterns would be transmitted in a poorly understood and garbled form, since there would be few, if any, properly trained women moving out of the old Carib hearth-land. It has already been noted that the transmission of Carib languages to the second and subsequent generations of these 'Carib' colonies was frequently imperfect or indeed minimal.

In view of the above conditions it is not surprising that there has been considerable difficulty in defining the precise archaeological equivalent of particular instances of Carib expansion known from the early chronicles. If we take a broad view of these problems, however, the situation appears more hopeful. Starting around AD 500 and continuing until the time of the first European contacts, certain stylistic and technological features are gradually spread out of the north-east quadrant of the Amazon Basin into adjacent parts of South America. These elements are sufficiently coherent for them to be perceived as a ceramic tradition, but it is a tradition which cross-cuts several of the other horizons and traditions recognized by other students of South American culture history.

On the technological level the most striking trait of this ceramic tradition is the use of *cauxí* as a tempering material. Its use was, of course, circumscribed by the distribution of the sponges which produce the material. They are not found in the lesser tributaries of the Amazon and Orinoco.

From the point of view of art style this wide-ranging ceramic tradition possessed two major characteristics. One was the use of thin, deep incision, executed with a sharply pointed stylus and quite unlike the broad U-shaped incision typical of all of the earlier Barrancoid styles. This mode of V-shaped incised lines is almost always organized into rectilinear designs, which also contrasts with the open, curvilinear scroll motif underlying much Barrancoid decoration. By far the most common germinal motif in all of the fine-line incised styles is a continuous band of contiguous isosceles triangles. The other artistic tendency is the

Fig. 41

Fig. 41 A series of incised and excised sherds showing the similarity in the organization of band designs over a wide range of late prehistoric cultures in the Amazon Basin and adjacent areas: Kondurí Complex, mouth of Río Trombetas, Central Amazon, a–b; Mound Masicito, Llanos de Mojos, Lowland Bolivia, c–d; Itacoatiara Phase, Itacoatiara, Central Amazon, e; Nericagua Phase, Upper Orinoco, Venezuela, f; Arauquín Style, Lower Río Aruaca, Llanos de Orinoco, Venezuela, g–h; Matraquero Style, Matraquero Site, Llanos de Orinoco, Venezuela, i–j; Camoruco Style, Middle Orinoco, Venezuela, k; Apostadero Style, Apostadero Site, Lower Orinoco, Venezuela, l–m; Valencia Style, Lake Valencia, Venezuela, n. The demonstrated range of this kind of design layout could be considerably expanded by including examples from the Quimbaya, Tairona, and Muisca Styles of Colombia

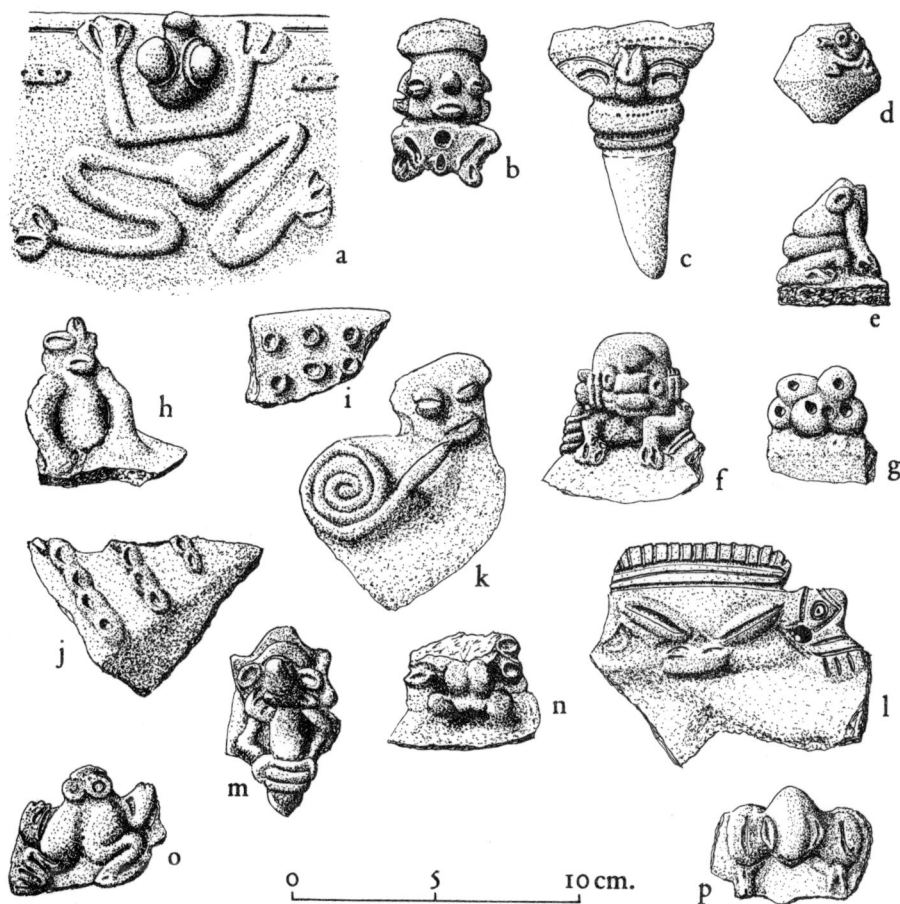

Fig. 42 Selection of ceramics with appliqué decoration showing the similarity in techniques and themes over a wide range of the Amazon Basin and adjacent areas in late prehistoric times. Santarém Style, Santarém, mouth of Río Tapajós, Lower Amazon, a–b; Konduri Style, Faro, Río Jamunda, Middle Amazon, c; Corobal Phase, Ventuari River, Southern Venezuela, d–g; Arauquín Style, Arauquín Site, Lower Río Aruaca, Llanos de Orinoco, Venezuela, h–i; Matraquero Style, Matraquero Site, Llanos de Orinoco, Venezuela, j–k; Camoruco Style, Middle Orinoco, Venezuela, l; Late Mabaruma Phase, Northwestern Guyana, m; Apostadero Style, Apostadero Site, Lower Orinoco, Venezuela, n; La Cabrera Style, Lower levels Los Tamarindos Site, Lake Valencia, Venezuela, o–p. The range could be considerably extended by including such Colombian styles as Quimbaya, Río de la Miel, and La Mesa, and the Milagro Phase of the Guayas Basin of Ecuador

The Upper Amazon

peculiar use of appliqué. Zoomorphic *adornos* and abstract designs are built up by plastering on thin rolls of wet clay in combination with lots of spherical blobs. The total effect could well be simulated by using the ribbon of cake icing exuded from a pastry tube.

Fig. 42

The subject matter represented in this singular style of additive sculpture is variable. Snakes, monkeys, caimans, and jaguars occur, rampant over various vessel forms; human representations are not infrequent. Abstract composition consisting of fields or clumps of pellets are wide-spread, but more than any other element, toads dominate the iconography of this tradition of plastic representation.

Fig. 42 b, c, f, h, k–n

Fig. 42, a, d, e, o

The most famous and elaborate of all of the ceramic styles which show the characteristics discussed above is Santarém, on the Lower Amazon. This style almost certainly represents the pottery of the historic Tapajos nation, one of the largest and most tightly organized political units in the Amazon Basin. The multiplicity of affixed elements in the Santarém style and their baroque organization somewhat masks the nature of the basic design motifs, but when these compositions are analysed in terms of their constituent elements, the affinities with this tradition are clear.

Fig. 42 a, b

Other styles in this fine-line incised tradition are so numerous that there is space to do little more than map them.

Fig. 43

In the Central Amazon around Manaus these tendencies are best represented by the Paredão Phase recently defined by Hilbert. More interesting from the point of view of determining the history of this fine-line incised stylistic tradition is the Itacoatiara Phase, during which fine-line angular incision occurs as an overlay on typically Barrancoid decoration. These designs and the related fine-line incision on some of the Jauarí Phase pottery are the earliest examples of this kind of decoration known from the lowlands of South America and suggest that it first developed on the north shore of the Middle to Lower Amazon.

Fig. 41 e

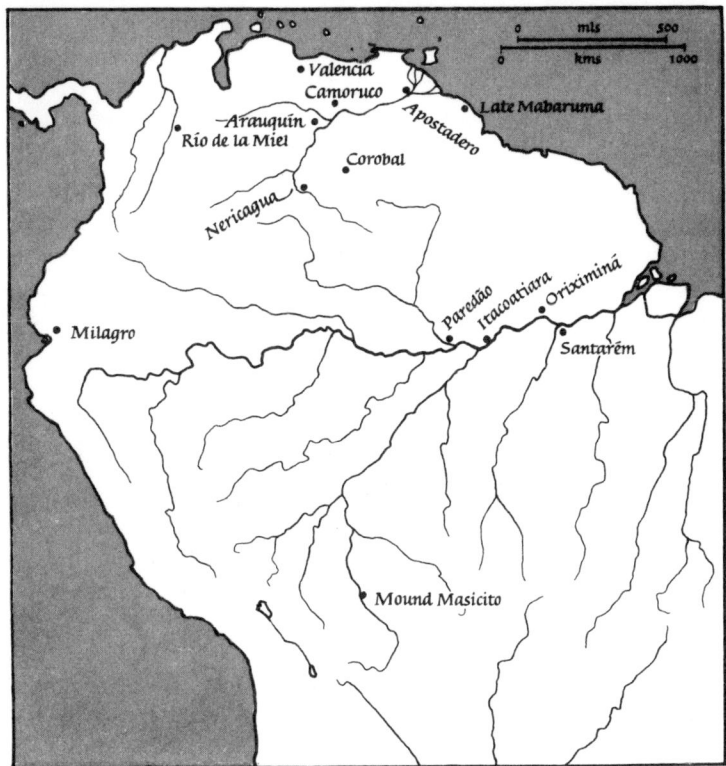

Fig. 43 Late sites in and around the Amazon Basin characterized by vessels having fine-line triangular incision and/or complex strip appliqué

Ceramic styles in the generalized tradition which we have been discussing extend to the west considerably beyond the Amazon and Orinoco Basins. There are several burial-urn styles from the Lowlands of Colombia which show most of the characteristics. One of these, Río de la Miel, occurs in the Middle Magdelena relatively close to the San Jorge Basin, the largest area of drained fields in Colombia. The modelled and incised elements in the Chibchan ceramic style are also related. As noted earlier, the modelled incised segment of Milagro cermics (the protohistoric

169

to historic culture in the Guayas Basin of Ecuador) is also of this tradition.

I do not wish to make the claim that all the fine-line incised styles I have discussed were made by Carib groups or that all Carib groups, as of contact time, made ceramics which could be accommodated within the broad stylistic tradition outlined above. None the less, the general timing and direction of the expansion of this stylistic tradition correspond remarkably well to the known fact of the Carib expansion. Various anthropologists, and most especially Paul Rivet, have suspected that the rather gross burial-urn styles of lowland Colombia were the leavings of Carib invaders. In Venezuela and Guyana the distribution of the late prehistoric to historic Guarguapo, Apostadero, and Late Mabaruma styles corresponds rather well to the late expansion of Caribs in this area at the expense of their Arawakan neighbours.

CHAPTER XI

Terracing and the Eastern Slopes of the Andes

FAR LESS ATTENTION has been paid to the history and extent of terraced land in the Central Andes than to the development of canal irrigation, but the former type of agricultural system may well have played a greater part in determining the pattern of population distribution at the time of the first European contacts.

As already indicated, the moist eastern slopes of the Andes have a reasonably high agricultural potential. The major problem was to retain the soil on precipitous slopes onces the dense *ceja* has been cleared. For this purpose some pattern of terracing or near-terracing was essential.

The shift from bottom-land farming to slope farming is likely to lead to a complete redistribution of farming communities. Thorough surveys in a number of the Highland Basins of the Central Andes should enable us to trace the expansion of agricultural communities from their initial position adjacent to the prime agricultural lands of the valley bottoms to locations progressively further up the sides of the valleys and onto the eastern Andean slopes running down towards the jungle. It is only for the Huánuco Basin that we come close to having this kind of detailed information. Agricultural occupation of the Basin started before 2000 B C with the major settlements, such as Kotosh, adjacent to the limited areas of self-irrigating bottom land. From this time on, the archaeological evidence suggests the continuous development of a single ethnic group until early in the Christian era. Agricultural activities were concentrated on the valley bottoms.

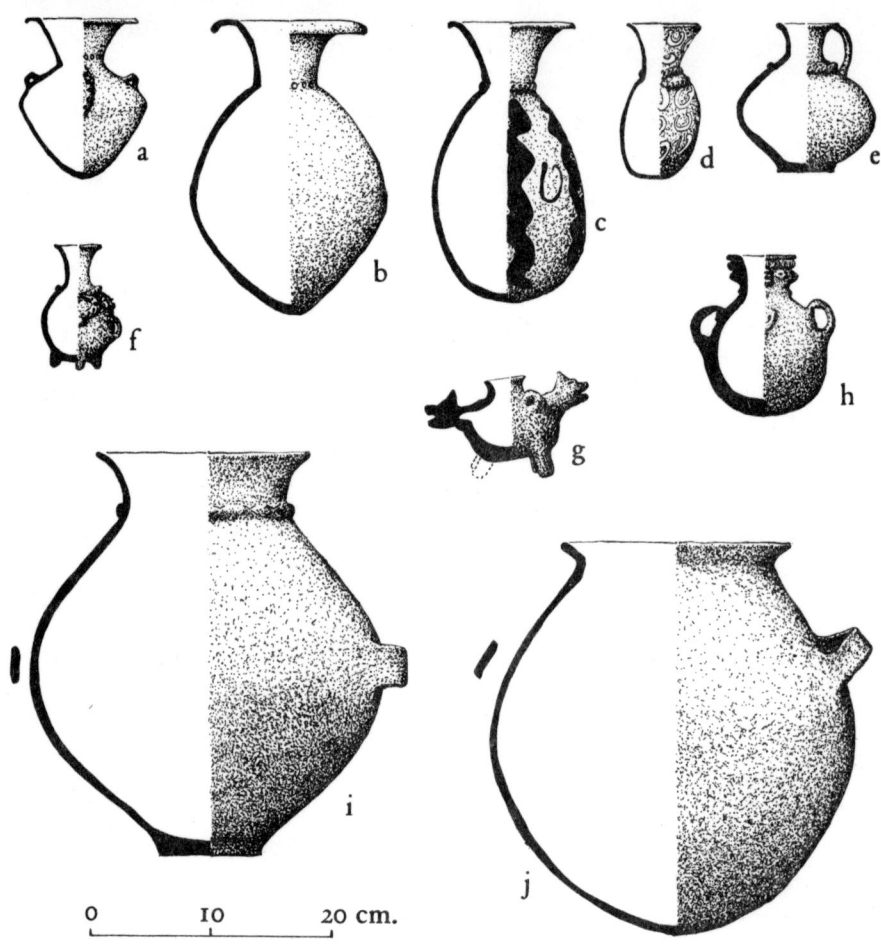

Fig. 44 Vessels from sites along the crest and eastern slopes of the Peruvian and Bolivian Andes: Late component at Marca Huamuchuco, Huamachuco, Peru, coarse brown ware with appliqué and reed punctation, a; Tantamayo Style, Tantamayo Region, Peru, plain brown ware, b; Tarmatambo, Tarma Basin, Peru, dark red paint on unslipped buff surface, c, white paint on unslipped buff surface, d; Burial cave T-9a, Tarma Basin, Peru, appliqué, on rough, red slipped surface, f, Higueras Red, the Higueras Component of Kotosh, Huánuco Basin, Peru, g–h, j; Eastern slope of the Bolivian Andes east of Lake Titicaca, site of Markopata, grave 2, i, site of Chulpani, grave 2, e

The Eastern Slopes of the Andes

Some time between 100 BC and AD 600 there is a complete change in ceramic tradition, suggesting a total replacement of population, and the valley-bottom sites are less intensively occupied or used mainly as cemeteries. The intrusive Higueras pottery is crude, poorly smoothed, and infrequently decorated. The surfaces are typically covered with an irregular, thin red wash; decoration, where it occurs, takes the form of carelessly applied rolls of clay or the crudest kind of modelled representations of men and animals.

Fig. 44 g, h, j

From the arrival of Higueras ceramics to the Spanish conquest there is a progressively greater tendency for large towns to be located on the high ridges surrounding the Huánuco basin at elevations of 12,000 to 13,000 feet. Vast areas of semi-terraced agricultural land were opened up on the slopes immediately below these fortified and easily defensible towns. Ceramics continue in the coarse and largely unembellished tradition introduced by the Higueras people. The recent studies of Murra and Thompson permit us to identify this ceramic tradition and this series of hill-top towns with the historic Chupachu, a Quechua-speaking group conquered by the Inca Empire only a short time before the coming of the Spanish.

The Higueras-Chupachu ceramics are just one of a series of related styles showing the same range of vessel form categories and poorly finished surfaces. Plain brown surfaces or a thin and irregular wash of red slip are standard.

Fig. 44

This coarse-ware ceramic tradition has not received the careful study it deserves. From the aesthetic point of view the ceramics are without interest; none the less, the similarities among these widely distributed styles and the abruptness with which they replace the previous ceramic traditions in the various areas of the eastern Highlands suggest that this coarse-ware tradition is of greatest significance as evidence of a major population expansion along the eastern edge of the Central Andean highlands. Even in the Huánuco Basin it is difficult to date precisely the invasion

Fig. 45

173

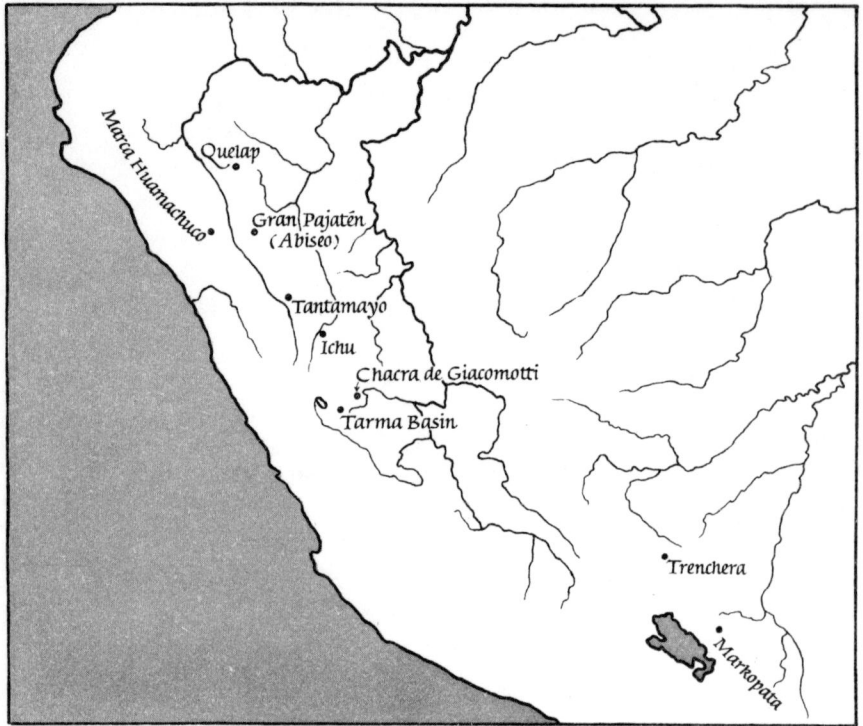

Fig. 45   Sites dominating the crest and eastern slopes of the Andes

of peoples bringing in the Higueras style; while elsewhere in the Peruvian Andes our chronological controls are even less precise. There are several lines of evidence which suggest that most of the major population movements responsible for the spread of the coarse-ware tradition took place before AD 600.

The distribution of the more divergent languages within Quechua—those not mutually intelligible with Cuzco Quechua (the language of the Inca Empire)—corresponds rather well with the distribution of the coarse-ware tradition. It seems highly probable, therefore, that the appearance of the Higueras style of ceramics in the Huánuco Basin, and of related ceramic styles

The Eastern Slopes of the Andes

throughout much of the Peruvian Andes, marks the arrival of Quechua-speakers.

The consistent pattern of association of the coarse-ware tradition with heavily fortified sites located at high elevations and dominating expanses of terraced or semi-terraced agricultural lands, suggests that it was the development of an agricultural system efficiently exploiting the steep eastern slopes of the Andes that both permitted and caused the pre-Incaic expansion of Quechua.

Our best evidence for the origins of the coarse-ware tradition comes from the Cochabamba Basin of Bolivia. The Chullpa Pampa style, now dated to the first couple of centuries AD, has great significance for an understanding not only of the culture history of the Central Andes but also of that of all of South America. Secondary adult urn burial in large urns with lids has its earliest securely dated South American occurrence in the Chullpa Pampa style; and the form of the burial urn in Chullpa Pampa is remarkably similar to urn shapes in such styles as

Fig. 46

Fig. 46 a

Fig. 46 Typical shapes of the red-slipped ware from Chullpa Pampa, Cochabamba area, eastern slope of the Bolivian Andes

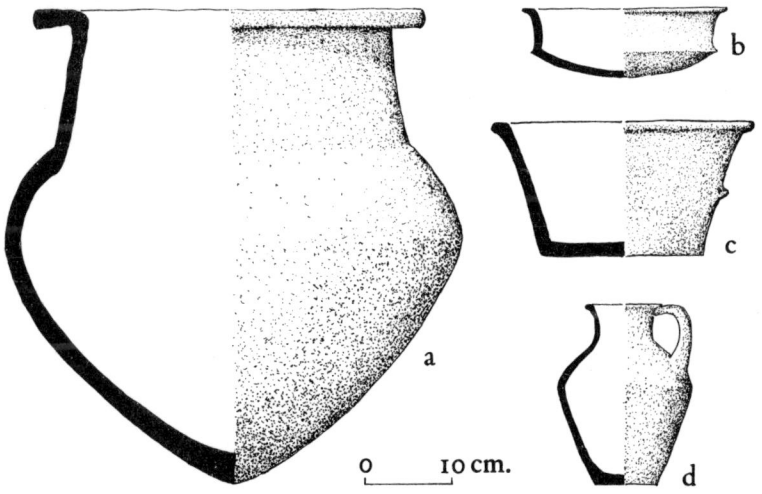

The Upper Amazon

Plate 56

Marajoara at the mouth of the Amazon, and the polychrome style of painted urn from north-west Argentina. These observations suggest that the Cochabamba Basin has long had important contacts with the eastern lowland of South America. (It has sometimes been counted as part of the Lowlands even though it has an elevation of more than 3,000 metres.)

In the range of coarse, red-slipped Chullpa Pampa materials illustrated by Walter are prototypes for all of the vessel forms and decorative techniques typical of Higueras and the other coarse-ware styles of the Eastern Andes. The dates for the Chullpa Pampa materials are considerably earlier than those for any comparable materials within the Central Andes proper. The coarse-ware tradition, the pattern of intensive farming on the steep Andean slopes, and Quechua languages all appear to have spread from south to north along the eastern slope of the Andes.

Steward has suggested that there was a sharp cultural boundary dividing the peoples of Tropical Forest Culture from the bearers of Central Andean civilization. He even went so far as to suggest that the zone of *ceja* vegetation on the eastern slopes of the Andes was largely uninhabited in Pre-Columbian times and served as an effective barrier to cultural interchange between the two areas. Earlier it was noted that the lower part of the *ceja* was occupied by Tropical Forest peoples from at least 1800 B C on. It is now clear that in late pre-contact times the precipitous upper slopes of the *ceja* were densely occupied by representatives of the coarse-ware ceramic tradition. The work of Rydén east of Lake Titicaca, the surveys of William Isbell in the Sandía region and of Bonavia to the east of Ayacucho, my own observations in the Chanchamayo, Thompson's work to the east of Huánuco, the recent explorations of Rojas and Bonavia at Gran Pajatén (Abiseo) all demonstrate that stone architecture, extensive agricultural terracing, and the coarse-ware ceramic tradition extend well down into the zone of *ceja* vegetation to an elevation of less than 1,500 metres.

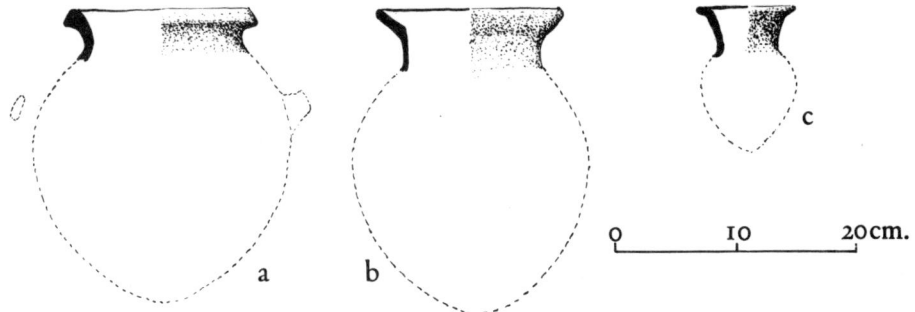

Fig. 47 Range of vessel shapes demonstrable for PER-8, Chacra de Giacomotti, on a ridge 1,300 metres above the town of La Merced, Chanchamayo, Peru. All pottery is of a coarse, brown ware

The situation in the Chanchamayo around San Ramón and La Mercéd may be taken as typical. In late times the floor of the valley was occupied by the Campa who were making Naranjal ceramics. On the ridges immediately above La Mercéd are sites producing a ceramic style which has been designated Chacra de Giacomotti. The foundations of numerous masonry houses are scattered along a knife-edge ridge and terraced agricultural lands are found immediately below. Though the ceramic remains from the Chacra de Giacomotti sites are fragmentary, they belong in the coarse-ware tradition. Cast, T-shaped axes of bronze are common on these sites, ground stone bowls with pouring spouts and carefully shaped stone mace-heads are also present. It is clear that Chacra de Giacomotti is a late culture probably extending into historic times. There was no empty buffer zone between the two very different ethnic groups sharing the Chanchamayo in late prehistoric times. So steep are the slopes of the Chanchamayo that the Chacra de Giacomotti peoples looked down almost directly on the towns of their Campa neighbours. It is certain that considerable trade and cultural exchange took place. Sherds of the Naranjal style occurred on the Chacra de

Fig. 47

The Upper Amazon

Fig. 48

Plates 51, 47

Plates 48–50

Giacomotti sites and vice versa. Elsewhere along the *ceja* zone there is further evidence that trade and cultural contact were the norm rather than the exception. Archaeological sites along the Lower Río Pachitea are said to produce bronze axes in quantity, and I have recently obtained concrete evidence that bronze axes are indeed common in archaeological sites along the Upper Río Pisqui. It is clear that these axes were not made in the jungle but were traded down from the eastern Andean slopes.

While the ceramics of these coarse-ware styles are uniformly dismal, other aspects of material culture are of considerable interest. The Tantamayo area is known for its highly stylized human figurines and spectacular multi-storied architecture.

Even more elaborate are the masonry mosaics decorating the walls of the various structures of Gran Pajatén (Abiseo). It is said that most of the precipitous slopes around the site are terraced and that there are many similar sites in the area. Here again is striking evidence of the dense occupation of the *ceja* in immediately pre-contact times.

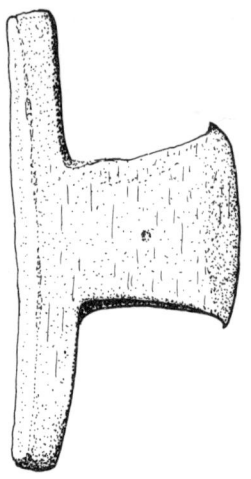

Fig. 48 Cast bronze axe from the Río Pisqui near the Pisquibo colony of Nueva Edén, Peru

0   5 cm.

The Eastern Slopes of the Andes

These communities of the eastern slopes are outstanding not only for the variety of their masonry but also for the ingenuity of their fortifications. This is true of the Chupachu sites above Huánuco; it is true of the large sites above Tarma investigated by Jensen; and it is especially true of the ruin of Trenchera above Sandía, which has been described by William Isbell. The houses were densely packed together on the crest of a high peak. Rows of houses shared common back walls which offered further obstacles to attackers attempting to storm the crest. The whole community was surrounded by a massive double wall breached by a single entrance. Both of the defensive walls were furnished with catwalks on their inner side, offering the defenders an excellent vantage point and maximum cover as they fought off an attack.

Plate 54

Plate 53

The defensible position of all of these tightly packed communities and their ingenious defence systems argue that warfare was extremely common in late prehistoric times and we can assume that such warfare was an expression of the competition for agricultural land.

The Inca Empire arose out of the state of constant warfare among these various small kingdoms of farming folk on the slopes of the Andes. It has already been suggested that all the Quechua-speaking peoples may have their point of origin on the eastern slopes of the Andes and considerably to the south. The origins of the highly distinctive ceramic style which served as a hallmark for the Inca Empire may also lie in that direction. Killke, the ceramic style from which the imperial Inca style is derived, shows more similarity to the Mollo style of the eastern slope of the Bolivian Andes than to the earlier styles of the Cuzco Basin. These ceramic similarities, though tenuous, suggest that the arrival of the Incas in the Cuzco Basin may have been part of a continuing population movement from south to north along the eastern slopes of the Andes.

Plate 52

CHAPTER XII

The Present Ethnographic Picture in the Ucayali Basin

Fig. 49

THE RECENT DISTRIBUTION of Indian groups on the Peruvian Amazon and in the Ucayali Basin is complex; and it is beyond the scope of this book to mention, let alone discuss, each of the known groups. In this brief final chapter I shall concentrate on the contrasts between the riverine groups and the tribes living on the old alluvial lands back from the rivers.

THE SHIPIBO AND CONIBO

Plate 55

The Shipibo and Conibo share a common art style and intermarry extensively. The degree to which these Indians are oriented to the rivers and lakes rather than to the forest cannot be overemphasized; fishing is still a major economic pursuit. They farm intensively both on the rich flood plains and on the poorer lands of the bluffs, with the more demanding crops such as plantains and maize planted on the former. Their farming methods are by no means casual, and the better agricultural lands are systematically planted and carefully weeded.

Most Shipibo-Conibo experienced missionization by the Franciscans for varying periods during the seventeenth to nineteenth centuries. All were completely caught up in the rubber boom during the first decade of this century. Individual family groups came under the total domination of particular *patrones* and there was a great displacement of population during this period. After the rubber boom had collapsed, communities established themselves in their old homeland, usually growing up around the nucleus of a school or mission station. While the Shipibo-Conibo may be sceptical about the details of Christian dogma, they are totally convinced of the virtues of literacy and Western medicine.

180

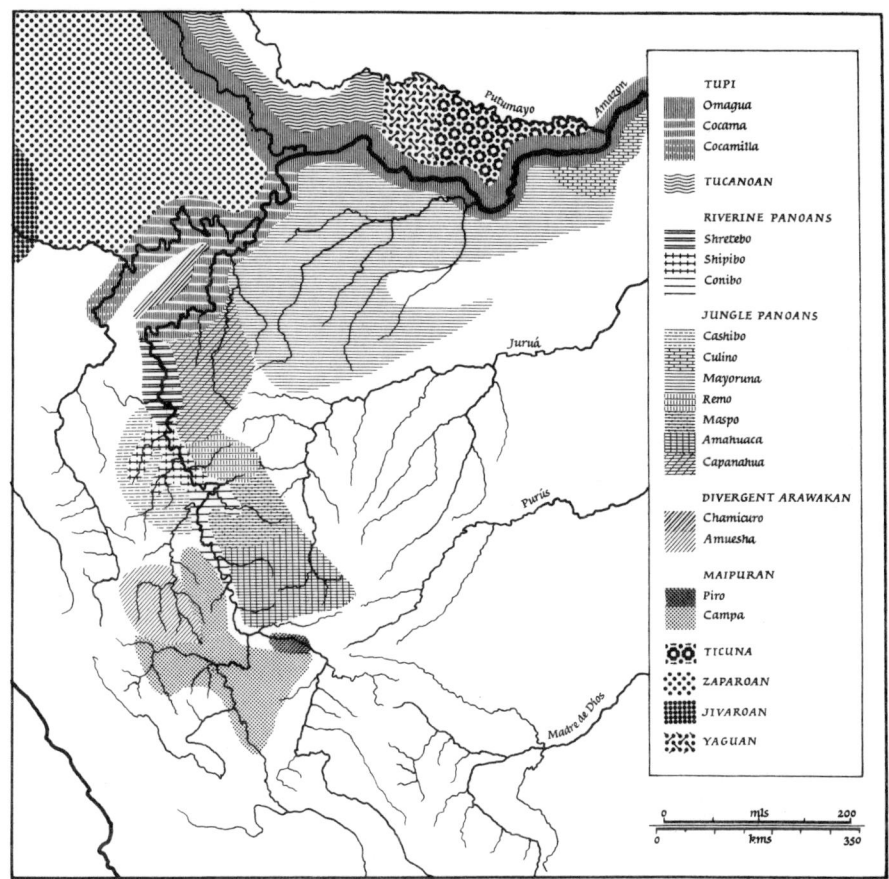

Fig. 49 Recent distribution of aboriginal groups in the Ucayali Basin.

The degree to which the large Shipibo-Conibo communities were broken down under the stress of missionization and the rubber boom, and reassembled under various strong Western influences, makes it difficult to assess the structure of the prehistoric community. It is clear that the basic unit of society is, and for a long time has been, the extended family. A number of these

The Upper Amazon

Shipibo-Conibo extended families, which have a strong bias towards matrilocality, are grouped together in named, localized communities.

From as far back as their own traditions reach, the Shipibo-Conibo have been in a state of constant warfare with the Panoan-speaking groups inhabiting the jungles away from the river. They attribute cannibalism and all manner of other loathsome habits to these forest tribes. Shipibo war parties would attack Cashibo, Amahuaca, or Remo households with the hope of wiping out the adult males and taking the females and children as slaves. There was a definite feeling of missionary zeal associated with these wars. The Shipibo regarded themselves as 'civilized' and the backwoods Panoan groups as 'sub-standard' from the cultural point of view. The Cashibo and Amahuaca maidens captured by the Shipibo were being 'saved' from a life of barbarism. Such captive girls were adopted into the family of their captor and gradually civilized. Many of the best Shipibo potters turn out to be civilized Cashibo or Amahuaca or the daughters of such redeemed savages.

Considering the vicissitudes which the riverine Panoan groups have endured, their art and material culture remain in a remarkable state of preservation to this day. This is particularly true of their pottery.

The modern Shipibo-Conibo potter thinks in terms of two basic wares; one for producing vessels which are to be placed in the fire, the other for making every other kind of vessel. These two distinct wares involve the use of different clays and different proportions of the two tempering materials which are added to the basic clays to improve their characteristics. The cooking ware is made with a black clay of high organic content to which is added a very high proportion of *cariapé* temper. The non-culinary ware is made with a mixture of red and white clays to which is added a much smaller proportion of *cariapé* and a much larger amount of finely ground potsherds.

Plate 63

Fig. 50 Band designs from the necks of Shipibo and Pisquibo quënti, *cooking pots, showing a range of decorative techniques; broad-line incision and finger-nail incision,* a*; finger-nail incision,* b*; pattern burnishing and finger-nail incision,* c

The fire-proof pot comes in three standardized sizes: small size, used mainly for the steaming of arthritic joints; standard size, used for the cooking of the family meals; and giant size, used for boiling-up manioc to be used in making beer for fiestas. The cooking ware is almost never painted, but is almost always decorated with a variety of techniques including true corrugation, finger-nail incision, pattern burnishing, fine-line incision, un-obliterated coils and broad-line grooving with the finger-tip, and punctation. All the kinds of decoration found on modern Shipibo-Conibo cooking pots and the form-category itself can be found in the ceramics of the Cumancaya tradition, giving us the strongest reasons for believing that the modern Shipibo and Conibo are the direct descendants of the makers of Cumancaya ceramics.

Plates 66, 67
Plate 65

Fig. 50
Plates 66, 67

Non-culinary ware is produced in three basic vessel shapes: the water jar, the beer mug, and the food bowl. The water jar and the beer mug also come in three distinct size-categories with specialized function, while the food bowl shows a number of functionally significant variations in form and interior finish. The large beer mug is circulated round and round the group of celebrants during a fiesta.

Plates 57, 58, 60, 61

Plate 58, 60

There are two basic colour schemes for the decoration of Shipibo-Conibo serving ware. Black and red on white, and white on red. The exteriors of jars and beer mugs tend to be decorated in black and red on white, while food bowls frequently have white on red decoration.

183

Whereas the style of decoration on the cooking ware derives entirely from the Cumancaya tradition, the roots of the Shipibo-Conibo painted style are more diverse. The fondness for straight lines and step motifs clearly derives from the Cumancaya style, while the two basic colour schemes and the insistence on two or three standardized widths of painted line have their clear antecedents in the Caimito and Napo styles. It is known that the Shipibo-Conibo and the Cocama shared the same missions during the seventeenth to nineteenth centuries and most likely the styles became amalgamated while these were active.

Other elements of Shipibo-Conibo technology are also remarkably preserved considering the long periods of Western contact. The rocker pestle of stone combined with the trough mortar of wood has been much praised as a labour-saving device in the preparation of maize. The stone rocker may also serve as a whetstone or as a mould for hammering-out conical ornaments of metal. This multiple usage indicates the great scarcity of stone on the alluvial flood plain of the Ucayali.

Plate 63

Plate 64

It was noted that ceramic pot-rests in groups of three became common on the Central Ucayali during the Pacacocha occupation of the area. Such fire-dogs have passed out of use along the mainstream of the Ucayali, but are still common in the households on the Río Pisqui.

Plate 68

Most Shipibo-Conibo women still cling to a traditional style of dress. The blouse is of obvious European inspiration, but the tubular skirt of hand-woven cotton is of purely Indian derivation. Most men now wear Western-style clothes for everyday use, but may put on the traditional hand-woven *cushma* for fiestas or as protection against mosquitos during the evening.

Plate 65

Plate 59

Fiestas are still an important part of Shipibo-Conibo life. The Indians are now nominally Catholic and a number of the important feasts of the Roman Catholic calendar are celebrated. Traditionally the girls' puberty ceremony was the most important social event, lasting for at least three days and involving the

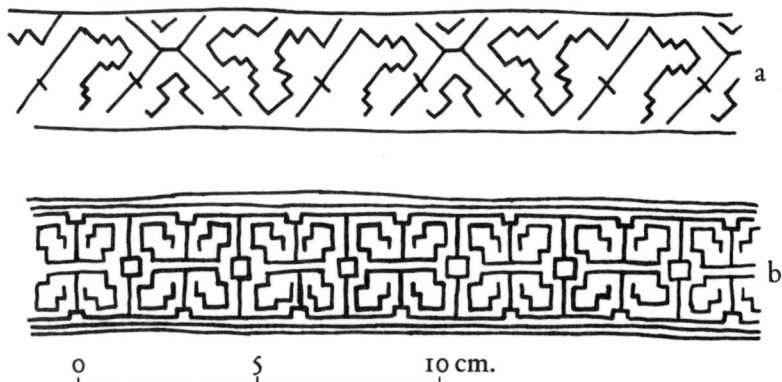

Fig. 51 Impressions from modern, carved wooden roller seals: Shipibo from the colony of Callería, a; Conibo from the colony of Painaco, b. These are used by young bachelors in painting their own faces for fiestas

production and consumption of prodigious quantities of manioc beer. Fights between the adult males of the community were a standard feature during the latter part of the celebration. The pretext for these fights was almost always adultery.

At such fiestas one sees the maximum use of traditional items of adornment. Labrets and nose ornaments are in evidence and both sexes wear complex designs painted on their faces in the semi-indelible, blue-black juice of *Genipa americana*. The face painting of the Shipibo-Conibo is second only to that of the Mbaya-Caduveo in its elaboration. It is carried out only by women; a young bachelor, having no one to paint his face, carves a cylinder seal of hard wood with which to apply the designs.

Plate 64

Fig. 51

THE COCAMA

Descendants of the Cocama Indians make up a large part of the rural population of eastern Peru. They tend to live in large towns, a pattern followed by their prehistoric ancestors. Whereas the Shipibo-Conibo affirm their adherence to older cultural patterns, the Cocama are to outward appearances just rural Peruvians. Twenty years ago some of the women still wore the traditional

The Upper Amazon

Plate 69

style of skirt but one never sees this today. Some Cocama women still make pottery but almost all the vessels are of the water-jar shape. Floral designs of obvious European derivation are the common form of decoration and only occasionally does one see a vessel with a traditional design. Forty years ago Cocama pottery was artistically more complex and showed a much wider range of shape and decoration. Specimens collected before the turn of the century show design layouts and motifs which are

Plates 69, 70

directly derived from the Napo-Caimito ceramic tradition.

Floral designs have spread to other tribal groups along the Upper Amazon and excellent examples can now be found on

Plate 71

the pottery of such peoples as the Ticuna.

THE PANOAN-SPEAKING TRIBES OF THE FOREST

It has been suggested earlier that, as population pressures built up on the flood plains of the larger rivers, various groups were pushed away from the rivers and back into the jungle. Also, that the poor soils of the old alluvium and the sparse hunting resources

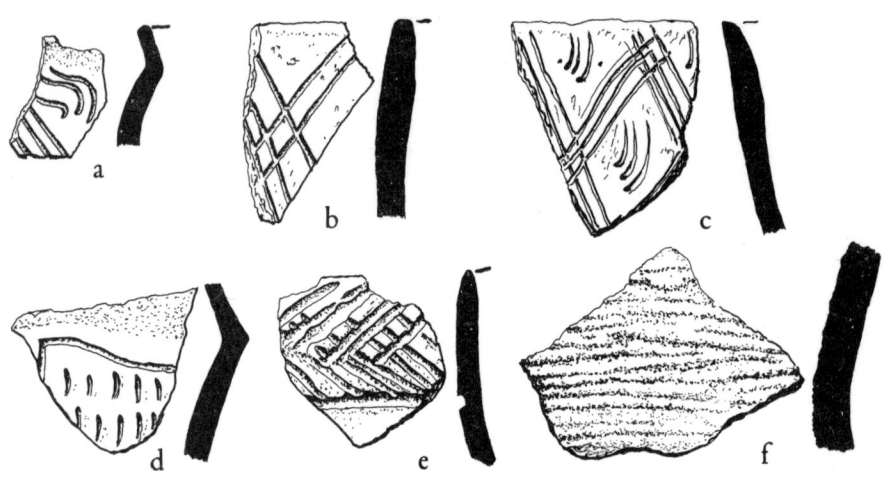

Fig. 52 Sherds of the Tournavista Complex from PAC-23, Kilometer 8 on the road from Tournavista to the Pucallpa road, showing a range of decorative techniques: fine-line incision, a–c; zoned finger-nail incision, d; broad-line incision, e; scraping, f; unobliterated coils, g–h; finger-

of the jungle quickly forced these groups to accept a more nomadic way of life and a general decline in their level of culture. The surviving Panoan-speaking tribes of the deep forests fully bear this out. These include the Cashibo to the west of the Ucayali and the Amahuaca, Remo, and Mayoruna to the east of the Ucayali. All speak languages which are obviously related to the one the Shipibo and Conibo have in common. It is likely that not much more than 1,000 years ago all these people shared the same language and had a common culture. It has already been argued that the Cumancaya complex can be taken as representative of this proto-Panoan culture. Whereas the culture of the modern Shipibo-Conibo has grown even more complex through the addition of elements from their Cocama neighbours, that of the backwoods Panoans has grown progressively simpler, as all but a few of the decorative and technological complexities of Cumancaya were lost.

As protection against their riverine neighbours, the Panoan tribes of the jungle lived well away from even the minor streams.

nail incised appliqué, i; finger-tip grooving, j–l. This complex almost certainly represents the protohistoric Cashibo.

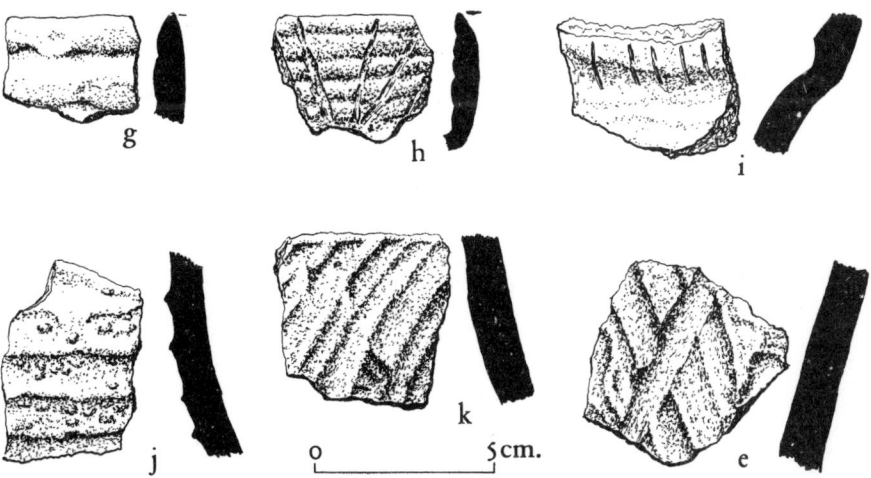

The Upper Amazon

The effective social unit was very small, often no more than a single family. These groups moved their homes and *chacras* frequently. Their agricultural practices were rudimentary and slipshod compared to those of the Shipibo-Conibo. It would be possible to compare every domain of Amahuaca or Remo culture with the corresponding segment of Shipibo-Conibo culture, thus demonstrating the complete poverty of the former. Plates 72–75 The four vessels representative of modern Cashibo and Isconahua pottery here reproduced are an accurate gauge of the technological and artistic poverty of these groups, especially when they are compared to the productions of the Shipibo-Conibo.

As yet it is impossible to present the full archaeological record of the cultural deterioration that resulted in the backwoods Panoan groups. The most common archaeological assemblage Fig. 52 known from the Tournavista area is almost certainly late prehistoric Cashibo. Its aesthetic quality is by no means impressive, but it shows a wider range of incised and plastic decoration than Plate 74 the starkly plain pottery collected from the hostile Cashibo near

Fig. 53 Fine-line incised sherds from a site at Kilometer 30 on the road from Tournavista to the Pucallpa road. All are of a fine orange paste with fine sand tempering, and are fragments of compoteras. The interior of e has a rectilinear design in red

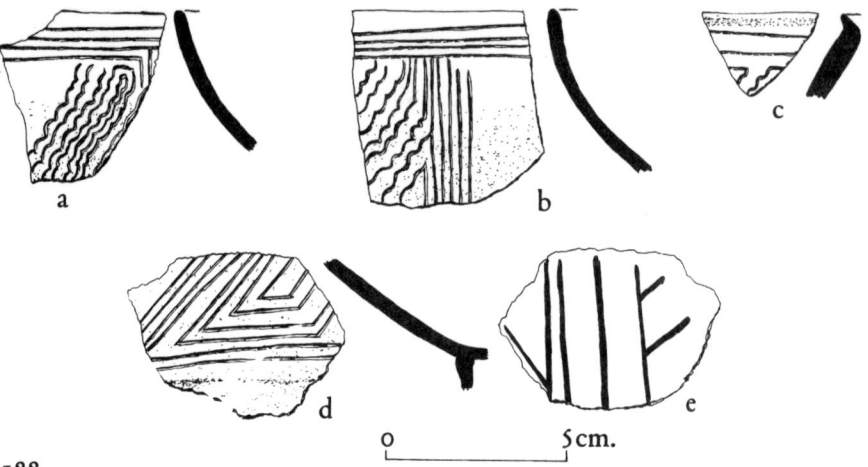

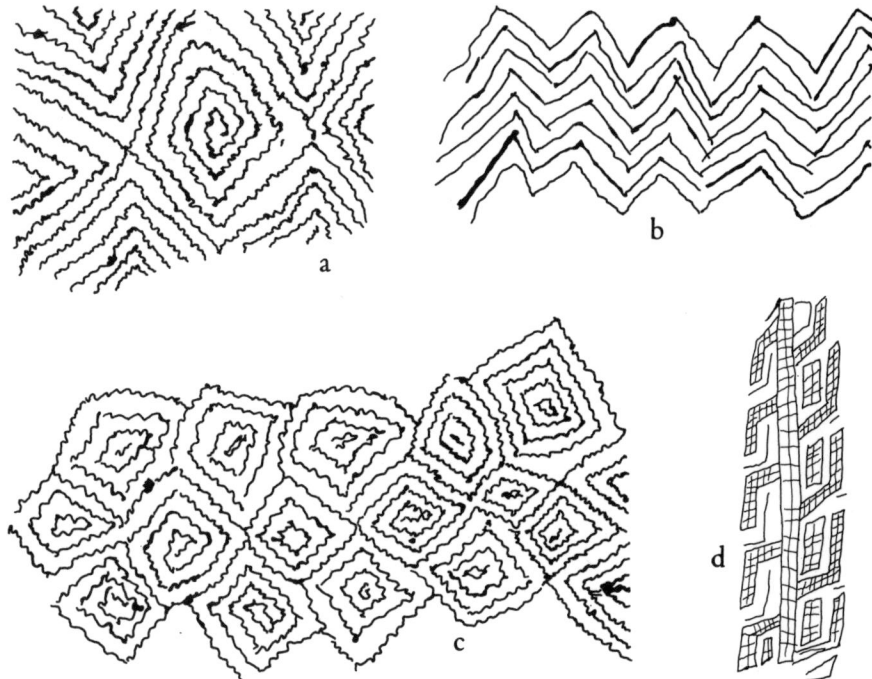

Fig. 54 Paintings made by Isconahua women of the colony on the Río Callería, who worked in the author's note-book using a native type paint-brush and achiote *dye, a–c. Painting from a cane arrowhead of the Tournavista band of Cashibo (Inunahua), collected in 1962 by H. Clifton Russell,* d

Tournavista in 1962. All the decorative techniques in these Tournavista ceramics have antecedents in the Cumancaya complex. Other late ceramic complexes which differ from the Tournavista materials are known from the territory occupied by the modern Cashibo. Given the thousand-year time span between the arrival of Cumancaya culture and the historic Cashibo such diversity is to be expected.

Even in the technologically undemanding area of painting, the artistic vocabulary of these backwoods Panoans is limited. The Isconahua band of the Remo paint their pottery, their dance paraphernalia, and their faces, but the three designs given to

Fig. 53

The Upper Amazon

Fig. 54 a–c

Fig. 54 d

me by elder women of the band just about exhaust the available motifs. In technical competence these paintings are below the level attained by a Shipibo child of ten. The hunting and war arrows of the Cashibo show more non-functional elaboration, and some are impressive in their bizarre forms. Yet the painting on these objects is at a simple level of organization compared to the painting of the Shipibo-Conibo.

While Shipibo-Conibo populations continue to expand and to borrow selectively from Western civilization, the backwoods groups are fast disappearing. Some are in a state of constant warfare with the Peruvian government. When these peoples are brought in and pacified, they show a high susceptibility to Western diseases, and those who survive show little pride in preserving their past way of life.

Bibliography

CHAPTER I

STEWARD, JULIAN H. 'Tribes of the Montaña,' in *Handbook of South American Indians,* Julian H. Steward, ed., vol. 3, 507–34. *The Tropical Forest Tribes,* Bureau of American Ethnology, Bulletin 143. Washington, D.C., 1948.

CHAPTER II

The river system of the Amazon Basin

LATHRAP, DONALD W. 'Aboriginal occupation and changes in river channel on the Central Ucayali, Peru,' *American Antiquity,* vol. 33, no. 1, 62–79. Salt Lake City, 1968.

LEOPOLD, LUNA B. AND LANGBEIN, W. B. 'River meanders,' *Scientific American,* vol. 214, no. 6, 60–70. New York, 1966.

MARBUT, C. F. AND MANIFOLD, C. B. 'The topography of the Amazon Valley,' *The Geographical Review,* vol. 15, no 4, 617–42. New York, 1925.

STERNBERG, HILGARD O'REILLY. 'Radiocarbon dating as applied to a problem of Amazonian morphology,' *Comptes Rendus du XVIII Congrès International de Géographie,* 399–425. Rio de Janeiro, 1960.

The vegetation cover

SAUER, CARL O. 'Geography of South America,' in *Handbook of South American Indians,* Julian H. Steward, ed., vol. 6, 319–44. Bureau of American Ethnology, Bulletin 143. Washington, D.C., 1950.

The fauna of the Tropical Forest

GILMORE, RAYMOND M. 'Fauna and ethnozoology of South America,' in *Handbook of South American Indians,* Julian H. Steward, ed., vol. 6, 345–464. *Physical Anthropology, Linguistics, and Cultural Geography of South American Indians,* Bureau of American Ethnology, Bulletin 143. Washington, D.C., 1950.

HOLMBERG, ALLAN R. *Nomads of the long bow,* Smithsonian Institution, Institute of Social Anthropology, publication no. 10. Washington, D.C., 1950.

The soils and their Agricultural Potential

CARNEIRO, ROBERT L. 'Slash-and-burn agriculture: A closer look at its implications for settlement patterns,' *Selected Papers of the Fifth International Congress of Anthropological and Ethnological Sciences,* Anthony F. C. Wallace, ed., 229–34. Philadelphia, 1960.

—, 'Slash-and-burn cultivation among the Kuikuru and its implications for cultural development in the Amazon Basin,' in *The Evolution of Horticultural Systems in Native South America, Causes and Consequences: a Symposium,* Johannes Wilbert, ed. *Antropológica,* suppl. publ. no. 2, 47–67. Caracas, 1961.

MARBUT, C. F. AND MANIFOLD, C. B. 'The soils of the Amazon in relation to agricultural possibilities,' *The Geographical Review,* vol. 16, no. 3, 414–42. New York, 1926.

MEGGERS, BETTY J. AND EVANS, CLIFFORD, 'The reconstruction of settlement pattern in the South American Tropical Forest,' in *Prehistoric Settlement Patterns in the New World,* Gordon R. Willey, ed. Viking Foundation Publications in Anthropology, no. 23, 156–64. New York, 1956.

STERNBERG, HILGARD O'REILLY. 'Land and man in the Tropics,' in *Economic and Political Trends in Latin America, Proceedings of the Academy of Political Science.* May 5, 1964.

—, 'Die Viehzucht in Careiro-Cambixegebiet, ein Beitrag zur Kulturgeographie der Amazonasniederung,' in *Heidelberger Geographische Arbeiten* Heft 15 (Festgabe für Gottfried Pfeifer), 171–97. Wiesbaden, 1966.

CHAPTER III

The definition of Tropical Forest Culture

GOLDMAN, IRVING. *The Cubeo Indians of the Northwest Amazon,* Illinois Studies in Anthropology, no. 2. Urbana, 1963.

LATHRAP, DONALD W. 'The "hunting" economics of the Tropical Forest Zone of South America: an attempt at historical perspective,' in *Man the Hunter,* Richard B. Lee and Irven DeVore, eds., 23–29. Chicago, 1968.

Bibliography

LOWIE, ROBERT H. 'The Tropical Forests: an introduction,' in *Handbook of South American Indians*, Julian H. Steward, ed., vol. 3, 1–56. Bureau of American Ethnology, Bulletin 143. Washington, D.C., 1948.

MEGGERS, BETTY J. 'Environmental limitation on the development of culture', *American Anthropologist*, vol. 56, 801–24. Menasha, 1954.

—, 'Environment and culture in the Amazon Basin: an appraisal of the theory of environmental determinism,' in *Studies in Human Ecology*. The Pan American Union, Washington, D.C., 1957.

MEGGERS, B. J. AND EVANS, CLIFFORD. *Archeological investigations at the mouth of the Amazon*, Bureau of American Ethnology, Bulletin 167. Washington, D.C., 1957.

NORDENSKIÖLD, ERLAND. 'The ethnography of South America seen from Mojos in Bolivia,' *Comparative Ethnographical Studies*, 3. Göteborg, 1924.

—, 'L'Archéologie du Bassin de l'Amazon,' *Ars Americana*, no. 1. Paris, 1930.

ROWE, JOHN H. 'Introduction to "The Tapajo," by Curt Nimuendajú,' *Kroeber Anthropological Society Papers*, no. 6, 1–25. Berkeley, 1952.

STEWARD, JULIAN H. 'Culture areas of the Tropical Forests,' in *Handbook of South American Indians*, Julian H. Steward, ed., vol. 3, 883–99. Bureau of American Ethnology, Bulletin 143. Washington, D.C., 1948.

The nature of the Tropical Forest agricultural system

JONES, WILLIAM O. *Manioc in Africa*. Stanford, 1959.

KAPLAN, LAWRENCE. 'Archeology and domestication in American Phaseolus (beans),' *Economic Botany*, vol. 19, no. 4, 358–68. Baltimore, 1965.

LANNING, EDWARD P. *Peru Before the Incas*. New Jersey, 1967.

LEEDS, ANTHONY. *The Evolution of Horticultural Systems in Native South America, Causes and Consequences: a Symposium*, Introduction. Johannes Wilbert, ed. *Antropológica*, suppl. publ. no. 2, 1–12. Caracas, 1961.

MACNEISH, RICHARD S. 'A summary of the subsistence', in *The Prehistory of the Tehuacan Valley*, vol. 1, *Environment and Subsistence*, Douglas S. Byers, ed., 290–309. Austin, 1967.

PICKERSGILL, BARBARA. 'The archaeological record of chili peppers (*Capsicum* spp.) and the sequence of plant domestication in Peru,' *American Antiquity*, vol. 34, no. 1, 54–61. Salt Lake City, 1969.

ROGERS, DAVID J. 'Studies of *Manihot esculenta* Crantz and related species,' *Bulletin of the Torrey Botanical Club*, vol. 90, 43–54. New York, 1963.

—, 'Some botanical and ethnological considerations of *Manihot esculenta*,' *Economic Botany*, vol. 19, no. 4, 369–77. Baltimore, 1965.

SAUER, CARL O. 'Cultivated plants of South and Central America,' in *Handbook of South American Indians*, Julian H. Steward, ed., vol. 6, 487–544. *Physical Anthropology, Linguistics, and Cultural Geography of South American Indians*, Bureau of American Ethnology, Bulletin 143. Washington, D.C., 1950.

—, *Agricultiral Origins and Dispersals*. New York, 1952.

WHITAKER, THOMAS W. AND CUTLER, HUGH C. 'Cucurbits and cultures in the Americas,' *Economic Botany*, vol. 19, no. 4, 344–49. Baltimore, 1965.

Technological aspects of Tropical Forest culture

BISCHOF, HENNING. Review of *Early formative period of Coastal Ecuador: the Valdivia and Machalilla Phases*, by Betty J. Meggers, Clifford Evans, and Emilio Estrada, *American Journal of Archaeology*, vol. 71, no. 2, 216–19. 1967.

COE, MICHAEL D. 'Directions of cultural diffusion': Review of *Ecuador*, by B. J. Meggers, *Science*, vol. 155, no. 3759, 185–86. Washington, D.C., 1967.

ESTRADA, EMILIO AND MEGGERS, BETTY J. 'A complex of traits of probable transpacific origin on the Coast of Ecuador,' *American Anthropologist*, vol. 63, 913–39. Menasha, 1961.

LATHRAP, DONALD W. Review of *Early formative period of Coastal Ecuador: the Valdivia and Machalilla Phases*, by B. J. Meggers, C. Evans, and E. Estrada, *American Anthropologist*, vol. 69, no. 1, 96–98. Menasha, 1967.

LOWIE, ROBERT H. 'The Tropical Forests: an introduction,' in *Handbook of South American Indians*, Julian H. Steward, ed., vol. 3, 1–56, Bureau of American Ethnology, Bulletin 143. Washington, D.C., 1948.

MEGGERS, BETTY J., EVANS, CLIFFORD, AND ESTRADA EMILIO.

Bibliography

Early formative period of Coastal Ecuador: the Valdivia and Machalilla Phases, Smithsonian Contributions to Anthropology, vol. 1. Washington, D.C., 1965.

QUIGLEY, CARROLL. 'Aboriginal fish poisons and the diffusion problem,' *American Anthropologist*, vol. 58, no. 3, 508–25. Menasha, 1956.

The origins of Tropical Forest culture

ANGULO VALDES, CARLOS. 'Evidencias de la Série Barrancoide en el norte de Colombia,' *Revista Colombiana de Antropología*, vol. 11, 75–87. Bogotá, 1962.

BISCHOF, HENNING. 'Canapote, an early ceramic site in Northern Colombia: preliminary report,' *XXXVI Congreso Internacional de Americanistas*, vol. 1, 483–91. Sevilla, 1966.

—, Review of *Early formative period of Coastal Ecuador: the Valdivia and Machalilla Phases*, by Betty J. Meggers, Clifford Evans, and Emilio Estrada, *American Journal of Archaeology*, vol. 71, no. 2, 216–19. 1967.

COE, MICHAEL D. 'Directions of cultural diffusion': Review of *Ecuador*, by B. J. Meggers, *Science*, vol. 155, no. 3759, 185–86. Washington, D.C., 1967.

ESTRADA, EMILIO AND MEGGERS, BETTY J. 'A complex of traits of probable transpacific origin on the Coast of Ecuador,' *American Anthropologist*, vol. 63, 913–39. Menasha, 1961.

LATHRAP, DONALD W. Review of *Momíl: Excavaciones en el Sinú*, by Gerardo and Alicia Reichel-Dolmatoff, *American Journal of Archaeology*, vol. 62, 360–62. 1958.

—, Review of *Early formative period of Coastal Ecuador: the Valdivia and Machalilla Phases*, by B. J. Meggers, C. Evans, and E. Estrada, *American Anthropologist*, vol. 69, no. 1, 96–98. Menasha, 1967.

MEGGERS, BETTY J., EVANS, CLIFFORD, AND ESTRADA, EMILIO. *Early formative period of Coastal Ecuador: the Valdivia and Machalilla Phases*, Smithsonian Contributions to Anthropology, vol. 1. Washington, D.C., 1965.

REICHEL-DOLMATOFF, GERARDO. *Colombia*. London and New York, 1965.

—, 'Excavaciones arqueológicas en Puerto Hormiga (Departamento de Bolivar),' *Antropología*, 2. Universidad de los Andes, Bogotá, 1965.

REICHEL-DOLMATOFF, GERARDO, AND DUSSAN DE REICHEL, ALICIA. 'Momíl: Excavaciones en el Sinú,' *Revista Colombiana de Antropología*, vol. 5, 109–334. Bogotá, 1956.

CHAPTER IV

The relationship between subsistence and population is, of course, complex rather than simple. The Flannery paper is an excellent discussion of the kinds of complications of which the archaeologist should be aware. Birdsell's paper remains a classic experiment in constructing models to elucidate past processes, and is the source for much of the present author's thinking on these problems.

BIRDSELL, J. B. 'Some implications of the genetical concept of race in terms of spatial analysis,' *Cold Spring Harbor Symposia in Quantitative Biology*, no. 15, 259–314. New York, 1950.

FLANNERY, KENT V. 'Archeological systems theory and early Mesoamerica,' in *Anthropological Archeology in the Americas*, Betty J. Meggers, ed., 67–87. Anthropological Society of Washington, Washington, D.C., 1968.

GREENBERG, JOSEPH H. 'The general classification of Central and South American languages,' *Selected Papers of the Fifth International Congress of Anthropological and Ethnological Sciences*, 791–94. Philadelphia, 1960.

SWADESH, MAURICIO. 'La lingüística de las regiones entre las civilizaciones Mesoamericanas y Andinas,' *Actas del XXXIII Congreso Internacional de Americanistas*, 123–36. San José, 1959.

VAYDA, ANDREW P. 'Expansion and warfare among swidden agriculturists,' *American Anthropologist*, vol 63, no. 2, 346–58. Menasha, 1961.

The Arawakan stock

NOBLE, G. KINGSLEY. *Proto-Arawakan and its descendants*, Indiana University Publication in Anthropology and Linguistics, no. 38. Bloomington, 1965.

TAYLOR, DOUGLAS AND ROUSE, IRVING, 'Linguistics and archaeological time depth in the West Indies,' *International Journal of American Linguistics*, vol. 21, no. 2, 105–15. Baltimore, 1955.

Bibliography

Tupí-Guaranian
RODRIGUES, ARION D. 'Classification of Tupí-Guaraní,' *International Journal of American Linguistics*, vol. 24, no. 3, 231–34. Baltimore, 1958.

CHAPTER V

Early Tutishcainyo; Late Tutishcainyo; Shakimu
LATHRAP, DONALD W. 'The cultural sequence at Yarinacocha, Eastern Peru,' *American Antiquity*, vol. 23, no. 4, 379–88. Salt Lake City, 1958.
—, *Yarinacocha: Stratigraphic Excavations in the Peruvian Montaña*. M.S. doctoral dissertation, Harvard University, Cambridge, 1962. (Available on microfilm.)
—, 'Los Andes centrales y la montaña,' *Revista del Museo Nacional*, vol. 32, 197–202. Lima, 1963.
—, 'The Tropical Forest and the cultural context of Chavín,' in *Dumbarton Oaks Conference on Chavín, October 26–27, 1968*, Elizabeth P. Benson, ed., 1970.

The Alto Pachitea
ALLEN, WILLIAM L. *A Ceramic Sequence from the Alto Pachitea, Perú.* M.S. doctoral dissertation, University of Illinois, Urbana, 1968.

The Cave of the Owls
LATHRAP, DONALD W. AND ROYS, LAWRENCE. 'The archaeology of the Cave of the Owls in the Upper Montaña of Peru,' *American Antiquity*, vol. 29, no. 1, 27–38. Salt Lake City, 1963.

The Huánuco Basin
IZUMI, SEIICHI AND SONO, TOSHIHIKO. *Andes 2, Excavations at Kotosh, Peru, 1960*. Tokyo, 1963.
LANNING, E. P. *Chronological and Cultural Relationships of Early Pottery Styles in Ancient Peru*. MS doctoral dissertation, University of California, Berkeley, 1960.
LATHRAP, DONALD W. 'Origins of Central Andean civilization: new evidence.' Review of *Andes 2*, by S. Izumi and T. Sono, *Science*, vol. 148, no. 3671, 796–98. Washington, D.C., 1965.
TELLO, JULIO C. 'Discovery of the Chavín culture in Peru,' *American Antiquity*, vol. 9, no. 2, 135–60. Salt Lake City, 1943.

The Upper Amazon

Ecuador

BUSHNELL, G. H. S. 'The archaeological collection from Macas, on the Eastern slopes of the Ecuadorian Andes,' *Man*, vol. 46, no. 2, 2-6. London, 1946.

EVANS, CLIFFORD AND MEGGERS, BETTY J. *Archeological investigations on the Río Napo, Eastern Ecuador*, Smithsonian Contributions to Anthropology, vol. 6. Washington, D.C., 1968.

The more distant cultural relationships of the Early Tropical Forest Cultures of the Upper Amazon

CRUXENT, J. M. AND ROUSE, I. *An archaeological chronology of Venezuela*, Pan American Union, Social Science Monographs, no. 6, vols. 1 and 2. Washington, D.C., 1959.

HOWARD, GEORGE D. *Excavations at Ronquín, Venezuela*, Yale University Publications in Anthropology, no. 28. New Haven, 1943.

ROUSE, I. AND CRUXENT, JOSE MARIA. *Venezuelan Archaeology.* Caribbean Series, 6. Yale University Press, New Haven, 1963.

CHAPTER VI

Northern Barrancoid

CRUXENT, J. M. AND ROUSE, IRVING. *An archaeological chronology of Venezuela*, Pan American Union, Social Science Monographs, no. 6, vols. 1 and 2. Washington, D.C., 1959.

EVANS, CLIFFORD AND MEGGERS, BETTY J. 'Archeological investigations in British Guiana,' *Bureau of American Ethnology*, Bulletin 177. Washington, D.C., 1960.

LATHRAP, DONALD W. 'An alternative seriation of the Mabaruma Phase, Northwestern British Guiana,' *American Antiquity*, vol. 29, no. 3, 353-59. Salt Lake City, 1964.

—, 'The Mabaruma Phase: a return to the more probable interpretation,' *American Antiquity*, vol. 31, no. 4, 558-66. Salt Lake City, 1966.

OSGOOD, CORNELIUS AND HOWARD, GEORGE D. *An archeological survey of Venezuela*, Yale University Publications in Anthropology, no. 27. New Haven, 1943.

ROUSE, IRVING. 'Prehistory of Trinidad in relation to adjacent areas,' *Man*, vol. 47, 93-98. London, 1947.

Hupa-iya
LATHRAP, DONALD W. *Yarinacocha: Stratigraphic Excavations in the Peruvian Montaña.* M.S. doctoral dissertation, Harvard University, Cambridge, 1962. (Available on microfilm.)

Barrancoid styles of the Central Amazon
HANKE, WANDA. 'Archäeologische Funde im oberen Amazonas-gebiet,' *Archiv für Völkerkunde,* vol. 14, 31–65. Vienna, 1966.
HILBERT, PETER PAUL. 'Archäeologische Untersuchungen am Mittleren Amazonas,' *Marburger Studien zur Völkerkunde,* no. 1. Berlin, 1968.

Eastern Bolivia and the Upper Xingú
NORDENSKIÖLD, ERLAND VON. 'Urnengräber und Mounds im Bolivianischen Flachlande,' *Baesslerarchiv,* vol. 3, 205–55. Berlin, 1913.
—, 'Finds of graves and old dwelling-places on the Río Beni, Bolivia,' *Ymer,* vol. 44, 229–37. Stockholm, 1924.

CHAPTER VII

Yarinacocha; Pacacocha
MYERS, THOMAS P. 'Reconocimiento arqueológico en el Ucayali Central,' *Boletín del Museo Nacional de Antropología y Arqueología,* no 6. Pueblo Libre, 1967.
—, *The Late Prehistoric Period at Yarinacocha, Peru.* M.S. doctoral dissertation, University of Illinois, Urbana, 1970.

Enoqui and the Modern Amuesha
ALLEN, WILLIAM L. *A Ceramic Sequence from the Alto Pachitea, Perú.* M.S. doctoral dissertation, University of Illinois, Urbana, 1968.

CHAPTER VIII

Cumancaya
EVANS, CLIFFORD AND MEGGERS, BETTY J. *Archeological investigations on the Río Napo, Eastern Ecuador,* Smithsonian Contributions to Anthropology, vol. 6. Washington, D.C., 1968.
MEJIA XESSPE, TORIBIO. 'Ceramica incisa y bicroma de Aspusana,

Huallaga Central,' *Boletín del Museo Nacional de Antropología y Arqueología,* no. 4, 6–7. Pueblo Libre, 1965.

REICHEL-DOLMATOFF, GERARDO AND DUSSAN DE REICHEL, ALICIA. 'Investigaciones arqueológicas en el Departamento del Magdalena, Colombia, 1946–1950,' *Boletín de Arqueología,* vol. 3, nos. 1–6. Bogotá, 1951.

Caimito, Napo, and the Polychrome Tradition

EVANS, CLIFFORD AND MEGGERS, BETTY J. 'Use of organic temper for carbon 14 dating in Lowland South America,' *American Antiquity,* vol. 28, no. 2, 243–45. Salt Lake City, 1962.

—, *Archeological investigations on the Río Napo, Eastern Ecuador,* Smithsonian Contributions to Anthropology, vol. 6. Washington, D.C., 1968.

GILLIN, JOHN. 'An urn from the Río Aguarico, Eastern Ecuador,' *American Anthropologist,* vol. 38, no. 3, 469–70. Menasha, 1936.

HOWARD, G. D. *Prehistoric ceramic styles of Lowland South America, their distribution and history,* Yale University Publications in Anthropology, no. 37. New Haven, 1947.

MEGGERS, BETTY J. *Ecuador.* London and New York, 1966.

MEGGERS, B. J. AND EVANS, CLIFFORD. *Archeological investigations at the mouth of the Amazon,* Bureau of American Ethnology, Bulletin 167. Washington, D.C., 1957.

—, 'An experimental formulation of Horizon Styles in the Tropical Forest area of South America,' *Essays in Precolumbian Art and Archaeology,* by S. K. Lothrop, et al., 186–92. Salt Lake City, 1961.

METRAUX, ALFRED. 'Tribes of the Middle and Upper Amazon River,' in *Handbook of South American Indians,* Julian H. Steward, ed., vol. 3, 687–712. The Tropical Forest Tribes, Bureau of American Ethnology, Bulletin 143. Washington, D.C., 1948.

NORDENSKIÖLD, ERLAND VON. 'Urnengräber und Mounds im Bolivianischen Flachlande,' *Baessler-archiv,* vol. 3, 205–55. Berlin, 1913.

CHAPTER IX

DENEVEN, W. M. 'The aboriginal cultural geography of the Llanos de Mojos of Bolivia,' *Ibero-Americana,* no. 48. Berkeley, 1966.

Bibliography

PARSONS, JAMES J. 'Ridged fields in the Río Guayas Valley, Ecuador,' *American Antiquity*, vol. 34, no. 1, 76–80. Salt Lake City, 1969.
PARSONS, JAMES J. AND BOWEN, WILLIAM A. 'Ancient ridged fields of the San Jorge River Floodplain, Colombia,' *The Geographical Review*, vol. 56, no. 3, 317–43. New York, 1966.
PARSONS, JAMES J. AND DENEVAN, WILLIAM M. 'Pre-Columbian ridged fields,' *Scientific American*, vol. 217, no. 1, 92–100. New York, 1967.

CHAPTER X

ESTRADA, EMILIO. 'Ultimas civilizaciones prehistóricas de la Cuenca del Río Guayas,' *Publicación del Museo Víctor Emilio Estrada*, no 2. Guayaquil, 1957.
EVANS, CLIFFORD, MEGGERS, BETTY J. AND CRUXENT, JOSE M. 'Preliminary results of archeological investigations along the Orinoco and Ventuari Rivers, Venezuela,' *Actas del XXXIII Congreso Internacional de Americanistas*, 359–69. San José, 1959.
HILBERT, PETER PAUL. 'A cerâmiça arqueológica da região de Oriximiná,' *Instituto de Antropología e Etnología do Pará*, publication no. 9. Belem, 1955.
—, Archäologische Untersuchungen am Mittleren Amazonas,' *Marburger Studien zur Völkerkunde*, no. 1. Berlin, 1968.
LINNE, SIGVALD. *The Technique of South American Ceramics*. Göteborg, 1925.
PALMATARY, HELEN CONSTANCE. 'The archaeology of the Lower Tapajós Valley, Brazil,' *Transactions of the American Philosophical Society*, n.s., vol. 50, pt. 3. Philadelphia, 1960.
REICHEL-DOLMATOFF, GERARDO AND ALICIA. 'La Mesa: un complejo arqueológico de la Sierra Nevada de Santa Marta,' *Revista Colombiana de Antropología*, vol. 8, 161–213. Bogotá, 1959.
RIVET, PAUL. 'La influencia Karib en Colombia,' *Revista del Instituto Etnológico Nacional*, vol. 1, no. 2, 55–87. Bogotá, 1943.
ROUSE, IRVING. 'The Carib,' in *Handbook of South American Indians*, Julian H. Steward, ed., vol. 4, 547–66. *The Circum-Caribbean Tribes*, Bureau of American Ethnology, Bulletin 143. Washington, D.C., 1948.

CHAPTER XI

BIRD, ROBERT M. 'El maiz y las divisiones étnicas en la Sierra de Huánuco,' *Cuadernos de Investigación, Universidad Nacional Hermilio Valdizán, Huánuco, Antropología* 1, 34–44. Huánuco, 1966.

BONAVIA, DUCCIO. 'Investigaciones en la Ceja de Selva de Ayacucho,' *Arqueológicas* 6. Museo Nacional de Antropología y Arqueología, Pueblo Libre, 1964.

—, *Las Ruinas del Abiseo*. Universidad Peruana de Ciencias y Tecnología, Lima, 1968.

IBARRA GRASSO, DICK EDGAR. *Prehistoria de Bolivia*. Cochabamba, 1965.

ISBELL, WILLIAM H. 'New discoveries in the Montaña of Southeastern Peru,' *Archaeology*, vol. 21, no. 2, 108–114. Brattleboro, 1968.

McCOWN, THEODORE D. *Pre-Incaic Huamachuco: survey and excavations in the Northern Sierra of Peru*, University of California Publications in American Archaeology and Ethnology, vol. 39, no. 4. Berkeley, 1945.

ROJAS PONCE, PEDRO. 'The ruins of Pajatén,' *Archaeology*, vol. 20, no. 1, 9–17. Brattleboro, 1967.

RYDEN, STIG. 'Chullpa Pampa—a pre-Tiahuanaco archaeological site in the Cochabamba region, Bolivia, a preliminary report,' *Ethnos*, vol. 17, 39–50. Stockholm, 1952.

—, *Andean excavations, II. Tupuraya and Cayhuasi: two Tiahuanaco sites*, Statens Etnografiska Museum, Monograph Series, publication no. 6. Stockholm, 1959.

—, 'Complementary notes on pre-Tiahuanaco site Chullpa Pampa in Cochabamba area, and notes on one Tiahuanaco site in La Paz, Bolivia,' *Ethnos*, vol. 26, 40–55. Stockholm, 1961.

THOMPSON, DONALD E. 'La Alfareria Inca de Huánuco,' *Boletín del Museo Nacional de Antropología y Arqueología*, no. 6, 8–9. Pueblo Libre, 1967.

—, 'An archeological evaluation of ethnohistoric evidence on Inca culture,' in *Anthropological Archeology in the Americas*, Betty J. Meggers, ed., 108–20. The Anthropological Society of Washington, Washington, D.C., 1968.

WALTER, HEINZ. *Beiträge zur Archäeologie Boliviens: Archäologische Studien in den Kordilleren Boliviens II*. Berlin, 1966.

CHAPTER XII

The Shipibo and Conibo

NIMUENDAJU, CURT. *The Tukuna,* trans. by W. D. Hohenthal and ed. by Robert Lowie. University of California Publications in American Archaeology and Ethnology, no. 45. Berkeley, 1952.

STEWARD, JULIAN H. AND METRAUX, ALFRED. 'Tribes of the Peruvian and Ecuadorian Montaña,' in *Handbook of South American Indians,* Julian H. Steward, ed., vol. 3, 535–656. *The Tropical Forest Tribes,* Bureau of American Ethnology, Bulletin 143. Washington, D.C., 1948.

TESSMANN, GÜNTER. *Menschen ohne Gott.* Stuttgart, 1928.

—, *Die Indianer Nordost-Perus.* Hamburg, 1930.

The Panoan Speaking Tribes of the Forest

CARNEIRO, ROBERT L. 'Shifting cultivation among the Amahuaca of Eastern Peru,' *Völkerkundliche Abhandlungen,* Band 1, 9–18. Hannover, 1964.

MOMSEN, RICHARD P., JR. 'The Isconahua Indians: a study of change and diversity in the Peruvian Amazon,' *Revista Geográfica,* vol. 32, no. 60, 59–81. Río Brasil, 1964.

WHITON, LUIS C., GREENE, H. BRUCE AND MOMSEN, RICHARD P., JR. 'The Isconahua of the Remo,' *Journal de la Société des Américanistes,* vol. 53, 84–124. Paris, 1964.

Sources of Illustrations

Grateful acknowledgment is made to the following persons and institutions who have provided photographs and permission to publish them:
Pedro Rojas Ponce, 8, 9, 11, 12 (bottom half), 18–27, 31, 33–38, 40–44, 47–51, 75; William M. Denevan, 45, 46; William H. Isbell, 53, 54; George Stuber, Museum of Anthropology, University of Michigan, Ann Arbor, 69, 70; Field Museum of Natural History, Chicago, 52, 56; all other photographs are by the author.

Figures 1–6, 16, 22, 40, 43, 45, 49 were drawn by Shalom Schotten; all other figures were drawn by the author. In addition to the results of the field work of the author and his students, the following published sources have been consulted in the preparation of the figures:
Fig. 2, Carl O. Sauer, *Geography of South America*, Map 8, C. F. Marbut and C. B. Manifold, *The Topography of the Amazon Valley*, Pl. V;
Fig. 3, Carl O. Sauer, *Geography of South America*, Map 10, Joseph A. Tosi, *Mapa Ecologico del Perú*;
Fig. 4, J. Alden Mason, *The Languages of South American Indians*, Distribution Map, G. Kingsley Noble, Jr, *Proto-Arawakan and Its Descendants*, Arion D. Rodrigues, *Classification of Tupí-Guaraní*;
Fig. 6, J. Alden Mason, *The Languages of South America*;
Fig. 17 a–b, J. M. Cruxent and Irving Rouse, *An Archeological Chronology of Venezuela*, Vol. 2, Pl. 93:16, 9; Fig. 17 c–d, Clifford Evans and Betty J. Meggers, *Archeological Investigations in British Guiana*, Pl. 29, a, i; Fig. 17 e–i, J. M. Cruxent and Irving Rouse, *An Archeological Chronology of Venezuela*, Vol. 2, Pl. 95:23; Pl. 97:6, Pl. 27:2, Pl. 28:23, 18; Fig. 17 j–l, Helen Constance Palmatary, *The Archaeology of the Lower Tapajós Valley, Brazil*, Pl. 84 d, c, a; Fig. 17 m–o, Peter Paul Hilbert, *A Cerâmica Arqueológica da Região de Oriximiná*, Figs. 29, 30; Fig. 17 p, Wanda Hanke, *Archäologische Funde im oberen Amazonasgebiet*, Fig. 31; Fig. 17 q–s, Peter Paul Hilbert, *Preliminary Results of Archeological Research on the Japurá River, Middle Amazon*; Fig. 1, i, o, 1; Fig. 17 t–v, Wanda Hanke, *Archäologische Funde im oberen Amazonasgebiet*, Figs. 14, 19, 15;

Sources of Illustrations

Fig. 20 a–e, Erland von Nordenskiöld, *Urnengräber und Mounds im Bolivianischen Flachlande*, Figs. 51, 63 and 66, 53, 62, 52;

Fig. 21 a–i, Erland von Nordenskiöld, *Urnengräber und Mounds im Bolivianischen Flachlande*, Figs. 77, 60, 57, 58, 47, 44, 48, 49, 76;

Fig. 30 a–c, Kalervo Oberg, *The Terena and the Caduveo of Southern Mato Grosso, Brazil*, Pls. 21b, 22b, a;

Fig. 31 a–b, Leonardo Branisa, *Un Nuevo Estilo de Ceramica Pre-Colombiana de Chuquisaca, Mojocoya Tricolor*, Figs. 97, 99; Fig. 31 c–e, Dick Edgar Ibarra Grasso, *Prehistoria de Bolivia*, pp. 218–9, Figs. 2, 4, 5;

Fig. 32 a–g, Erland von Nordenskiöld, *Urnengräber und Mounds im Bolivianischen Flachlande*, Figs. 2, 21, 19, 6, 4, 9, 7;

Fig. 38a, Jacinto Jijón y Caamaño, *Antropología Prehispánica del Ecuador*, Fig. 498;

Fig. 39 a–f, Erland von Nordenskiöld, *Urnengräber und Mounds im Bolivianischen Flachlande*, Figs. 38, 36, 37, 96, 124, 120b;

Fig. 40, James J. Parsons and William M. Denevan, *Pre-Columbian Ridged Fields*;

Fig. 41a, Helen Constance Palmatary, *The Archaeology of the Lower Tapajós Valley, Brazil*, Pl. 87a and Peter Paul Hilbert, *A Cerâmica Araqueológica da Região de Oriximiná*, p. 36; Fig. 41b, Helen Constance Palmatary, *op. cit.* Pl. 90 and Peter Paul Hilbert, *op. cit.*, p. 30; Fig. 41 c–d, Erland von Nordenskiöld, *Urnengräber und Mounds im Bolivianischen Flachlande*, Figs. 144, 139; Fig. 41e, Peter Paul Hilbert, *Preliminary Results of Archeological Investigations in the Vicinity of the Mouth of the Río Negro, Amazonas*, Fig. 2h; Fig. 41f, Clifford Evans, Betty J. Meggers, and José M. Cruxent, *Preliminary Results of Archeological Investigations along the Orinoco and Ventuari Rivers, Venezuela*, Fig. 2g; Fig. 41 g–n, J. M. Cruxent and Irving Rouse, *An Archaeological Chronology of Venezuela*, Vol. 2, Pl. 78:2, Pl. 77:25, Pl. 81:16, 19, Pl. 88:5, Pl. 103:2, 17, Pl. 69:4;

Fig. 42 a–b, Helen Constance Palmatary, *The Archaeology of the Lower Tapajós Valley, Brazil*, Pl. 4a, Pl. 72d; Fig. 42c, Peter Paul Hilbert, *A Cerâmica Arqueológica da Região de Oriximiná*, Fig. 14:3; Fig. 42d–g, Clifford Evans, Betty J. Meggers, and José M. Cruxent, *Preliminary Results of Archeological Investigations along the Orinoco and Ventuari Rivers, Venezuela*, Fig. 3 d, j, p, k; Fig. 42 h–l, n, J. M. Cruxent and Irving Rouse, *An Archaeological Chronology of Venezuela*, Vol. 2, Pl. 74:7,

Pl. 76:7, Pl. 80:21, 20, Pl. 87:4, Pl. 102:4; Fig. 42m, Clifford Evans and Betty J. Meggers, *Archeological Investigations in British Guiana*, Pl. 19 i, Fig. 32 a, b; Fig. 42 o–p, Alfred Kidder, II, *Archaeology of Northwestern Venezuela*, Pl. III, 12, Pl. II, 7;

Fig. 44a, Theodore D. McCown, *Pre-Incaic Huamachuco*, Fig. 15, n; Fig. 44b, specimen in collection of the Museo Nacional de Antropología y Arqueología, Pueblo Libre, Lima, Perú, redrawn from photograph by author; Fig. 44 c–d, f, drawn from Kodachrome slides taken by Harald P. Jensen; Fig. 44 g–h, j, Seiichi Izumi and Toshihiko Sono, *Andes 2: Excavations at Kotosh, Perú, 1960*, Pl. 37 d, c, Pl. 34a; Fig. 44 e, i, Stig Rydén, *The Tiahuanaco Era East of Lake Titicaca*, Fig. 69:3, Fig. 49:1;

Fig. 46, Stig Rydén, *Complementary Notes on Pre-Tiahuanaco Site, Chullpa Pampa, in Cochabamba Area*, Fig. 1;

Fig. 49, Günter Tessmann, *Die Indianer Nordost-Perus*, Distribution Map.

THE PLATES

2
3

4

5

6

7

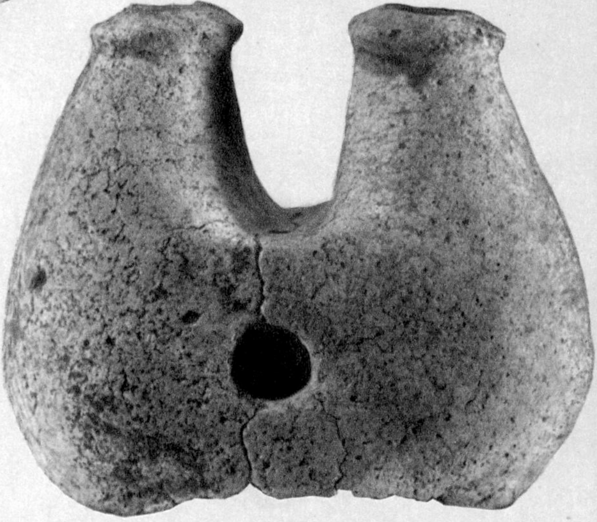

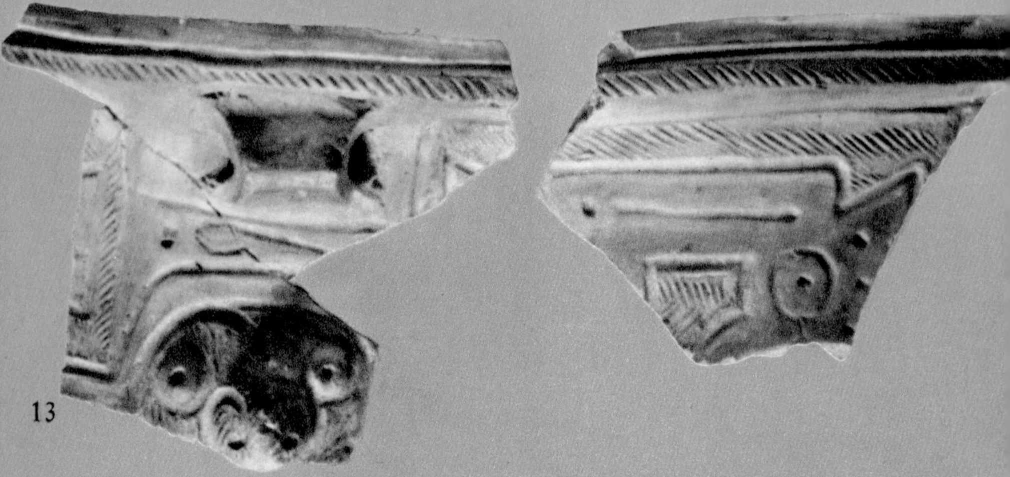

13
15 
16
17

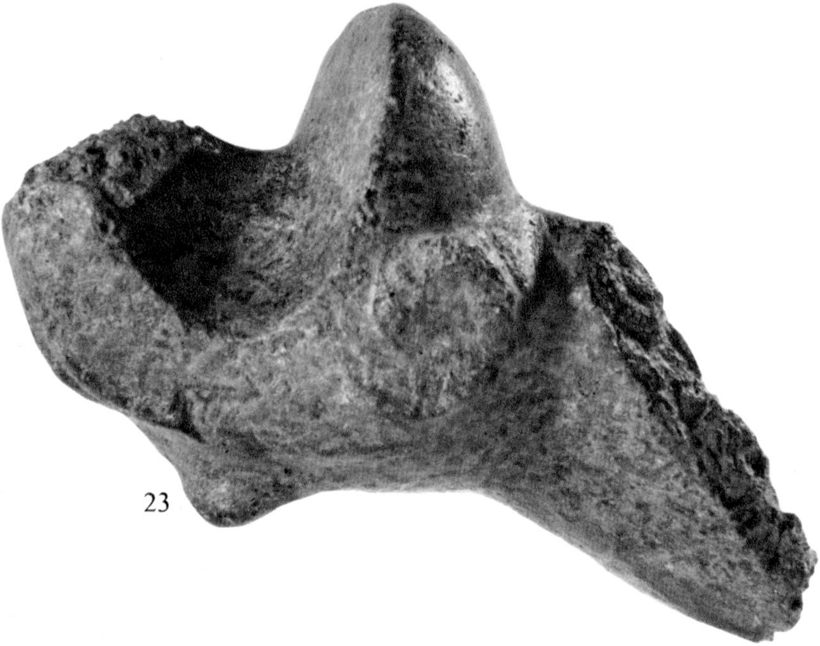

23

26

24

25

27

31

32

40

41

45, 46

49

50

51

52

53

57

58

59

60

61

62

63

64

65

66

67

68

Notes on the Plates

1 The mainstream of the Ucayali River below Pucallpa, Peru. A forest of young balsa trees is already growing on the most recent point-bar formation at the left of the picture.

2 An air view of the flood plain of the Ucayali River near Requena, Peru, from an elevation of about 3,000 metres. The meanders of the active channel of the river dominate the whole left half of the picture while ox-bow lakes from previous channels extend to the right edge. The river is about a kilometre wide in this area.

3 Canoe travel on Yanayacu, an *igapó* (side channel), paralleling the mainstream of the Amazon River in Ticuna country near Caballococha, Peru.

4 The ox-bow lake of Yarinacocha, an old channel of the Ucayali River near Pucallpa, Peru. The view is from the Shipibo Indian colony of San Francisco de Yarinacocha located on the bluff of old alluvial deposits bounding the active flood plain of the Ucayali. The multi-component archaeological site of Hupa-iya, UCA-2, underlies the modern village.

5 Imaríacocha, a large lake drowning the valley of the Río Tamaya, an eastern tributary of the Ucayali. The Caimito Complex archaeological site, TAM-1, underlies the whole plaza of the Conibo Indian household and extends below the present level of the lake.

6 The easternmost range of the Peruvian Andes rising in a 2,000-metre escarpment behind the Pisquibo Indian village of Nueva Edén on the upper Río Pisqui. The collision of westwardly moving air masses against this face causes almost daily rain-storms.

241

The Upper Amazon

7   Lush tropical rain-forest along the Río Pisqui at the eastern foot of the Andes in Peru. Tree ferns 6 metres tall dominate the lower canopy of vegetation.

8   The precipitous terrain and dense *ceja* vegetation typical of the eastern slopes of the Peruvian Andes in the zone between 600 and 2,000 metres elevation. The view is from the ruins of Gran Pajatén in the drainage of the Huallaga River.

9   Sherd of an elaborately excised bowl, Early Shakimu Complex, from the archaeological site UCA-34, Jose's Hill, near Yarinacocha, Peru. Collection of the Museo Nacional de Antropología y Arqueología, Pueblo Libre, Lima, Perú. The bowl was 7 cm. high.

10 Cup with excised decoration, Early Shakimu Complex, from UCA-34, Jose's Hill. Collection of the Museo Nacional de Antropología y Arqueología, Pueblo Libre, Lima, Peru. 8 cm. high.

11 The top part of a double-spout-and-bridge bottle from the Early Shakimu component at UCA-34, Jose's Hill. Collection of the Museo Nacional de Antropología y Arqueología, Pueblo Libre, Lima, Peru. 10.5 cm. wide.

12 Bottom and side view of a bowl from the Early Shakimu component at UCA-34, Jose's Hill. The excised design was covered with a thick, highly burnished, dark red slip. Collection of the Museo Nacional de Antropología y Arqueología, Pueblo Libre, Lima, Peru. Diameter 18 cm.

13 Sherds of a zoned incised bowl, Cave of the Owls Fine Ware. From the limestone cave, Gruta de las Lechusas, near Tingo María in the upper Montaña of eastern Peru. Collection of the Robert H. Lowie Museum of Anthropology, University of California, Berkeley. Left-hand sherd 10 cm. wide.

14 Fragments of two bowls of Cave of the Owls Fine Ware, from the Gruta de las Lechusas, Tingo María, Peru. Collection of the Robert

Notes on the Plates

H. Lowie Museum of Anthropology, University of California, Berkeley. Left-hand sherd 13 cm. wide.

15 Excised sherds of the Pangotsi Complex, from the multicomponent site PAC-14, Casa de la Tía, on the Nazaratequi River in the upper Montaña of eastern Peru. Upper left-hand sherd 4.5 cm. wide.

16 Fragment of a roller stamp, Nazaratequi Complex, from PAC-14, Casa de la Tía, Nazaratequi River. About 5 cm. long.

17 Examples of incised decoration typical of the Nazaratequi Complex, with the sherd in the upper left showing zoned red painting. From the multicomponent site PAC-14, Casa de la Tía, Nazaratequi River. Sherd in upper left 7 cm. wide.

18 The Crossed Hands, a relief sculpture in a temple structure 10 construction levels below the surface of the Kotosh ruin, but still well above the earliest occupation levels there. A date of 2000 B C is probable, making this the earliest known architectural use of sculpture in the New World. The llama bones in the niche above were probably placed as a sacrificial offering.

19 The ruin of Kotosh adjacent to the flood plain of the Higueras River, in the Huánuco Basin at an elevation of about 2,000 metres on the eastern slope of the Peruvian Andes.

20 Junction of the Tabaconas and Chinchipe Rivers in the Lower Marañón Valley, north-eastern Peru. The site of Huayurco lies in the triangle of land between the rivers.

21 Necklace of shell beads from a burial in the lower component of the Huayurco site. Collection of the Museo Nacional de Antropología y Arqueología, Pueblo Libre, Lima, Peru.

22 Bottle of burnished black-ware from the lower component of the Huayurco site. The form and finish are typical of bottles from Early Horizon sites in the Andes to the south and west of Huayurco. About 20 cm. high.

The Upper Amazon

23 *Adorno* off a sculptured stone bowl, the lower component of the Huayurco site. The head is that of a male howler monkey in the act of vocalizing. Collection of the Museo Nacional de Antropología y Arqueología, Pueblo Libre, Lima, Peru.

24 Sherd with appliqué decoration, Huayurco site. Probably associated with the lower component there. Collection of the Museo Nacional de Antropología y Arqueología, Pueblo Libre, Lima, Peru.

25 Small bowl of heavily veined, translucent onyx from the lower component of the Huayurco site. Collection of the Museo Nacional de Antropología y Arqueología, Pueblo Libre, Lima, Peru. About 15 cm. in diameter.

26, 27 Sculptured stone bowls from the lower component of the Huayurco site. Collection of the Museo Nacional de Antropología y Arqueología, Pueblo Libre, Lima, Peru. About 30 cm. in diameter.

28 Sherds of the Hupa-iya component at the Hupa-iya site, UCA-2, on Yarinacocha, Eastern Peru. The broad-line, curvilinear incision is typical of all ceramics of the Barrancoid Tradition.

29 Decorated spindle whorls of the Hupa-iya component at the Hupa-iya site, UCA-2. Specimen in upper left is 2.7 cm. in diameter.

30 *Adornos* of the Hupa-iya component at the Hupa-iya site, UCA-2. The use of appliqué pellets with deep central punctations is characteristic of ceramic complexes of the Barrancoid Tradition. Central specimen in lower row is 4.2 cm. long.

31 Typical vessel of the Yarinacocha Complex from the multicomponent site UCA-34, Jose's Hill, Yarinacocha, Eastern Peru. Collection of the Museo Nacional de Antropología y Arqueología, Pueblo Libre, Lima, Peru. Diameter 22 cm.

32 *Adornos* from Cumancaya Complex vessels, excavated at UCA-22, the Cumancaya site, in the Central Ucayali Basin to the south-east of Pucallpa, Peru. Central sherd is 7.5 cm. wide.

Notes on the Plates

33 Fragment of an *olla* with scraped surface from the mass of smashed pots covering a Cumancaya Complex burial at TAM-2, Caimito.

34 Fragment of an *olla* with typical Cumancaya-style incised decoration from the mass of smashed pots covering a Cumancaya Complex burial at TAM-2, Caimito, on Imaríacocha to the south and east of Pucallpa, Peru.

35 Fragment of an *olla* with corrugated surface from the mass of smashed pots covering a Cumancaya Complex burial at TAM-2, Caimito.

36 Large corrugated burial urn of a late variant of the Cumancaya Tradition, from the Santa Rosa site, UCA-23. Collection of the Museo Nacional de Antropología y Arqueología, Pueblo Libre, Lima, Peru. Diameter 46 cm.

37 Small ceramic head from the Aspusana River, an eastern tributary of the Huallaga River to the north of Tingo María, eastern Peru. Collection of the Museo Nacional de Antropología y Arqueología, Pueblo Libre, Lima, Peru.

38 Zoned bichrome sherd, with very hard, well polished white and maroon slips, from the Aspusana River. Collection of Museo Nacional de Antropología y Arqueología, Pueblo Libre, Lima, Peru.

39 A ceramic colander and a ceramic pestle of the Cumancaya Complex, from UCA-22, the Cumancaya site. Diameter of colander 11 cm., length of pestle 6.5 cm.

40 Zoned red and white bichrome bowl of the Naneini Complex from the multi-component site PAC-14, Casa de la Tía, on the Nazaratequi River in the upper Montaña of eastern Peru. Collection of the Museo Nacional de Antropología y Arqueología, Pueblo Libre, Lima, Peru. Diameter 22 cm.

41 Squarish bowl with appliqué used to indicate human face, Caimito Complex from TAM-2, the Caimito site, on Imaríacocha to the south-

east of Pucallpa, Peru. Traces of black and red on white decoration can be noted, though most of the white slip has eroded away. Collection of the Museo Nacional de Antropología y Arqueología, Pueblo Libre, Lima, Peru. Maximum diameter 23.5 cm.

42 Squarish *olla*, with broad-line incision and appliqué decoration, and human face at one corner. From TAM-2, Caimito. Collection of the Museo Nacional de Antropología y Arqueología, Pueblo Libre, Lima, Peru. Diameter 26 cm.

43 Frog effigy, Caimito Complex from TAM-1, Casa de Guillermo, on Imaríacocha, eastern Peru. Collection of the Museo Nacional de Antropología y Arqueología, Pueblo Libre, Lima, Peru. Length about 5 cm.

44 Miniature four-lobed bottle, Caimito Complex, from TAM-11, the Bella Flor site, Imaríacocha, eastern Peru. Incised decoration on unslipped surface. Collection of the Museo Nacional de Antropología y Arqueología, Pueblo Libre, Lima, Peru. Height 10 cm.

45, 46 Air views of aboriginal, ridged agricultural fields in the Llanos de Mojos, eastern Bolivia.

47 The central structure of the ruin of Capash, in the Tantamayo area east of the Marañón River in the Department of Huánuco, Peru.

48 General view of the ruins of Gran Pajatén partially cleared of the *ceja* vegetation which had covered it. Eastern slope of the Andes, Huallaga River drainage, Peru.

49 Mosaic masonry on round structure at Gran Pajatén, depicting condors and humans.

50 Detail of mosaic masonry, Gran Pajatén.

51 Ceramic figurine, Tantamayo style. Collection of the Museo Nacional de Antropología y Arqueología, Pueblo Libre, Lima, Peru (108.C/ 41322 T. C.). About 25 cm. high.

Notes on the Plates

52 Pitcher of the Killke series, black and red on buff surface, from the Cuzco area. In Montez collection purchased in 1893 by Field Museum of Natural History, Chicago, Cat. #2789, Neg. #100923. Height 17.5 cm.

53 View of the inside of the double defensive wall around the ruined city of Trenchera showing the cat-walks for defenders, and the expanse of *puna* surrounding the city. Above the modern city of Sandía, on the eastern slope of the Andes near the Bolivian border in south-eastern Peru.

54 General view of the ruined city of Trenchera showing outer defensive wall and rows of houses extending to the crest of the mountain. Near Sandía, south-eastern Peru.

55 Highly productive field of maize at the Conibo colony of Painaco, near Juancito on the Lower Ucayali in eastern Peru. The man is about 158 cm. tall.

56 Large funerary urn, Calchaqui region of north-west Argentina. Zabeleta collection, Field Museum of Natural History, Chicago, Cat. #102258, Neg. # 18342.

57 Shipibo *chomo*, water jar, from the colony of San Francisco de Yarina-cocha, 1967. Neck, black on white; body, black, white, red, and un-slipped surface. Collection of the Department of Anthropology, University of Illinois, Urbana. Maximum diameter 37 cm.

58 Pisquibo *quënpo aní* (large drinking vessel made for communal use at a fiesta), from the colony of Nueva Edén on the Upper Río Pisqui, 1967. Black and red on white. Collection of the Department of Anthropology, University of Illinois. Maximum diameter 38.5 cm.

59 Shipibo *cushma* (men's garment), colony of San Francisco de Yarina-cocha, 1967. Painted design mainly in black and yellow on hand spun, hand woven, cotton cloth. Collection of the Department of Anthropology, University of Illinois, Urbana. About 100 cm. wide.

The Upper Amazon

60 Conibo *quënpo aní* (large drinking vessel made for communal use during a fiesta), from the colony of Painaco on the Lower Ucayali, 1967. Black and red on white. Collection of the Department of Anthropology, University of Illinois, Urbana. Maximum diameter 31.5 cm.

61 Bottom view of a particularly fine Conibo *quëncha* (food bowl) from the colony of Caimito on Imaríacocha, to the south-east of Pucallpa in eastern Peru, 1967. White painting on a red slip. Collection of the Department of Anthropology, University of Illinois, Urbana. Maximum diameter 23.5 cm.

62 Pisquibo strainer for *masato* (manioc beer), colony of Manco Capac, 1967. About 50 cm. wide.

63 Shipibo rocker pestle of stone with trough mortar of wood used for grinding food and ceramic materials, colony of San Francisco de Yarinacocha, 1967. In this instance potsherds are being ground for use as temper in making ceramics. The conical depressions in the pestle are used for hammering out metal nose ornaments (see Plate 67). The *pishín*, palm-leaf mat, is the most frequently used ground cover. Impressions from the bottoms of archaeological pots show that exactly this kind of mat has been in use in the area for at least the last 700 years.

64 Young Shipibo woman fully dressed for a fiesta. The nose ornament and labret are of aviation aluminium. San Francisco de Yarinacocha, 1967. The face painting is done with the blue-black dye, *Genipa*.

65 Shipibo women making *masato* (manioc beer) for a fiesta, San Francisco de Yarinacocha, 1964. Manioc is boiled in the large ceramic pot, *quënti aní*, then placed in a canoe and beaten to a pulp. A wild sweet potato is chewed up and spat into the mash to speed fermentation. The mixture is then returned to the cooking pots for further boiling and fermentation.

66 Pisquibo *quënti* (cooking pot) from the colony of Nueva Edén, 1967. Decoration by stick punctation and finger-nail incision. Maximum diameter 28 cm.

Notes on the Plates

67 Pisquibo *quënti* (cooking pot) from the colony of Nueva Edén, 1967. Incised decoration. The bottom had been broken from this particular piece and it was in use as a *mapu ëiti* (a closed kiln for firing small fine ware vessels). Maximum diameter 35.5 cm.

68 Typical hearth in Pisquibo cook-house at Manco Capac on the Upper Río Pisqui in eastern Peru, showing the arrangement of firewood in star form and ceramic firedogs of a type in use in the Central Ucayali Basin for over 1,000 years. Cooking-bananas are being grilled.

69 Cocamilla water jar. Collected by Beal-Steere in 1871 before Cocama and Cocamilla style was completely dominated by European derived floral motifs. Black and red on white. Collection of the Museum of Anthropology, University of Michigan, Ann Arbor, Cat. #7344, Neg. #16367. Maximum diameter 22.5 cm.

70 Cocamilla bowl. Beal-Steere collection 1871. Black and red on white. Double-headed serpent motif closely parallels examples of same motif on Napo Phase pottery from the Río Napo in Ecuador. Museum of Anthropology, University of Michigan, Cat. #7358, Neg. #16368. Maximum diameter 23.5 cm.

71 Ticuna water jar, colony of Cushillococha, near Caballococha, eastern Peru, 1964. Black painting and incision on unslipped brown surface. Showing the application of European derived floral motifs to a vessel of aboriginal shape and technology. Maximum diameter about 35 cm.

72 Cooking-pot of the Isconahua band of Remo, Isconahua colony of the Río Callería, near Pucallpa, eastern Peru, 1967. Striations were made by scraping the surface of the moist pot with a split seed. Diameter 23 cm.

73 Drinking vessel of the Isconahua band of Remo. Scraped, unslipped surface, with the decoration consisting of a nicked appliqué strip. Collected by H. Clifton Russell. Mouth diameter 14.5 cm.

74 Vessel of the wild band of Cashibo (Inunahua) in the Tournavista area, Lower Pachitea River, eastern Peru. Collected from inside the house

The Upper Amazon

when the group was pacified by H. Clifton Russell in 1962. It contained a package of burned bones. Collection of the Department of Anthropology, University of Illinois. Mouth diameter 15.5 cm.

75 Small bowl from a cache of pottery at the late archaeological site UTO-1 on the Lower Utoquinea River near Pucallpa in eastern Peru. The coils used in manufacturing the vessel were left unobliterated on the outer surface as a decorative technique. It probably can be attributed to the protohistoric Remo. Collection of the Museo Nacional de Antropología y Arqueología, Pueblo Libre, Lima, Peru. Maximum diameter 12.4 cm.

Index

achiote *(Bixa orellana)*, 59
aggression, 54, 164, 185
agricultural land, 17–20, 27, 36–44, 59, 67, 103, 123, 128, 160–2, 173, 179, 180, 186
agriculture, 17, 36–44, 47–60, 63, 65, 104–5, 116, 160, 171, 180, 188
Aguarico River, 151–3
Aguatía River, 84
Alaka complex, 64
alluvial soils, 18, 26–9, 39–42, 64, 74–5, 114, 122, 124, 126, 128, 161, 171
Alto Pachitea, 95–102, 122, 128–9, 136, 144
Amahuaca, 140, 182, 187, 188
Amazon Basin, 19–22, 24–8, 31–6, 39–47, 53, 59, 62, 63, 67, 70, 73, 84, 94, 108, 112, 116, 120, 128, 131, 135, 151, 155, 157 160, 165, 168
Amazon River, 17, 19, 22–6, 28, 30, 31, 40, 46–7, 73–5, 78–80, 83, 109, 111–12, 116, 120–1, 127–8, 136, 143, 149–50, 154–5, 157, 159, 163, 168, 186
Amuesha, 72, 75, 96, 112, 135
Ananatuba complex, 112
Andes, 20, 25, 26, 28, 31, 34, 39–42, 48, 59–60, 70, 74, 80, 82, 94, 104–5, 107, 110, 126, 128, 140, 142–5, 155, 161, 163, 171–9
Andean culture, 46, 104–5, 107, 176
Apostadero complex, 170
Apurimac River, 122
Archaic (Meso-Indian), 63–7, 116
architecture, 104–5, 178–9
Argentina, 49, 58, 143, 176
arrowroot, 37, 57

art style (general), 17, 64–5, 86–7, 89–90, 93–5, 98–100, 102–3, 106–11, 113–27, 129–30, 137–44, 146–59, 163, 164–70, 172–8, 179, 180, 182–5, 186–90; floral motifs, 155, 186; scroll motifs, 86, 98, 108, 111, 114, 117, 120, 121, 126, 138, 141–3, 156, 159, 165; step motifs, 137–43, 182–5, 188–9
Aspusana River, 143
atlatl, 61
axes, 62–3, 89, 123, 149–50, 177–8

balsa trees, 29
bananas, 18, 49, 59, 180
bark cloth, 33
Barlovento, 65–6
Barrancas complex, 56, 86, 113–16
Barrancoid tradition, 64, 109, 113–27, 128, 156–9, 165, 168
basketry, 52, 54, 62
beans, 37, 58
beer, 18, 51, 54–6, 88, 101, 139, 183–5
Bení River, 123
Bolivia, 41, 82, 104, 123–6, 142, 175, 179
Bororo, 133
bottle-gourd, 58
bow, 61
Brazil, 22, 25, 63–4, 78, 80, 82, 141–2, 150, 155
Brazilian Highlands, 24, 25, 31, 41–2, 58, 81, 126
bronze, 62, 177–8
Bucarelia, 65
burials, 108, 138, 148, 159, 163

Caiambé site, 156–7
Caimito complex, 145–51, 153–6, 184, 186

251

Index

Caimito site, 138–9, 147–9
Campa, 121–3, 177
Canapote complex, 65
cannibalism, 20, 164, 182
canoes, 24, 32, 36, 54, 61, 73–5
caña brava, 29, 62
Caribbean, 45, 64–6, 82, 116, 145
Caribs, 164–70
Casa de la Tía site, 96–8
Cashibo, 140, 182, 187–9
Cashibocaño complex, 131–2
Cashinahua, 140
Casiquiare Canal, 24, 73, 75, 121
Cave of the Owls, 102–3, 107
ceja, 34, 39, 42, 95, 102, 171, 176, 178
ceramics (general), 17, 19, 32, 48, 52–6, 58, 62–7, 84, 92–5, 96–102, 102–3, 105–19, 120–1, 121–3, 123–7, 129–33, 134–5, 136–45, 146–59, 163, 164–70, 172–8, 179, 182–4, 186–9
ceramics, decorative techniques: adornos, 98, 108, 118, 120, 121, 124–7, 131–3, 138, 148–9, 167–8; appliqué, 90, 103, 109, 113–14, 117–18, 123–4, 138, 147, 158, 163, 166–8, 172–3; corrugation, 108, 109, 122, 132, 133, 136–7, 142, 144, 183, 186–7; excision, 94–5, 98–9, 108, 149–50, 155; modelling, 90, 103, 113–14, 117–18, 120–1, 124–7, 156–7, 169; pattern burnishing, 106, 183; post-fired paint, 87, 98, 100, 103, 107; punctation, 95, 98, 100, 109, 114, 183; resin glaze, 32, 139; resist, 139; slip painting, 90, 94–5, 96–100, 110, 121, 126, 130, 131, 136, 139–40, 147, 173, 183; zoned painting, 100, 109, 138–40, 143, 144
ceramics, tempering (general), 87, 90–2, 96–7, 123, 129, 155, 182; *cariapé*, 155–6, 182; *cauxí*, 155–6, 165; sand tempering, 96–9; shell tempered pottery, 87, 96; sherd tempering, 129, 182
ceramics, vessel appendages: handles, 91, 98, 103, 119–20, 172, 175, 177; labial flanges, 85–6, 91, 102, 106, 111, 114, 121, 156; lugs, 93, 95, 98, 114, 117, 120, 126; tetrapods, 124; tripods, 138, 167
ceramics, vessel form: bowls, 85, 91, 94, 102, 108, 110–11, 117–18, 120, 123, 127, 149, 156, 177; buck pots, 52, 118–19, 123, 127; burial urns, 132, 144, 147, 155, 157, 158–9, 169–70, 175; colanders, 139, 143; *comals* (griddles), 52, 56, 64, 100, 119, 130, 131, 134–5; cooking pots, 85, 97, 106, 182–3; cups, 85, 88, 97, 183; double-spout-and-bridge bottles, 85–6, 90, 92, 93, 102, 106, 109, 110, 114, 116; fermentation vessels, 55, 88, 100–1, 114, 131–2, 183; water jars, 100, 183, 186
Chacra de Giacomotti complex, 177
chacras, 17, 31, 59, 188
Chanchamayo Basin, 40, 122–3, 176–7
Chavín, 87, 94–5, 109
chile peppers, 58–9
Chimay site, 123–4
Chorrera complex, 109
Chullpa Pampa complex, 175
Chupachu, 173, 179
Circum-Caribbean culture, 45–6
clothing, 17, 119, 184–6
Cobichanique complex, 96–8
coca, 60
Cocama, 17, 19, 79, 136, 150–4, 157, 184, 185–6
Cocamilla, 79, 152
Cochabamba Basin, 34, 104, 175
Colombia, 41, 56, 64–6, 82–3, 86, 101, 117, 145, 150, 164, 169–70
cotton, 49, 58–9, 62, 119, 184
Cruxent, José María, 64, 111
Cumancaya complex, 108, 109, 122, 136–8
Cumancaya site, 92, 136–8
Cumancaya tradition, 133, 136–45, 183–4, 186–9
cushma, 119, 184
Cuzco, 179

disease, 18, 47, 190

Index

Early Mabaruma complex, 114–16
Early Tutishcainyo complex, 84–9, 102, 106–7, 112, 114
economic surplus, 51–5, 59, 91, 114
Ecuador, 66–7, 91, 101, 107, 109, 117, 151, 153, 161, 163, 170
El Palito complex, 115–16
Enoqui complex, 135–6
Estilo-Globular, 120
Estrada, Emilio, 66–7, 163
ethnic indentity, 17, 19, 182, 185, 190
Evans, Clifford, 66–7, 91, 143, 150–1, 155

face painting, 101, 141, 185
fauna, 27, 31, 35–6
fertilizing of soils, 37–9, 44, 161
fiestas, 18, 53, 54, 61, 101, 183–5
figurines, 144, 149, 178
fire dogs, 52, 56, 131, 184
fishing, 18, 19, 35, 36, 61, 65, 88, 128, 180
fish poisons, 33, 50, 60
flooding, 29, 30, 37–42, 160–2
flood plains, 26–30, 34, 35, 39, 40, 44, 49, 56, 57, 62, 64–7, 74, 75, 103, 107, 110–11, 113, 120, 129, 131, 152, 157–8, 160–1, 187
flora, 29, 31–5
food grinding, 61, 184
food processing, 51–53, 110, 119, 184
fortifications, 173, 175, 179
Franciscans, 123, 154, 180, 184

geology, 25–30
Genipa, 59, 185
Gran Chaco, 24, 70, 75, 80, 142
Gran Pajatén (Abiseo) site, 176, 178
grasslands, 34, 41–2, 49, 160
grater board, 51, 54
Greater Antilles, 57, 70, 72–3, 75, 110, 128
Guaporé River, 80, 82
Guarguapo complex, 170
Guaribe complex, 145
Guarita complex, 121, 155–6, 159

Guayas Basin, 108–9, 162–3, 170
Guiana, 53, 64, 75, 114, 116, 164
Guiana Highlands, 24–5, 31, 41–2, 46, 82–3
guinea-pig (domesticated), 105
Guyana, 24, 25, 64, 113–14, 170

Hacha complex, 58
head hunting, 20
Higueras complex, 172–4, 176
Hilbert, Peter Paul, 120–1, 150, 155–7, 168
houses, 18, 19, 32, 59, 88, 104, 119, 133, 177, 179
Huallaga River, 28, 40, 107, 122, 143, 152
Huánuco Basin, 34, 40, 87, 89, 103–7, 109, 171–3, 179
Huayurco site, 108–9
hunting, 35–6, 47, 63–5, 128, 186
Hupa-iya complex, 92, 113, 117–20, 121–2, 129, 131, 136

Ica Valley, 94
Imaríacocha, 18–19, 138, 145, 151
Inca, 62, 173–5, 179
irrigation, 103, 171
Isconahua (Remo), 138, 189
Itacoatiara complex, 120–1, 155, 167–8

jaguar, 87, 168
Jamunda River, 120
Japurá complex, 121
Japurá River, 26, 121, 157
Jauarí complex, 120, 168
Jívaro, 83, 109
José's Hill site, 92, 94, 129
Juruá River, 74–5, 80–1, 83, 140, 152, 159

Killke style, 179
Kondurí complex, 120, 163, 166–7
Kotosh site, 87, 89, 102–7, 109, 171

labrets, 185
La Mercéd, 122, 177

253

Index

Lanning, Edward P., 55, 67, 106
Late Mabaruma complex, 170
Late Tutishcainyo complex, 89–93, 103, 109
leaching of soils, 39, 43, 161
Lesser Antilles, 82, 110, 116, 128, 164
Lima bean, 58
linguistic groupings, 20, 54, 68–83; Arawakan, 70–81, 83, 96, 112, 127, 170; Aymaran, 80; Cariban, 81–3, 126, 165; Chibchan, 82, 169; Equatorial, 83; Gě, 81–82, 126, 133; Guaycuruan, 80, 142; Maipuran, 72–7, 79, 82, 116, 123, 127; Panoan, 79–81, 135, 139–40, 142, 144–5, 180–90; Quechuan, 80, 173–6, 179; Tacanan, 80; Tupí-Guaranían, 17, 52, 63, 78, 79, 81, 83, 126, 136, 151
linguistic relationship, 68–9, 187
llama (domesticated), 105, 243
Llanos de Mojos, 24, 34, 41, 75, 159, 160–1
Los Barrancos complex, 113–15, 117

macana, 61
Macás, 109
Machalilla complex, 91, 92
Madeira River, 23, 24–6, 74–5, 78, 82–3, 112, 159
Madre de Dios River, 73, 80–1
Magdalena River, 56, 65–6, 169
maize, 18, 38, 39, 44, 49, 55, 58–9, 61, 67, 133–4, 180, 184
Malambo complex, 56, 66
Mamoré River, 124
Manacapurú complex, 121, 156–7
manatee (sea cow), 35
Manaus, 25, 26, 31, 74, 120, 121, 168
Mangueiras site, 121, 157
manioc, 18, 38–9, 44, 48–57, 60, 65–6, 88, 100, 114, 119, 130, 131, 134–5, 139, 183–5
Maracá, 157
Maracaibo, Lake, 64–7
Marajó Island, 112
Marajoara complex, 149–51, 157, 175

Marañón River, 22, 28, 30, 75, 107–9
masonry, 103, 176–7
Mayoruna, 140, 187
Mbaya-Caduveo, 141–2, 185
meanders, 28–30, 39
Meggers, Betty J., 66–7, 109, 143, 150–1, 154–5
Mesoamerica, 39, 46, 48, 55–60, 101
middens, 51–2, 56, 62, 64–6, 84, 88–9, 92, 96, 98, 102, 103–4, 109, 113, 116, 119, 124, 129, 133, 136, 145
migration, 18–20, 24, 25, 45–6, 56, 61, 63–4, 68–83, 102, 112, 113, 116, 117, 119–20, 121–3, 127, 128, 131, 135, 136, 139–40, 142, 144, 150, 153–5, 157, 158, 160, 163–4, 173
Milagro complex, 161–2, 169
Miracanguera complex, 155–7, 159
Misque, 126
missionization, 47, 72, 123, 152, 154, 180–2, 184
Moche, 144
Mojocoya complex, 142–3
Mojos, 72
Mollo style, 179
Momíl, 56, 66
monkeys, 36, 108, 168
Montaña, 70, 72, 109
mosquito bars, 89, 119
mosquitoes, 88, 119, 184
Mound Hernmark, 158–9
Mound Velarde, 124–6, 139, 158–9

Naneini complex, 135, 144
Napo complex, 145, 150–1, 153–6, 184, 186
Napo River, 109, 143, 150–5, 157–9
Naranjal complex, 121–3, 177
narcotics, 33, 60
natural levees, 29, 30, 41, 136
Nazaratequi complex, 96, 98–102, 135
Nazaratequi River, 95–7
Nazaratequi tradition, 96–102, 111–12, 128, 135, 144

Index

Negro River, 22–4, 28, 31, 73, 75, 83, 112, 116, 121, 127
Noble, G. Kingsley, 72–4, 78
Nordenskiöld, Erland, 124, 142
Nueva Esperanza complex, 131, 133

Omagua, 79, 136, 150–3, 157
Orellana, Francisco de, 19, 151–3
Orinoco River, 24, 41, 56, 64, 72–3, 75, 85, 86, 110, 111, 113, 114, 116, 117, 121, 123, 127, 128, 145, 165, 169
ox-bow lakes, 29, 35, 84, 87, 136

Pacacocha complex, 131–2, 184
Pacacocha tradition, 131–3
Pachitea River, 18, 74, 96, 128, 178
Painaco, 17–19
Pangotsi complex, 96–9
Paracas, 87
Paredão complex, 159, 168
peach palm, 57
peanuts, 38, 40, 58, 60
Perené River, 122
Peru, 17, 22, 42, 48, 55, 57–9, 70, 72, 80, 83–4, 87, 92, 94, 101, 105–7, 117, 123, 127, 153, 155, 171–9, 180, 185
Pilcomayo River, 142
pile dwellings, 30, 88
pineapple, 18, 57
pirañha fish, 35, 62
Pirapitinga complex, 155–6
Pisqui River, 178, 184
Pleistocene Period, 26, 63
point bar formations, 29, 30, 39, 160
political control, 37, 45–6, 63, 94, 114, 151–3, 161, 168
Polychrome tradition, 121, 145–59, 183–6
population, 18, 20, 27, 31, 32, 36, 45–7, 69, 73–5, 83, 84–5, 97, 114, 119, 128–9, 152, 157, 160–1, 163–4, 171, 179, 190
Portacelli complex, 145
potatoes, 49, 104
priests, 45–6, 161

projectile point, 61, 189–90
protein, 27, 35, 49, 58, 67, 128
puberty ceremonies, 18, 62, 184
Pucallpa, 17, 26, 29, 84
Puerto Hormiga, 64–6
Purús River, 74, 75, 80–81, 140–59

Quebeno River, 152

rainfall, 34–5, 40–3
Rancho Peludo, 56, 64
Recuay, 144
religion, 17, 18, 45–7, 94, 105, 129, 161, 184
Remo, 141 182, 186, 188
rice, 17, 37, 40, 49
ridged fields, 160–4, 169
Río de la Miel, 169
Río Guapo complex, 111–12
Río Palacios complex, 142–4
riverine resources, 19, 27, 31, 35–6, 47, 60–1, 87
Rivet, Paul, 170
rocker mortars, 61, 184
roller stamps, 101, 185
Ronquín site, 111–12
root crops, 47–8, 63, 88, 128
rubber, 33, 180–1

Saladero, 56, 111–12
Saladoid tradition, 111–12, 113, 128
San Agustín site, 145
Sandía, 179
San Jorge Basin, 164, 169
San Ramón, 122, 177
Santarém complex, 120, 163, 168
Sao Joaquim complex, 155
Sarayacu, 153–4
Sauer, Carl O., 49, 104, 107
sculpture, 105, 108, 149–51
selective propagation, 48–50, 57
settlement pattern, 29–31, 36, 44, 84, 103, 113, 119, 124, 128, 133, 145, 151, 173, 180–1, 184, 187

255

Index

Shakimu, 92–5, 102, 108, 117, 129–31, 136
shell-fish, 63–7, 88, 96, 108
Shipibo-Conibo, 17–19, 92, 119, 136, 139–40, 180–5, 187–90
Sinú River, 57, 66
slash-and-burn agriculture, 17, 44
slaves, 47, 182
snuff, 60
social organization, 37, 45–7, 53, 114, 129, 133, 161, 164, 180, 181, 188
soils, 18, 36–44
Solimoes River, 22
spindle whorls, 62, 119, 149, 244
squashes, 58
statues, 45–6
Steward, Julian H., 20, 70, 176
stone working, 52, 62–3, 89, 108, 123, 149–50, 177, 184
sweet potato, 57, 60

Taino, 72, 74–5, 112
Tamaya River, 145
Tantamayo, 178
Tapajóz River, 120
Tarma, 172, 179
Tefé complex, 155, 157
Tejár complex, 163
Temple of the Crossed Hands, 104–5
temples, 45–6, 104
terraces, 39, 171–9
textiles, 62, 119, 247
Thompson, Donald E., 173, 176
thorn forest, 34, 35, 40, 107, 243
Tiahuanaco horizon, 126, 142
Ticuna, 186
Tingo María, 40, 102–3, 107, 143
tipití, 52
Titicaca Basin, 70, 142, 176
Tivacundo complex, 143
toads, 138, 148–9, 167–8
tobacco, 17, 60
Tournavista complex, 186–8
towns, 17, 45, 119, 124, 173, 183

trade, 32, 35, 53, 56, 62–3, 90–2, 108–9, 126, 177–8
trans-oceanic contact, 63, 66–7
Trenchera site, 179
Trombetas River, 120
Tropical Forest Culture, 20, 45–67, 73–4, 82, 87, 89, 91, 100, 104, 107, 110–12, 119, 126–7, 128, 160, 176
tropical forests, 29, 31–4, 40, 43, 49, 84, 107, 128, 129, 186–7
turtles, 35, 148–9
Tutishcainyo site, 84, 88–90, 92
Tutishcainyo tradition, 88, 94, 102–3, 110–12, 119, 128

Ucayali River, 17, 18, 20, 22, 25–6, 29–30, 40, 58, 73–5, 79–81, 90, 92, 102–3, 108, 109, 113, 117, 119–20, 121–3, 128–31, 133, 135, 136–8, 140, 142–5, 151, 154, 157–9, 180–90
Urubamba River, 122
Uru-Chipaya, 72–4

Valdivia complex, 66–7, 91
Valencia, Lake, 67
Venezuela, 25, 41, 56, 64, 67, 75, 110–16, 127, 128, 145, 164, 170

Waira-jirca, 103, 105–7
Wai-Wai, 46
warfare, 20, 45, 54, 69, 79, 82, 102, 121–3, 129, 151–2, 160, 164, 177, 182, 187, 190
water transport, 24, 70, 73–5, 81, 111, 145, 152
wattle-and-daub-construction, 88, 119
wood working, 61–2, 101, 185

Xanthosoma, 37, 57
Xingu River, 70, 75, 79, 126, 133

Yampara stlye, 126
Yarinacocha complex, 119, 129–31
Yarinacocha (lake), 84, 133, 154
Yasuní complex, 109